THE
LAST RAID

THE
LAST RAID

THE COMMANDOS,
CHANNEL ISLANDS
AND FINAL NAZI RAID

WILL FOWLER

The
History
Press

Cover illustrations. Front: Germans making use of innovative inflatable craft, often used for local movement around the Channel Islands. (Bundesarchiv) *Back:* A German MG34 machine-gun post in an improvised anti-aircraft position. (WF Collection)

First published 2016

The History Press
The Mill, Brimscombe Port
Stroud, Gloucestershire, GL5 2QG
www.thehistorypress.co.uk

British Library Cataloguing in Publication Data.
A catalogue record for this book is available from the British Library.

ISBN 978 0 7509 6637 5

Typesetting and origination by The History Press
Printed and bound in Great Britain by TJ International

CONTENTS

FOREWORD

He picked up the Colt M1911A1 .45 pistol with a smile of recognition.

'This was my personal weapon.'

He turned it over, looked at its functional lines and felt its familiar weight.

Training and the harsh test of war had given him a confidence with weapons that was instantly recognisable to the group of soldiers gathered around him.

The pistol was part of a display of Second World War weapons used by British commandos. The speaker – a veteran of No. 4 (Army) Commando – was addressing officers and non-commsioned officers (NCOs) of the Infantry Trials and Development Unit (ITDU) Warminster before they embarked on a battlefield study of Operation Jubilee.

I was to be their guide, taking them to the beaches around Dieppe where, on 19 August 1942, men of the Canadian 2nd Infantry Division fought and died in Operation Jubilee, a brief and disastrous amphibious assault on the French port.

The only part of the operation that was a success was Operation Cauldron, the attack by No. 4 Commando on a flanking German coastal battery code-named Hess. It was a well-planned and superbly executed attack. At the time James Dunning, the speaker at Warminster, was the 22-year-old Troop Sergeant Major of C Troop, No. 4 Commando – armed with a Colt 45.

The men of the ITDU hung on his words as he described the formation of commandos and their role in the Second World War. In 1940, commandos were a new and untried force made up of volunteers prepared to undertake hazardous but unspecified operations against the enemy.

It was a chance to hit back.

In 1940, many British soldiers of the British Expeditionary Force (BEF) had escaped from France over the beaches of Dunkirk only months before – they were proud men who felt that they had been driven off the continent of Europe in what had not been a fair fight. Now the enemy had turned the towns and cities of Britain into a battleground as *Luftwaffe* bombers pounded these vulnerable targets, and their families and friends were forced into the front line.

Many saw the air attacks as a precursor to a massive German amphibious assault on the British Isles and its occupation by an alien and cruel power.

Across the Channel there was already a miniature version of what life under German occupation would be like. The Channel Islands, which had resisted the French for centuries, had been captured by the Germans without a fight in June 1940, and now the Prime Minister, Winston Churchill, wanted to challenge these complacent occupiers of this small part of Britain.

Following the evacuation from Dunkirk, he demanded that the armed forces should take the war back to the enemy. One of the most dramatic developments in this fightback would be the formation of commandos – volunteers from the army and later the Royal Marines who would raid the coastline of German-occupied Europe.

It was obvious, therefore, that Churchill would insist that the Channel Islands were on the commandos' target list.

In all there would be seven raids on the Channel Islands. The first, Operation Ambassador on 15 July 1940, was so ineffective, with men and equipment being abandoned for absolutely no tactical gains, that there was talk among senior army officers that the fledgling commandos should be disbanded.

In contrast, Operation Dryad on 3 September 1942 was a well-planned and very effective attack that captured the entire crew of seven men on the Casquet lighthouse, along with their code books and other documents.

Though in itself a small-scale action, Basalt in October 1942 would have repercussions that no one could have anticipated. Because there were reports that German prisoners had been tied up and shot, an enraged Hitler issued the secret 'Commando Order'; this required that any captured Special Forces were to be executed – a fate that befell members of the SAS and commandos later in the war.

There are some less well-known plans for operations against the Channel*
Islands that were proposed in 1943 by Admiral Lord Louis Mountbatten, then
heading combined operations. Some were large-scale raids, even landings
with armour and paratroops supported by naval gunfire and bombers. Had
the operation been launched, the casualties would have been worse than the
losses suffered by the Canadians at Dieppe in August 1942.

During the war the Channel Islands would become an obsession for three
powerful men: Churchill, who was angered that British territory was now
under enemy control; Mountbatten, who proposed the potentially costly and
impractical operations; and Hitler, who was determined that the Channel
Islands would remain German forever and was the driving force behind a
massive programme of fortification.

Allied commando raids were launched against the islands between 1940
and 1943. However, the most unusual raid was that launched by the Germans
from Jersey in March 1945, which saw a mixed force of soldiers, *Luftwaffe*
gun crews and sailors land at the Allied-controlled French port of Granville.
Their main mission was to capture British colliers and bring them and their
valuable cargo back to the Channel Islands to ensure that the power stations
were kept fuelled. They captured one collier and destroyed port installations,
as well as taking prisoners. These German servicemen on the raid were to be
some of the last men to be awarded the Knight's Cross during the Second
World War.

Following the Granville raid, the enraged Americans proposed that Allied
bomber forces should pound the islands' harbours to deter any further
seaborne attacks – but fortunately for the civilian population the war ended
a couple of weeks later and the garrison on this last outpost of the Third
Reich went quietly into captivity.

INTRODUCTION

Visit the Commonwealth War Graves Cemetery at Bayeux in Normandy and you will see the neat rows of distinctive British and Commonwealth headstones, with the name, age, rank, service number and cap badge of the young man or woman buried in the ground below. At the foot of the headstone is a short personal tribute from the wife or more often the parents who had been listed in the soldier's documents as next of kin.

It is over seventy years since D–Day and the fighting in Normandy, but these tributes still resonate with the surge of pain, resignation and tearful pride felt when the reluctant telegraph boy delivered the buff envelope, and parents or wives picked out the typed phrases such as 'killed in action' or 'missing presumed dead'.

Some 4,648 servicemen and women are buried at Bayeux, including 466 German soldiers. In a block on the right is the grave of a 38-year-old lieutenant in the Royal Naval Volunteer Reserve (RNVR) named Fredrick Lightoller. He was killed in action on the night of 9 March 1945 at the small northern French port of Granville. He was one of six British sailors, both Merchant and Royal Navy, and seventeen men of the US Navy and Army to die in a German amphibious raid launched from the Channel Island of Jersey.

Across the road from the cemetery is the pillared Memorial for the Missing. On it are listed the names, ranks and regiments of 1,805 servicemen and women who were killed, but whose bodies were never recovered. At the top of the memorial is the proud motto: '*NOS A GUILIEMO VICTI VICTORIS PATRIAM LIBERAVIMUS*' ('We, once conquered by William, have now set free the Conqueror's land').

At the far right-hand end of the memorial, high on one of the limestone panels, are the names of men from the Special Air Service (SAS), killed in France in the bloody fighting after D-Day. Some may have been captured and murdered by the Germans and their bodies dumped into unmarked graves: they were the victims of Hitler's notorious 'Commando Order' – an order prompted by a commando raid on the German-held Channel Islands. This is the story of that raid and its tragic consequences, and of others against these islands, the first of which went so badly wrong that it nearly spelled the end of the fledgling commando idea.

Following D-Day and the liberation of France, the islands were isolated and there was no longer any requirement to raid them to capture prisoners, gain intelligence or keep the garrison on edge. Then, only weeks before the end of the war in Europe, the German garrison launched its own commando raid on the French port of Granville.

1

OPERATION *GRÜNE PFEIL*: THE INVASION, 30 JUNE 1940

The Channel Islands – in Norman Îles d'la Manche, in French Îles Anglo-Normandes or Îles de la Manche – are an archipelago of British Crown Dependencies in the English Channel, off the French coast of Normandy. They include two separate bailiwicks, that of Guernsey and Jersey, with their respective capitals of St Peter Port and St Helier.

The main islands of the Channel Islands are Jersey, Guernsey, Alderney, Sark and Herm, the smaller inhabited islands being Jethou, Brecqhou (Brechou) and Lihou; all except Jersey are in the Bailiwick of Guernsey. There are also uninhabited islets: the Minquiers, Ecréhous, Les Dirouilles and Les Pierres de Lecq, also known as the Paternosters, part of the Bailiwick of Jersey; and Burhou and the Casquets, which lie off Alderney. These uninhabited islands can be visited but are a valued nature reserve and secure stopover point for migrating birds.

The Channel Islands were originally part of the Dukedom of Normandy; after 1066, when the Norman prince William conquered Anglo-Saxon Britain, the islands became part of this larger domain. With the passage of time, England won and lost portions of France but the islands remained secure, protected by the fast currents, rocky coastlines and difficult seas that surround them. The advent of steam power in the nineteenth century saw this protection diminished and, with France still the main enemy, forts, barracks and batteries were built to cover the harbours and protect the coastline.

War first came to the Channel Islands on 1 May 1779 when, in support of the American colonists then in rebellion against the British, the French attempted a landing on Jersey at St Ouen's Bay. Early that morning, British lookouts sighted five large vessels and a large number of smaller craft 9 nautical miles off the coast, on a course that made it obvious that they were intent on making a landing. Cutters and small craft supporting the landing fired grapeshot at soldiers of the 78th Regiment Highlanders and Jersey Militia who, together with some field artillery that they had dragged through the sand, had arrived in time to oppose the landing. The defenders suffered a few men wounded when a cannon burst but prevented the landing. The French vessels withdrew, first holding off 3 nautical miles from the coast before leaving the area entirely.

They would be back.

Two years later, on 5 January 1781, a new, more powerful force set out for Jersey. It consisted of 2,000 soldiers in four formations loosely called 'divisions'. Like later commando operations against the islands, the force commander, Baron Phillipe de Rullecourt, was relying on surprise. He held the rank of colonel in the French Army, but was seen in France as an adventurer and the sort of renegade that professional soldiers despise. However, the Baron knew that citizens and soldiers on Jersey would be off their guard celebrating 'Old Christmas Night' on 6 January.

French officers with a more rational approach saw an attack on Jersey as a waste of resources and believed that any lodgement on the island would be short-lived – there would be echoes of this in the assessment by the Chiefs of Staff of Admiral Mountbatten's plans for landings by the British in the Second World War.

Despite this, King Louis XVI was keen to embarrass the British in any way possible and promised de Rullecourt that if he succeeded and captured St Helier he would be promoted to general and awarded the Order of St Louis – better known as the Cordon Rouge because of its distinctive red sash. His second in command was an Indian prince known as Prince Emir, who had been captured by the British during the Anglo-French wars in India. He had been sent to France as a repatriated prisoner of war and remained in French service. Reflecting the attitudes of the times, a British veteran recalled that: 'He looked quite barbarian, as much as his discourse; if our fate has depended on him, it would not have been of the most pleasant; he advised the French General to ransack everything and to put the town to fire and to blood.'

What makes the expedition sound very modern was that it was not officially sanctioned by the French government, and so if it failed it was 'deniable'. Though it had no official backing, funding, equipment, transport and troops were provided by the government. In order to conceal its involvement, the government went so far as to order the 'desertion' of several hundred regular troops to de Rullecourt's forces.

It looked as if the plan might work when 800 men of the First Division landed undetected by the local guard post on the night of 6 January at La Rocque, Grouville. A subsequent trial by the British authorities found that the guards had deserted their post to go drinking. The First Division remained in place during the night awaiting reinforcements. Now the plan began to unravel; 400 men of the Second Division did not make landfall when their ships were lost among the rocks – in British accounts the ships were listed as four transports escorted by a privateer. The winter weather also played a part when the shipping for the Third Division – some 600 men – became separated from the main body and so was unable to land. However, the Fourth Division of 200 men landed early the next morning at La Rocque, bringing the total strength of the French force to only 1,000 – but they still had surprise on their side.

On the morning of 6 January the First Division moved stealthily into St Helier and established defensive positions while the population were still asleep. At 8 a.m. a French patrol entered Le Manoir de la Motte and captured the governor, Major (Maj) Moses Corbet, in bed. De Rullecourt tried to bluff the governor that the French were on the island in overwhelming strength, and threatened to sack the town if the governor did not sign a capitulation. Under the circumstances, Corbet showed considerable moral courage when he said that, as a prisoner, he had no authority and that any signature would be 'of no avail'. However, under pressure from de Rullecourt he eventually signed.

The bluff looked as if it might work when, under escort, Corbet was then pressurised to order Captains Aylward and Mulcaster, the young officers in command at Elizabeth Castle, to surrender. If the castle was secured, St Helier would be under French control. However, not only would Aylward and Mulcaster not surrender, but they opened fire, causing two or three French casualties. The French withdrew.

Though the governor was a prisoner, 24-year-old Maj. Francis Peirson, in command of the garrison at St Peter's Barracks, was beginning to build up a picture of the strength of the invading forces – in modern terminology the information was coming in from 'Humint', or human intelligence: what the locals had seen and heard. Peirson had joined the army in 1772 and was a veteran of the American War of Independence. As he assembled his force at Mont es Pendus (now known more prosaically as Westmount), he knew that his mixed force of regular soldiers and militia had grown to 2,000 men and outnumbered the French two-to-one. He would counter-attack.

In St Helier, the French had camped in the market and positioned captured British guns to cover the likely approaches. Though these guns were a valuable enhancement to their firepower, they had not located the British howitzers that were later to play a significant part in the Battle of Jersey.

Peirson worked fast. He sent the 78th Highland Regiment of Foot, who were part of the Regular Army garrison, to secure Mont de la Ville (now Fort Regent) to block any French withdrawal. When he reckoned they were in position, he ordered the main body to attack. Bluffing, and trying to play for time, de Rullecourt sent the governor to offer capitulation terms, with the threat that if the British did not sign in sixty minutes St Helier would be put to fire and the sword.

He had not reckoned with Peirson and Captain Campbell, commanding the Grenadier Company of the 83rd Regiment of Foot, who simply gave the French commander twenty minutes to surrender.

In Grouville, the 83rd Regiment of Foot had also refused to surrender, and in a somewhat overdramatic but prescient outburst, de Rullecourt is reported to have said: 'Since they do not want to surrender, I have come here to die.'

The French were outnumbered, but would also be outfought. Though they were able to fire the captured cannon once or twice, the British howitzer crew in the Grande Rue directly opposite the market, in the words of an eyewitness, 'cleaned all the surroundings of French'.

If men had not died in the action that followed, the Battle of Jersey would be remembered as a slightly farcical episode. It lasted about fifteen minutes. Many of the British soldiers were so confined in the streets of St Helier that, with no clear view of their enemies, they fired their muskets into the air. Finally, while some of the British regiments, such as the 78th Regiment,

95th Regiment of Foot and South-East, had obviously 'British' titles, the Battalion of St Lawrence and the Compagnies de Saint-Jean sound as if they should have been in the French order of battle.

Using Corbet as an intermediary, de Rullecourt tried bluffing the British commander, saying that the French had two battalions of infantry supported by a company of artillery at La Rocque, only fifteen minutes' march away. Through local intelligence, the British knew the true strength of the French forces. Forty-five elite grenadiers from the 83rd Regiment of Foot held off 140 French soldiers until reinforcements from the South-East Regiment arrived, and this proved to be the tipping point. The French broke, suffering thirty dead and wounded and seventy prisoners. Survivors fled through the countryside, trying to reach their boats, but many were caught.

The fight went out of the French when, through the clouds of gun smoke, they saw de Rullecourt tumble to the ground, hit by a musket ball. Some of the invaders threw down their weapons and ran, but others took up positions in the houses around the market and continued to trade shots.

For de Rullecourt, it was perhaps for the best that his fatal wish was granted and he died from his wounds on 7 January. Earlier, Maj. Peirson, leading from the front, had also been fatally wounded by a sniper in the battle in the square, but his troops, led by Lieutenant Dumaresq, had held their nerve and fought on.[1] Peirson's servant, Pompey, located the sniper and shot him dead. The British took 600 prisoners, who were shipped to England. British Regular Army losses were eleven dead and thirty-six wounded, among them Captain Charlton of the Royal Artillery, wounded while he was a prisoner of the French. The Jersey Militia suffered four dead and twenty-nine wounded.

To forestall similar attacks during the Napoleonic Wars, Martello[2] Towers were constructed along the coast. Twenty were built on Jersey and fifteen on Guernsey. They were intended both as lookouts and gun platforms to prevent landings, and can be found at St Ouen's Bay, St Aubin's Bay and Grouville Bay on Jersey and the northern part of Guernsey. One tower, at L'Etacq on Jersey, was demolished by the German occupation force to give a better field of fire for more modern weapons.

Older fortifications were improved, among the most imposing of which is Castle Cornet on Guernsey, which covers the approaches to St Peter Port. The castle used to be the residence of the governor, and indeed during the last throws of the English Civil War, it was the final remaining Royalist stronghold, having in the process lobbed cannonballs into the town. Partly for that reason, apart from the town church, many of today's buildings are of eighteenth-century origin. It was superseded by Fort George, which was completed in 1812, during the Napoleonic Wars.

The castle occupies such a tactically significant location that the Georgians built a barracks and battery close by and incorporated the castle into these defences. In surveying many of the existing fortifications in 1940, the Germans pronounced them tactically soundly positioned and went on to improve them further.

In 1852, Fort Hommet on Guernsey, which had begun as a Martello Tower, was expanded, with additional batteries and barracks, the 24pdr cannon replaced with more powerful 68pdr and 8in shell guns. During the Second World War, the Germans recognised the enduring utility of the site and fortified it further, creating the *Stützpunkt* (Strongpoint) Rotenstein. They also used Fort Albert on Alderney, Fort George and Castle Cornet in Guernsey, while on Jersey, Elizabeth Castle and Fort Henry found new garrisons.

As with all communities in the United Kingdom, the First World War left its mark on the islands. Some 2,298 young men gave their lives in the conflict from the 12,460 (6,292 from the Bailiwick of Jersey and 6,168 from the Bailiwick of Guernsey) who rallied to the colours. Two islanders would win the Victoria Cross (VC) and 212 decorations for gallantry were awarded to islanders. In the Second World War, islanders would fight and die in both the Merchant Marine and the Armed Forces of Great Britain. For infantry soldiers there was a strong affinity with the English county regiments that were the closest to their home islands, such as the Hampshire and Dorset Regiments.

In 1939, at the outbreak of the Second World War, the approximate populations of the Channel Islands were: Jersey, 50,000; Guernsey, 40,000; Alderney, 1,500; Sark, 500.

The islands, known collectively as The States, voted for conscription of men aged 18 to 41, to match the mainland's conscription law. A Defence Corps, the Insular Defence Corps and Royal Guernsey Militia, was formed. In the period known as the Phoney War, the islands made a substantial contribution to the war effort. Guernsey voted £180,000 (the equivalent of

£8,533,069 in 2012) towards the cost of the defence of the island, and to do so doubled income tax. In March 1940, Jersey raised a loan of £100,000 (£4,740,594) as a 'first instalment'. In a letter to *The Times*, Lord Portsea, who would defend the interests of the islands throughout the war, referring to them not as The Channel Islands but The Royal Islands, said that if these figures per head of population were extrapolated to the mainland of Britain they would represent £118 million in 1940.

As in 1914–1918, there seemed to be little threat to the islands following the outbreak of war in 1939. However, with the fall of France following the German invasion in May 1940, the British government decided that the Channel Islands were of no strategic importance and would not be defended. Perhaps through a sense of misguided pride, they decided to keep this a secret from the Germans. So, in spite of the reluctance of the new Prime Minister, Winston Churchill, the British government gave up the oldest possession of the Crown without firing a single shot. The Channel Islands served no purpose to the Germans, other than the propaganda value of having occupied a very small bit of British territory. The two battalions who had been stationed in the islands were withdrawn. The island's two lieutenant governors departed on 21 June 1940 with the last of the British troops.

Interestingly, the reasons for the evacuation of troops from the Channel Islands would be ignored by Mountbatten and Churchill when, later in the war, they began formulating ideas for major raids or even the recapture of the islands. The whole *raison d'être* for the British decision was that they regarded the Channel Islands as being too difficult to defend from German occupation. In coming to this decision, the British government took into account:

1. Difficulties of maintaining supply lines from England, which they knew would be subject to disruption by German sea and air attacks.
2. The likelihood that British garrisons would ultimately have to surrender the islands due to lack of supplies and the propaganda this would provide Germany.
3. Maintaining garrisons on the islands would tie up manpower needed for the war effort, manpower which could be better employed defending England.
4. The likelihood that actively defending the islands would have resulted in German military attacks, causing significant loss of civilian life.[3]

The British government had consulted the islands' elected government representatives in order to formulate an evacuation policy. Opinion was divided and, with no clear policy, there was disorder, with each of the islands adopting their own policies. The government concluded the best course was to make available as many ships as possible so that islanders had the option to leave if they wanted to. The authorities on Alderney recommended that all islanders evacuate, and nearly all did so. The Dame of Sark encouraged everyone to stay. Guernsey evacuated all children of school age, giving the parents the option of keeping their children with them or evacuating with their school. In Jersey, the majority of islanders chose to stay. In all, 6,600 left Jersey and 17,000 Guernsey. The trauma of evacuation was not confined to people – animals, including pets, suffered terribly in all three islands. In Jersey, over 5,000 cats and dogs were killed in five days at the Animal Shelter. In Alderney, cattle and pigs were left shut up and without food and fodder – dairy cows were abandoned unmilked. When men came over from Guernsey on Tuesday 25 June they found the body of a horse in the main street of St Annes. It had broken its neck as it attempted to jump a fence.

Out on the Casquets, the hazardous rocky feature 8 miles to the west of Alderney, the Trinity House vessel *Vestal* arrived on 22 June to evacuate the lighthouse crew. The light had been turned off at 2.45 p.m. on the previous day. Documents and the clocks were removed by the crew and, when they reached England, along with the keys they were forwarded to London.

Since the demilitarisation of the islands had been kept secret, the Germans assumed they would be defended and approached them with some caution. There were, after all, the many barracks and military installations built in the nineteenth century on the islands, as well as castles and fortifications from earlier times. Reconnaissance flights over these positions proved inconclusive. On 28 June 1940 a squadron of German bombers from detachments of *Luftflotte* III based at Villacoublay south-west of Paris attacked the harbours of Guernsey and Jersey. In St Peter Port, what the reconnaissance aircraft mistook for columns of troop carrying vehicles, '*LKW – und PKW – Kolonnen*', were in fact lorries and horse-drawn carts that were loaded with tomatoes for export to England. About 180 bombs were dropped and forty-four islanders were killed in the raids. An eyewitness quoted by Peter King in *The Channel Islands War* recalled grimly that the lorry drivers took cover under their vehicles:

only to be crushed as the fires started and the vans and trucks collapsed. The blood of the wounded and dying mingled with the juice of the tomatoes and when I came on the scene just as the last Hun plane faded into the distance the sight was one I shall never forget; the flames, the bodies the cries of the dying and injured, and the straggling line of people emerging from their shelter under the pier jetty.

Molly Bihet, who lived in St Peter Port at the time of the bombing, recalled the day: 'We were in Les Canichers walking home and these three planes came very low from the north … my mother pushed us into the closest house and we went down to the basement and we were hearing the noise, terrified we were really.' The youngest to die that day was 14 and the oldest 71. The only anti-aircraft defences on the islands was a Lewis gun on the steamer *Isle of Sark* that was in St Peter Port.

To prevent any further loss of life, an unofficial announcement was made on the BBC that night that the islands had been demilitarised, and formal notification was made via the US Ambassador in London on 30 June.

The Germans had in fact included invasion of the Channel Islands as part of their strategy long before they attacked Poland in 1939. In July 1938, they had sent at least one agent there and his report was sent to the *Oberkommando der Wehrmacht* (OKW), the Armed Forces High Command. Though the loss of the islands by the British would not have a significant strategic impact on the defence of the mainland, the Germans could not leave them as a potential base for British operations. At 3 p.m. on Thursday 20 June 1940 a signal was transmitted from Berlin: 'The capture of the British Channel Islands is necessary and urgent.'

The plans for capturing the islands, Operation *Grüne Pfeile* (Green Arrows), were in place and men of the 216th Infantry Division were standing by in nearby French ports ready for an assault landing. There was a fear among senior officers that the British might make a determined stand to hold the islands, and if the Germans sustained heavy losses in their fight for this little bit of Britain it would detract from the relatively bloodless victories they had enjoyed so far in Europe.

The plan involved the landing of six battalions, accompanied by naval assault troops and two companies of engineers. They would carry only light weapons and would take with them a small amount of captured French artillery. It would have to be a phased operation due to lack of sufficient shipping. Alderney and Guernsey would be taken first, then Jersey a day later. Aircraft from *Luftflotte* III would provide protection for the unarmed landing craft and Ju 87 Stuka dive bombers suppress the onshore defences. Admiral Karlgeorg Schuster, naval commander in France, was convinced that the Victorian fortifications covering the ports would be manned. The lack of reaction to the *Luftwaffe* attacks failed to convince him, but the *Luftwaffe* were prepared to take a gamble and test out the demilitarisation claim.

Hauptman Liebe-Pieteritz of the *Luftwaffe* landed at Guernsey with three Dornier aircraft flying top cover. He had to make a quick getaway when a flight of three Royal Air Force (RAF) Bristol Blenheim bombers appeared, and in the air battle that followed the *Luftwaffe* reported that two of the Blenheims were shot down – though RAF sources have no record of losses. Liebe-Pieteritz made his report and between 7 p.m. and 8 p.m. on 30 June a Ju 52 transport aircraft flew a platoon of *Luftwaffe* troops under command of Maj. Dr Albrecht Lanz to Guernsey. They were met at the airport by Inspector Sculpher, head of the island's police. The German officers were escorted in police cars and a commandeered taxi to the Royal Hotel to meet senior island officials. German instructions and regulations were read out. Few people on Guernsey realised that they had been occupied until they received their newspapers free on Monday 1 July – the lead story for the papers were orders from the first island Commandant.

On Friday 28 June, the German aircraft attacked Jersey. Two houses at La Rocque were damaged and three people were killed. The Havre-des-Pas slopes of Fort Regent were hit, and a stick of bombs was dropped on Norman's, which was gutted, Le Sueur's and Raffray's buildings, and in one of the little bays where yachts were kept, smashing some of those. More air activity followed, and on 1 July German aircraft piloted by *Leutnant* Kern flew low over the island, dropping messages for the authorities, demanding the surrender of the island. The messages were in pouches made from the bed linen of a French captain who had commanded a squadron of the *L'Armée de L'air*. The bags were weighted with sand and had red and blue ribbon streamers, while the surrender ultimatum was in a cardboard tube. The message said that white flags were to be flown and white crosses marked out at several key places like the airport. The States met urgently and agreed to the terms of surrender, as they had been advised to do by the British government.

By the end of that day about 100 men were on the island. The German commander had met with the Bailiff, and Jersey was under German rule. The force was reinforced when about 1,750 German soldiers flew in, and marched into St Helier. In the end about 11,500 German soldiers occupied Jersey, setting up their first HQ in the Town Hall in St Helier.

On the island, the occupying forces were quick to stamp their authority with orders issued to the population:

1 All inhabitants must be indoors by 11 p.m. and must not leave their homes before 5 a.m.

2 We will respect the population of Jersey; but, should anyone attempt to cause the least trouble, serious measures will be taken.

3 All orders given by the Military Authority are to be strictly obeyed.

4 All spirits must be locked up immediately, and no spirits may be supplied, obtained, or consumed henceforth. This prohibition does not apply to stocks in private houses.

5 No person shall enter the Aerodrome at St Peter [sic].

6 All Rifles, Airguns, Revolvers, Daggers, Sporting Guns, and all other Weapons whatsoever, except Souvenirs, must, together with all Ammunition, be delivered to the Town Arsenal by 12 (noon) tomorrow, July 3rd.

7 All British Sailors, Airmen, and Soldiers on leave, including Officers, in this Island must report at the Commandant's Office, Town Hall, at 10 a.m., tomorrow, July 3rd.

8 No boat or vessel of any description, including any fishing boat, shall leave the Harbours or any other place where the same is moored, without an Order from the Military Authority, to be obtained at the Commandant's Office, Town Hall. All Boats arriving in Jersey must remain in Harbour until permitted by the Military to leave. The crews will remain on board. The Master will report to the Harbour Master, St Helier, and will obey his instructions.

9 The Sale of Motor Spirit is prohibited, except for use on Essential Services, such as Doctors' Vehicles, the Delivery of Foodstuffs, and Sanitary Services, where such vehicles are in possession of a permit from the Military

Authority to obtain supplies. THE USE OF CARS FOR PRIVATE PURPOSES IS FORBIDDEN.

10 The Black-out Regulations already in force must be obeyed as before.

11 Banks and Shops will be open as before.

12 In order to conform with Central European Time all watches and clocks must be advanced one hour at 11 p.m. TONIGHT.

13 It is forbidden to listen to any Wireless Transmitting Stations, except German and German-Controlled Stations.

14 The raising of Prices of Commodities is forbidden.

The German Commandant of the Island of Jersey

July 2nd, 1940

On 2 July, German forces landed at Alderney, which had already been evacuated. The airfield had been obstructed but was soon cleared by the crews of two Fieseler *Storch* (Stork) liaison and observation aircraft that had superb Short Take Off and Landing (STOL) capability. They landed between the obstacles and, after they had been cleared, Ju 52 transports brought in more troops. A day later, Maj. Dr Albrecht Lanz, commanding officer of II Regiment 396 of 216th Infantry Division, and Dr Maas, his chief of staff and interpreter, arrived on Sark. Maas spoke excellent English, having studied tropical diseases for eight years in Liverpool.

It was here that the Germans found themselves faced by a remarkable woman, the feudal governor of the island, Seigneur Dame Sibyl Mary Hathaway. She had decided not to evacuate when faced by the prospect of German occupation, and urged all 500 of the population to remain on the island as well. She was much respected by the islanders and would soon be by the Germans, whose language she spoke perfectly. In her first encounter with the two officers, she achieved a small but significant psychological victory. When Maas discovered that she spoke German, he said, 'You do not appear to be the least afraid,' to which Sibyl Hathaway – in her words 'looking as innocent as possible' – replied, 'Is there any reason why I should be afraid of German officers?' This completely disarmed the two officers, and Lanz said if there were any difficulties in the future she could contact the Commandant of the Channel Islands in Guernsey direct – bypassing the chain of command. It would allow her to 'put a stop to any petty tyranny in Sark'.

For her leadership during this period, the British Home Secretary commented that she remained 'almost wholly mistress of the situation' throughout the occupation. On 4 July, a date that the Dame's American husband, Robert 'Bob' Woodward Hathaway, noted wryly was 'a hell of a day on which to be occupied', *Obergefreiter* Obenhauf and a section of ten men arrived to garrison the island.

For the Germans, there was considerable propaganda value in publishing photographs of the men of their armed forces – *Wehrmacht* – against classically British backgrounds of shops and banks or even talking to British policemen. When these pictures first appeared in the summer of 1940, they sent the tacit message that mainland Britain would soon be occupied.

One of the iconic pictures from the occupation shows a *Luftwaffe* officer in conversation with a police constable on Jersey. When it appeared in the British press, an effort was made to make the best of a bad thing with the caption 'This is Jersey Now – and this is still the law'. Eventually the corrupting effect of an occupation lasting almost five years would see the police involved in criminal activities.

For those on the mainland who remembered holidays on the Channel Islands in the 1930s, there were poignant pictures of a German soldier buying an ice cream from a 'stop me and buy one' tricycle ice cream vendor in Charing Cross, St Helier, Jersey. The photograph of a German Army band leading a column of soldiers past the very British architecture of Lloyds Bank on Pollet in St Peter Port, with an arrogant young officer at its head, was also disconcerting.

Within three months, civilian-owned cars were requisitioned – the owners receiving notification of which depot they were to deliver their cars to and the price they required. A few days later, the German authorities informed the owner if their vehicle had been acquired. On 23 October 1940, Mr A.A. Gould learned that the German authorities had paid 25,000 francs – roughly £7,000 in today's values – for his car. Continental road signs, along with a plethora of German tactical signs indicating headquarters and hospitals, were introduced and drivers were required to drive on the right. While these were inconveniences for the few islanders who could still use their cars, the speed at which some of the young German soldiers drove meant that it was safer to obey these new rules of the road. During the occupation there were improvements – some dangerous corners were straightened out, roads were widened and junctions improved to accommodate large military vehicles.

Horse-drawn ambulances carried the sick to hospital and horse buses moved islanders around – though one recalled in the latter years of the war that lack of fodder meant that the gaunt horse looked as underfed as her fellow islanders. Horses were also used by senior officers, who rode around inspecting work on the defences.

By mid-August 1940, the German civil and military administration had begun to take over on the islands. *Feldkommandantur* 515 – FK 515 – established its HQ in Jersey, with the Army HQ in Guernsey. Guernsey was a *Nebenstelle* – a branch of FK 515 that also ran Sark, while Alderney was an *Aussenstelle* – Outpost, and on the mainland the French port of Granville was the *Zufuhrstelle* – Stores Assembly Point.

British territory was now occupied by the armed forces of Nazi Germany and would endure almost five years under their control. For the first German soldiers who arrived on the Channel Islands, the people did not seem hostile and the well-stocked shops were a revelation; they quickly bought up luxury goods to send home – using *Reichkreditkassen* (Occupation Marks). This new currency would later become useful when official Channel Islands buying commissions went to France to purchase supplies for the islands.

Carel Toms, writing in *Hitler's Fortress Islands*, sums up the summer months of 1940:

> The troops were in paradise. The weather was perfect and the islands looked their best. The beaches were empty and the shops full. The 'visitors' bought as much as they wanted for themselves and to send home. They commandeered, placarded, paraded, marched, sang victory songs and held band concerts. They were going to be in England before the end of August.

Notes

1 The battle was reported in the *London Gazette*, where it was read by John Boydell, an alderman of the City of London. Boydell, a successful engraver, knew and admired the work of John Singleton Copley (1738–1815), a fashionable London-based American artist, who had settled in London and made a considerable reputation for himself painting historic subjects on a grand scale. Boydell's imagination had been captured by the report of the Battle of Jersey and he persuaded Copley to paint it. Copley's painting, entitled *The Death of Major Peirson*, was unveiled in London in 1784.

2 Martello Towers trace their name and origins back to a round fortress, part of a larger Genovese defence system built in Corsica at Mortella – Myrtle Point. Typically, a Martello Tower stands up to 40ft (12m) high (with two floors) with a garrison of one officer and fifteen to twenty-five men. Their round structure and thick solid masonry walls made them resistant to cannon fire, while their height made them an ideal platform for a single heavy artillery piece, mounted on the flat roof and able to traverse a 360° arc. A few towers had moats or other batteries and works attached for extra defence. The towers, which also served as observation points, were sited to give interlocking fields of fire.

3 Three years later, when British forces occupied the Dodecanese islands of Kos and Leros, the Germans were able to concentrate air and naval resources and recapture the islands. The operation was the brainchild of Churchill, who was convinced that it would bring Turkey into the war on the side of the Allies. In fact it cost the Allies losses of 4,800 men killed or captured, 113 aircraft, six destroyers sunk, four cruisers moderately damaged, four cruisers severely damaged, two submarines sunk, and ten minesweepers and coastal defence ships sunk. German losses were 1,184 men killed and fifteen landing craft sunk.

2

OCCUPATION, RESISTANCE AND DEPORTATION, 1940–45

During August 1940 the German military government organisation took over the administration from the army. The Channel Islands now became part of the Départment de la Manche, a sub-district of German Military Government Area A centred at Saint-Germain-en-Laye. For the first time since the days of William the Conqueror, the islands were now nominally part of France.

It is said that the OKW was anxious to study the behaviour of the Channel Islanders under occupation to learn how best they might govern Britain – a country they were confident would come to terms with the Reich. Berlin felt, therefore, that the occupying forces should be led by individuals who would create, as far as possible in the circumstances, a favourable and sympathetic impression on the local population. They could not have made a wiser choice of commander-in-chief than Maj-General Rudolph Graf von Schmettow.

Von Schmettow was an urbane aristocrat, head of an ancient Silesian family with long military traditions and nephew of Field Marshal Gerd von Runstedt,. A wounded veteran of the First World War, von Schmettow was respected by the troops under his command, but also quickly gained that of the local population, including Alexander Coutanche, the Bailiff of Jersey, and Ambrose Sherwill, the Attorney General in Guernsey, who described the general as a man of great charm and humanity, someone who, according to the official history of the occupation, earned the reputation of favouring the Channel Islanders whenever he could.

In a further move to create the right kind of impression, the general brought with him Maj. Prince Georg von Waldeck to take command of all the regular troops, Graf Hans von Helldorf as his chief-of-staff and, in 1942, Graff Max von Aufsess to handle the liaison between the military government and the Jersey authorities.

None of these cultured and aristocratic men were Nazis, and consequently, as the war progressed, von Schmettow became increasingly suspect in the eyes of his masters in Berlin. Baron von Helldorf would later come under suspicion for his leniency towards the local civilians and for failing to carry out orders he received from Berlin, and be banished to the little island of Herm, pending court martial. The wife of von Aufsess, who was still in Germany, was declared an enemy of the state and arrested by the Gestapo.

In June 1941, a detachment of the *Geheime Feldpolizei* (GFP) Secret Field Police was posted to the islands. It consisted of 131 uniformed personnel and 312 civilians. Headquarters were established at Silvertide, St Helier, Jersey, and The Albion Hotel, St Peter Port, Guernsey. The role of the GFP was security work, including counter-espionage, counter-sabotage, detection of treasonable activities, counter-propaganda and to provide assistance to the German Army in courts martial investigations.

What came as a surprise to the GFP personnel was that the islanders were prepared to inform on one another. Immediately after the war it was suggested that they were isolated individuals; however, in the 1990s it was revealed that they were a substantial group. The motives for informing were extremely varied: the hope of personal gain, the wish to stand well with the Germans, fury at injustice in the distribution of food or the extraction of penalties, concealment of their own illegal activities and a wish to avoid being involved in reprisals. Interestingly, though these acts assisted the forces occupying the Channel Islands they were not covered by the Treason Act of 1940, and so after the war none of the informers were punished.

The most notorious example of the informer's work was that of a man called Paddy, who was a friend of Charles Machon, a newspaper printer on the *Guernsey Evening Star* and one of the producers of the underground newspaper *GUNS – Guernsey Underground News Service*. *GUNS* began publishing on 2 May 1942 and lasted until February 1944. It was a 13½in by 8in sheet with a heading bearing the illegal V-sign. Circulation reached about

300, but Paddy took copies of the newspaper that Machon had given to him to distribute directly to the GFP. Paddy was subsequently seen with the GFP when they raided Machon's house in St Peter Port. Members of the *GUNS* organisation were put on trial on 6 April 1944. Ernest Legg, Cyril Duquemin and Francis 'Frank' Falla were imprisoned in Frankfurt and Naumberg, where Charles Machon and Joseph Gillingham died.

On Jersey, as on Guernsey, women who walked out with the young occupiers were known as 'Jerrybags'; it was said that this was because of the distinctive quality handbags that their German boyfriends brought back from visits to France. Some had sexual relations and children were born. Documents released in 1996 suggested that there may have been 900 such babies. One of the documents referred to the Westaway Creche in St Helier as 'full up with those little bastards'. What became of them has remained a secret. Some are thought to be still living on the island. Guernsey had an illegitimacy rate of 5.4 per cent before the war, but the figure jumped to 21.8 per cent in 1944 and this statistic included both married and single women. The German garrison were not permitted to marry local girls, but after the war some men returned to the islands, married and settled.

When the islands were liberated there were was little of the brutal settling of scores that took place on mainland Europe. However, a number of families fled to the local police cells for their security. Some of the Jerrybaggers found themselves ostracised by their community and there were cases of women being pursued by angry crowds. One notorious informer on Jersey, Mme Baudains, known as 'Mimi the Spy', hid with her son in prison and then, in the face of considerable protests, in a convent, before escaping secretly to mainland Britain at 6.15 a.m. on 23 March 1946.

However, as in the rest of Occupied Europe, there was a good deal of 'live and let live'. In some cases, men found employment constructing the sea walls that doubled as anti-tank barriers or farming to produce food for the occupiers. The upper strata of the islands' society and the administration who had remained found it necessary to sustain a working relationship with the senior officers that over the years was not unfriendly. There were changes that were difficult to adjust to – children had to learn German in schools and road traffic drove on the right. But there was resistance – mostly passive.

Among the acts of resistance that could lead to a stint in prison, on the islands or in France, was owning a radio, painting 'V' for victory signs, hiding runaway slave workers or simply giving them food. To avoid arrest, and also to prevent workers being punished, islanders worked out ingenious ways of leaving food in locations hidden from the German overseers, where workers could discreetly retrieve it.

That there was no obvious organised resistance movement on the islands is easy to understand, not least because of the density of German troops; roughly one to every three civilians – a higher density than in Germany itself.

Confiscation of radios became a punishment and also a means of isolating the Channel Islanders from news about the war. The first time radios were confiscated was following the commando landings in late 1940. However, by Christmas that order had been rescinded. In June 1942, complete confiscation of radios was ordered – but there were exceptions. Irish residents, as neutrals, could retain their radios, as could German officials. Islanders who refused to hand over their radios ran the risk of three months' imprisonment and even death. Confiscation was in breach of the Hague Convention, but using rather twisted logic the Germans claimed that with modifications a receiver could be turned into a transmitter and cited Article 53.[1]

On Sark, when radios were confiscated someone pinned to a tree in the Avenue a list of all those who had not handed in their sets. The Commandant was informed of the notice, but, saying it was the work of a traitor, decided to ignore it. Sibyl Hathaway retained hers – hidden in a trunk behind luggage left by friends. The radio was wrapped in a moth-eaten carpet 'to which we added moths from time to time'. Ironically, the German doctor on Sark would leave his portable radio for her to listen to when he was on his rounds.

Concealing a radio and listening to the BBC news became a small but significant act of defiance. Radios were hidden under floorboards, in false cupboards, in the bottom of armchairs, unused water tanks, even bricked into walls. What the occupiers failed to realise was that crystal sets could be constructed – redundant telephone booths were raided for earpieces – and the components of the compact sets were easier to conceal.

All news had a propaganda slant. However, even if the news was grim the BBC emphasised patriotism and optimism, and for those who could only get their news through the cinemas on Jersey and Guernsey, *Die Deutsche Wochenschau*, the heavy-handed Nazi propaganda, was depressing.

The islands' cinemas were also a place where resistance could be shown. After 'The Funnies' came the German news *Die Deutsche Wochenschau*, and this was a cue for the civilians sitting in the designated left-hand section of the stalls to boo and catcall. In an attempt to catch the catcallers, guards were posted and the house lights would be switched on. This then became a cue for a mass exit to the cinema's lavatories. One of the most telling moments in the cinema was when the dramatic propaganda film *Sieg im Westen*[2] was shown in the islands' cinemas. When men of the BEF were seen on-screen – albeit as prisoners captured at Dunkirk – the civilian audience cheered.

The 'V' sign campaign, a passive resistance movement, had spread across Europe.[3] 'V' stood for victory, and Prime Minister Winston Churchill had popularised it with his cheeky 'V' sign. The repeated symbol was supposed to make Germans feel surrounded by a hostile resistance army. 'V' was painted over German signs and on houses, a reminder of island solidarity. The symbol was also incorporated into art and everyday objects. It was engraved in cups, stitched in clothes and embroidery and hidden in paintings. The 'V' took on an aural connotation as well; besides the BBC overseas news broadcasts, the Morse 'V' could be clapped or incorporated into hammering as a covert signal of defiance. Some of these subtle acts of resistance were passed over by German guards, but were tremendous morale-boosters for Channel Islanders. The risk was not small, however; people were fined or even served prison time for painting 'V' signs.

On 3 July 1941, a notice was published by *La Gazette Officielle* under the signature of Victor Carey, stating that anyone found guilty of marking any gate, wall or other place with the letter 'V' – 'or any other sign or any word or words calculated to offend the German authorities or soldiers' – would be fined £25; in today's values over £1,000. After this, a cartoon circulated depicting Carey in the role of Judas Iscariot – the betrayer of Jesus who committed suicide following the betrayal – hanging from a tree. On Jersey, a stonemason repairing the paving of the Royal Square incorporated a 'V' into the paving stones. This was later amended to refer to the Red Cross ship *Vega*. The addition of the date 1945 and a more recent frame has now transformed it into a monument.

One Guernsey woman, Mrs Winifred Green, who was a waitress at the Royal Hotel, was court martialled and sent to prison in Caen for four months in 1941 for uttering the words '*Heil* Churchill'. Here, Mrs Green joined Kathleen Le Norman and Mrs Kinnaird from Jersey, who were in prison for painting 'V' signs. With time on her hands, the enterprising Mrs Green borrowed a needle, and with a corner of a bed sheet produced an embroidered handkerchief – with the words '*Heil* Churchill, RAF, Caen Prison, 1941' and a 'V' sign. She then smuggled this incriminating piece of needlework back to Guernsey in the lining of her coat. Back at work at the Royal Hotel, she gained the nickname 'Mrs Churchill'.

In 1941, Edmund Blampied designed banknotes issued by the State of Jersey. When folded in a specific way, the design revealed a 'V' symbol. He created a series of postage stamps in 1942 which hid the initials 'GR' for 'Georgius Rex,' symbolising loyalty to Britain and King George VI.

Artists Claude Cahun and Suzanne Malherbe created rhythmic poems, critiques and anti-German fliers from BBC reports. They then distributed these by placing them in the pockets and on the chairs of German soldiers, and throwing them into cars and windows. In 1944, the pair were arrested and sentenced to death, although this sentence was never carried out.

Then things began to turn nasty.

In 1941, the British government started to intern 500 Germans living in neutral Persia (modern-day Iran), fearing German control or sabotage of Persian oilfields that were a vital strategic resource. Hitler responded by personally ordering the deportation of Channel Islanders as retribution. He stated that for every one German held by the British, ten islanders were to be deported. He asked for the names of any Iranians living on the islands – and surprisingly there was one. Negotiations involving Swiss Red Cross authorities delayed the deportation, or, as the Germans called it, 'evacuation'. Then, on 15 September 1942, an order was published under the signature of the *Feldkommandant Oberst* Friedrich Knackfuss in the *Jersey Evening Post* and the following day in the *Guernsey Evening Press*. It read:

> By order of Higher Authorities the following British subjects will be evacuated and transferred to Germany (a) Persons who have their permanent residence not on the Channel islands, for instance, those who have been caught here by

the outbreak of war (b) All those men not born on the Channel Islands and 16 to 70 years of age who belong to the English people, together with their families. Detailed instructions will be given by the *Feldkommandantur* 515.

The Berlin authorities had a somewhat deluded idea that the Channel Islands were a sort of British colony, and consequently the removal of these 'foreigners' would cause the least disruption. Hitler said that the homes and properties of the deportees should be distributed among islanders of French descent. As for the deportees, they were to be sent to camps in the Pripet marshes in Eastern Europe. There was a slight delay in the implementation of the deportation order because of departmental uncertainty and inter-departmental confusion, since the German Foreign Office as well as the *Wehrmacht* were jointly involved. Following protests by Alexander Coutanche, the marshalling and assembly of the deportees was undertaken by German soldiers, not the island's police.

On 16,18 and 29 September, a total of 1,186 people were deported from Jersey, and on the 26th and 27th 834 more were deported aboard the *Minotaur* from Guernsey and Sark.

Instructions for the deportees read grimly like those issued to European Jews who were destined for 'resettlement in the East'; in reality the gas chambers of Poland. The Channel Island deportees were to take with them 'warm clothes, solid boots, some provisions, meal dishes, drinking bowl and if possible a blanket'. They were told: 'Your luggage must not be heavier than you can carry, and must bear a label with your full address.'

On Sark, Mrs Julia Tremayne, who kept a secret record of the occupation, received a visit from Maj. John and Mrs Skelton, who had been among eleven people from the little island listed for deportation. They asked her to look after some jewellery and three letters. It was only when the couple failed to report at the harbour that the Germans realised that something was amiss. It was the Skeltons' dog, now agitated and running free, that led them to the major and his wife lying side by side in a corner of the Common. The old soldier was dead – he had stabbed himself in sixteen places. Mrs Skelton had attempted suicide but survived, and later returned to the island. Theirs would not be the only suicide attempts among the deportees. Such was the atmosphere of fear and suspicion on the island that Mrs Tremayne hid the letters, knowing that the Germans thought that Maj. Skelton worked for British Intelligence. Only after liberation were they delivered to their addressees.

On the larger islands, the departure of the deportees was one of the significant moments in the history of resistance to the German occupation. On Jersey, Arthur Kent recalled: 'Many ex-servicemen among the deportees proudly wore their war medals. I saw hats and parasols in the national colours. I saw families from the country drive up in farmer's vans, the horses gaily bedecked with ribbons.'

In an earlier deportation, the watching crowds at the harbour started singing 'There'll always be an England'. As the chorus swelled, the watchers heard the deportees aboard their ship joining the song. This was followed by 'Jersey, Jersey', and finally the voices of the two groups blended in the National Anthem.

Bob Le Sueur, a clerk on Jersey, recalled: 'Whatever scenes there had been at home, such as breaking down and tears, by the time they got to the quayside the stiff upper-lip was showing. It was almost as if it was a Bank Holiday, and the people who looked the glummest were the Germans.'

On Guernsey, Mrs Cortvriend watched the deportees depart:

> My heart ached as I saw so many whom I knew, some of them close friends, crossing the gangway. One little fellow of 6 held my hand until the last minute … I learnt, some weeks later, that he had contracted asthma as a result of being housed in damp and unhealthy premises.

The deportees now began a journey into the unknown. For many, their first destination was Dorsten, a former prisoner-of-war (POW) camp in the heart of the industrial Ruhr. They were not to know that this was only a staging post and they would be held here for only six weeks. The air was thick with fumes from local factories. While women and children were housed in a barrack block, the men were in wooden huts where holes in the floors and walls had been stuffed with cardboard. The accommodation was crude but the camp commandant, who had been well treated by the British when he was taken prisoner in the First World War, returned this kindness to the islanders. He used his own money to buy milk for the children, and though food was poor and in short supply he ensured that Red Cross food parcels were delivered promptly and that there was no pilfering. He was a small man who carried a large cavalry sabre – but to the grateful prisoners he was simply 'Rosy Joe'. The camp closed on 11 November 1942.

Single men were then sent to Laufen, a camp that had been set up in a *Schloss* – the former residence of the Archbishop of Salzburg – close to the town of Obendorf, where the iconic Christmas carol 'Silent Night, Holy Night' had first been performed on Christmas Eve 1818. Laufen produced a memorial volume, *The Bird Cage*, that was written in 1944 and published in 1945. The cover featured two cartoon birds on a barbed-wire perch; one moustachioed creature with a flat cap in the colours of the Union flag, the other a bespectacled and slightly ill-tempered creature with spectacles and the Stars and Stripes on its breast.

Since Laufen was for men only, it was possible to enforce clear rules, with a committee and internal discipline structure elected by the inmates. Frank Stroobant was the first commandant, but his place was taken by Ambrose Sherwill in June 1943. Sherwill was not popular, one internee describing him as a petty dictator who played on the fears and hatreds of the more timid internees. Ironically, it was the Germans who were more relaxed and accommodating. The commandant, *Oberst* Kochenberger, was 'a very decent German Colonel' who disliked the Nazis. His security *Hauptman* had spent years in America and there was a *Sonderführer* who had been educated in Midhurst, Sussex. The elderly German military doctor 'really did his best for the sick', coping with outbreaks of scarlet fever, typhoid and septicaemia caused by mosquitoes in the summer. The camp sergeant major, Ertl, earned the inmates' respect since he 'put up with a great deal more than any English NCO would have stood'. Perhaps most tellingly, the commandant knew that the inmates had built a radio and consequently could follow the course of the war in BBC news broadcasts, but warned them if the Gestapo were about to conduct a search.

The bulk of the deportees, married couples with children, were sent to Biberach in the Bavarian Alps, not far from Laufen and close to the Swiss border. It had been built as a POW camp and was surrounded by a high wire fence with observation towers. While this looked pretty grim, the deportees were to discover that the camp was well built in other ways. For the first time in their lives, they encountered windows that were double-glazed; however, the windows were peg-hinged so with the warm weather they were able to remove them completely and allow air to circulate freely. Each barrack had its own water, electricity and communal bathrooms. The deportees arrived in the height of summer and wondered why they had been told to bring warm clothing. As the fuel supply was restricted and the winter and spring proved particularly cold, they were grateful that they had struggled across Europe with their sweaters and overcoats.

Biberach would hold the bulk of the deportees sent from the islands in 1942 and 1943. Under Garfield Garland's leadership, the internal administration of the camp was efficient and, once a reliable supply of Red Cross food parcels had been established in the middle of 1943, it flourished with amateur dramatics, keep fit and educational classes. Perhaps appropriately, the camp was liberated on St George's Day, 23 April 1945. It took four weeks for the inmates to be interviewed by intelligence officers and issued with identity cards before they boarded USAAF Dakotas and flew home.

Wurzach, or Bad Wurzach, also housed families with children. It was a *Schloss* that had been a Catholic monastery, but the most recent inmates had been French Corsican POWs, who had left a disgusting mess that took a week to clear up. Accounts of life at Wurzach are conflicting. According to Asa Briggs in *The Channel Islands Occupation and Liberation 1940–1945*, 'there was a holiday atmosphere' in the camp. Peter King describes a less than effective internal organisation: 'The atmosphere in this camp, cramped by admissions of other categories of prisoners – like Jews – was the least satisfactory of all.'

Pat Holt recalled the surreal experience of being housed in this former *Schloss* and discovering a room with a beautifully painted ceiling. Friendships were struck up with the residents of the neighbouring village – a community that was described by Barry Turner as 'straight out of a Franz Lehar operetta – all church bells and ox wagons'. Pat Holt's father, who on the Channel Islands was a plumber and heating engineer, had such a good relationship with his opposite number in the village that he was able to borrow tools to clear blocked lavatories and repair the boiler.

The Jews referred to by King arrived in December 1944. There were thirty, who were Dutch by origin but had been spared the ghastly fate of many of their European counterparts because each of them had British grandparents, and in the skewed logic of the Nazis this made them partially British and therefore they were to be interned as 'enemy aliens' and not exterminated. To the islanders in Wurzach, their arrival was a shock. One remembered: 'They were really only skin and bone – very badly treated, very badly dressed.' The little group kept to themselves but confidence grew with the kindness of the islanders and the arrival of Red Cross food, and it was then that the British internees began to learn more about the concentration camps.

On Saturday 28 April 1945, Sherman tanks crewed by men of the Free French Army entered Bad Wurzach, with their guns traversed towards the *Schloss*, which the crews had been told was a German headquarters. The inmates were spared death or injury only by the prompt surrender of the men of the village *Volksturm*. These elderly residents emerged with white flags and, at 12.15 p.m., the first French tank reached the *Schloss*. There was a huge cheer from the inmates, who unfurled a Union flag from the balcony.

It is a bitter irony that the deportees had been receiving Red Cross parcels before the islanders, and as the Allies overran Germany they would be liberated before their friends and neighbours at home on the islands.

Other camps that held islanders were Spittal and Kreuzberg for men only, and Compiègne, which held 130 women, children and men aged over 64 until August 1943. The inmates of Compiègne were unable to send mail, and consequently for several months their friends and relatives had no idea of what had happened to them. The accommodation was grim and one woman had a nervous breakdown.

Some islanders were spared the full period of internment when, following negotiations through a third party, interned nationals were repatriated between Germany and the United Kingdom. There are conflicting versions of how this process was initiated. Charles Cruikshank, author of *The German Occupation of the Channel Islands*, says that it was the UK that made the first contacts in December 1943, proposing an exchange of 600 islanders, but according to Roger Harris in *Islanders Departed Part 1*, it was camp leaders like Stroobant and Hilton who raised the issue and discussions began in February 1944. Home Office bureaucracy intervened in the process, with civil servants asserting that Channel Islanders would not have a 'home' on mainland Britain and consequently other British nationals should have preferential treatment. Following questions in Parliament, 125 islanders were included in the second batch, arriving in Liverpool on 15 September 1944, with a second batch on 23 March 1945.

Though most of the internees were liberated and found their way home via mainland Britain, there were some who never saw VE Day. Some forty-six died in Germany. At Wurzach there were twelve deaths and they were buried in the local cemetery, where there is now a monument in Jersey stone. At Laufen ten deaths were recorded, while at Biberach there were twenty deaths that spanned the age range from a 2-year-old girl to a man of 74.

For the Germans, the presence of British men and women within the Reich was a propaganda asset they were keen to exploit. A Jersey man, 20-year-old John Lingsham, decided to side with the enemy and left Laufen to work for the *Büro Concordia*.[4] On 16 August 1943, he was released to travel to Berlin, where he taught English to a group of fifteen women working in the German propaganda service. He subsequently went on to work on minor duties for the New British Broadcasting Service unit of the *Reichs-Rundfunk-Gesellschaft*, the German State Radio, monitoring and recording the wartime news bulletins of the BBC. After the war, he was convicted under the Defence Regulations and served five years' penal servitude. He died in Sheffield in 1975.

When German soldiers uncovered in 1943 the mass graves at Katyn near Smolensk of over 20,000 Polish officers captured in 1939 by the Red Army, and who on the orders of Stalin had been executed by the *Narodnyi Komissariat Vnutrennikh Del* (NKVD), the news was used as a propaganda weapon to discredit the Soviet Union. In a drive to give the massacre maximum publicity and hopefully cause a split between the Soviet Union and Western Allies, the Nazis brought neutral observers and interned Allied nationals to the site. Two people were selected from the internees from the Channel Islands, Frank Stroobant and Wynne Sayer. They joined a party of foreigners who were transported to Smolensk, where they were well looked after and photographed before, after a few days, they were driven 15 miles to the woods at Katyn. After witnessing the grim sight of the bodies of Polish officers stacked up in mass graves, the party was driven back to Smolensk for a grand evening meal.

The islanders recalled that the diners seemed to include every English-speaking German east of the Rhine. One of them told Stroobant that he had been born in north London and was an Arsenal supporter. The conversation may have been an attempt to win over Stroobant and persuade him to enlist in the *Britisches Freikorps.* [5] Peter King identifies him as Dennis John, the son of a German baker in north London, who had visited Jersey. This man is probably 23-year-old *SS-Mann* Dennis John Leister of Camden Town, who would later serve three years' penal servitude for his membership of the *Britisches Freikorps.* He died in Stevenage in 1990.

Life under military rule on the islands became increasingly harsh for the civil population. On Sark, Tremayne noted: 'The walls are all posted with notices about what we are not to do, and it all ends with death penalties.' In August 1941, the *Guernsey Evening Post* published under the signature of the Bailiff, Victor Carey, the order:

> Attention is called to the fact that under the Order relative to protection against acts of sabotage, dated October 10th 1940, any person who hides or shelters escaped prisoners of war shall be punished with death. The same applies for the hiding or sheltering of members of enemy forces, for instance, crews of landing aircraft, parachutists etc. Anyone lending assistance to such persons in their escape is also liable to the death sentence.

Notes

1 Hague Convention Article 53: 'An army of occupation can only take possession of cash, funds, and realizable securities which are strictly the property of the State, depots of arms, means of transport, stores and supplies, and, generally, all movable property belonging to the State which may be used for military operations. All appliances, whether on land, at sea, or in the air, adapted for the transmission of news, or for the transport of persons or things, exclusive of cases governed by naval law, depots of arms, and, generally, all kinds of munitions of war, may be seized, even if they belong to private individuals, but must be restored and compensation fixed when peace is made.'

2 *Sieg im Westen* was produced by the OKH, the German Army High Command, rather than the Propaganda Ministry of Dr Joseph Goebbels. As such, the film did not attempt to belittle the French and British troops, who were described as fighting hard. The programme provided states that it is to show the audacity of the German offensive and the superiority of German arms, required because they will not be permitted to live in peace. It did not give Hitler or the Nazi party a central role, thus ensuring its disfavour with Goebbels.

3 On 14 January 1941, Victor de Laveleye, the former Belgian Minister of Justice and director of broadcasts on the BBC Belgique service (1940–1944), suggested in a broadcast that Belgians use a V for *victoire* (French for 'victory') and *vrijheid* (Dutch for 'freedom') as a rallying emblem. In the BBC broadcast, de Laveleye said that 'the occupier, by seeing this sign, always the same, infinitely repeated, [would] understand that he is surrounded, encircled by an immense crowd of citizens eagerly awaiting his first moment of weakness, watching for his first failure.' Indeed, within weeks, chalked-up Vs began appearing on walls throughout Belgium, the Netherlands and northern France.

By the summer of 1941, the emblematic use of the letter V had spread through occupied Europe, and on 19 July, Winston Churchill put the British government's stamp of approval on the V for Victory campaign in a speech, from which point he started using the V hand sign. Early on, he used it with the palm in (sometimes with a cigar between the fingers). It has been suggested that when the vulgar, almost obscene connotations of the V sign made with the palm facing inwards was pointed out to Churchill, he adopted a V sign with the palm outwards. The chances are that Churchill had a shrewd grasp of popular sentiment, and making a V sign in effect towards Nazi Germany was read as both defiant and insulting.

4 *Büro Concordia* was a 'black propaganda' operation that broadcast from radio stations within Germany and occupied Europe. The stations purported to be based within the United Kingdom and included among their staff Leonard Banning, Frank McLardy and, most famously or infamously, William Joyce, who became known to British listeners as Lord Haw Haw.

5 The *Britisches Freikorps* – British Free Corps – was a unit of the *Waffen-SS* recruited from British and Dominion POWs. The men were told that their enemy was the Soviet Union. The *Britisches Freikorps* was originally known as The Legion of St George. It came into existence in late 1943 and, like other foreign *Waffen-SS* units, had a distinctive arm shield, cuff title and collar insignia. However, at full strength there were only about fifty-nine men who belonged to this unit at one time or another, some for only a few days. In reality it had a strength of twenty-seven men, smaller than a contemporary German platoon. Though there are some reports of individuals fighting in the defence of Berlin in 1945 as a formation, it was too small to have any significant role other than propaganda.

3

INSELWAHN: ISLAND MADNESS, 1941–44

The fortification of the Channel Islands would become such an obsession with Hitler that, behind his back, senior officers described it as *Inselwahn* – island madness.

As early as May 1941, he ordered that the 319th Infantry Division be allocated to their defence and that the division should be reinforced with troops and weapons over and above the strength of a normal first line division (see Appendix IV). All this was confirmed on 20 October 1941, when Hitler issued the directive that laid down that the Channel Islands were to be converted into 'impregnable fortresses'.

The small area and confined roads on many of the islands did not make them ideal tank country – but as part of the defences of the islands the garrison was assigned its own tank battalion. The first armour to arrive were ex-French First World War vintage two-man Renault FT17 light tanks. Obsolete by even the 1930s, the tank was armed with an 8mm Hotchkiss machine gun in a fully rotating turret – the first armoured fighting vehicle (AFV) in the world to be so equipped. When Hitler published his Fortification Directive for the islands, it included sending heavier armour to reinforce the FT17s. These were captured French Char B1 bis; very different beasts, with a hull-mounted 75mm gun and turret-mounted 47mm gun and two machine guns. The tank was well armoured and had a top speed of 28km/h. Following conversion training, the men who crewed them were formed into *Panzer Abteilung* 213.

They had been told that they were to be posted to North Africa to reinforce the *Afrika Korps*, but instead were sent to the Channel Islands. In addition to tanks, self-propelled anti-tank guns, *4.7-cm Pak 36(t) auf GW Renault R35(f)*, were deployed on the islands; remarkably, there were two on Sark and one on Alderney. The vehicle was an amalgam of a French tank chassis with a Czech anti-tank gun in a box-like armoured superstructure. Following the liberation, one of the Char B1 bis was taken back to the United Kingdom and became part of the collection at the Bovington Tank Museum – but the tank is now back on the islands, on loan to the Jersey War Tunnels Museum.

Sometime before the Fortification Directive, experts of the German Army's Fortress Engineer Staff began conducting a tactical, geographical and geological survey to determine the requirements for the anticipated fortification programme (see Appendix I). In the course of this survey, it was soon realised that the proximity of the Channel Islands to France meant that by placing artillery batteries of sufficient range on the islands, as well as on the French coast, it would be possible to seal off the entire Bay of St Malo and thus dispense with the need to heavily fortify many kilometres of the adjacent French coastline. Shortly afterwards, the *Organisation Todt*[1] (OT) arrived in the islands with all their construction equipment and a work-force consisting of thousands of foreign workers, either voluntary or forced labour. Eventually some 16,000 OT workers would come to the islands. In November 1941, Dr Fritz Todt himself visited the islands to inspect the construction programme. He issued construction orders identifying the following areas of responsibility:

1. Individual troops – field fortifications (trenches, foxholes etc.).
2. Divisional Engineers – distribution of landmines and flame throwers.
3. Army Construction Battalions – reinforced field order defences.
4. Fortress Engineers/Construction Battalions – supplying and installing fortress weapons, some tunnelling, transport of heavy loads, compiling construction progress reports and maps, ordering and supervising O.T. tasks.
5. *Organisation Todt* – quarrying, construction of roads, power stations, most tunnelling, supervising civilian building firms, sea transport, controlling non-military labour and building fortress standard defences.

Work on the fortifications was designated Operation Adolf on Alderney, Gustav on Guernsey and Jakob on Jersey.

Hitler decreed that 10 per cent of the steel and concrete used in the Atlantic Wall, the coastal defences that ran from the border with Spain to the North Cape in Norway, should go to the Channel Islands. The plans called for 414 reinforced concrete structures for Guernsey, 234 for Jersey and 153 for Alderney. Tunnels and underground chambers would provide 50,000 square metres (m^2) of cover, while 20,000m of anti–tank walls and field railways would protect and serve the islands.

It was a tough objective, but at the height of operations in May 1943, 25,500 cubic metres (m^3) of rock had been excavated; in September that year, 40,881m^3 of reinforced concrete had been produced. By the end of the war, the defences had consumed over 613,000m^3 of concrete. Underground tunnels and galleries were constructed for ammunition storage and as shelters. On Jersey, 23,495m^2 were excavated, 19,216m^2 on Guernsey and 4,795m^2 on Alderney. In 1944, when construction stopped, 244,000m^3 of rock had been extracted collectively from Guernsey, Jersey and Alderney (the majority from Jersey). At the same point in 1944, tunnelling work on the entire Atlantic Wall, excluding the Channel Islands, had extracted only 225,000m^3.

Narrow gauge railway tracks were laid in Jersey and Guernsey to move construction material and hard core from quarries to fortification sites, and to supply them. In Jersey, a 1m-gauge line was laid following the route of the former Jersey Railway from St Helier to La Corbière, with a branch line connecting the stone quarry at Ronez in St John. A 60cm line ran along the west coast, and another was laid heading east from St Helier to Gorey. The first line was opened on 15 July 1942. The ceremony was witnessed by Leslie Sinel, who recalled that, with a band playing, the Commandant blew a whistle and the engine, after a couple of attempts to get away, began its journey after a decorated tape had been cut. The front of the locomotive was decorated with a large cut-out *Reichsadler* eagle and swastika flag. The proceedings ended with a grand dinner at the Pomme d'Or Hotel. Afterwards, islanders were reprimanded for their frivolous behaviour when the German national anthem was played. For local Jersey children, the tracks were an irresistible target for strategically placed stones – though whether this caused any derailments is unknown.

The Alderney Railway was built by the British government in the 1840s and opened in 1847. Its original purpose was to carry stone from the eastern end of the island to build the breakwater and the forts. It was taken over by the Germans, who lifted part of the standard-gauge line and replaced it with a 1m-gauge line, worked by two Feldbahn 0-4-0 diesel locomotives. Today, restored to standard gauge, it is the only working railway on the Channel Islands.

On Jersey, coastal *Panzermauern*, or anti-tank walls, were installed where defensively weak points had been identified. The builders of the Atlantic Wall had realised that the seawall at Dieppe had effectively prevented the Canadian Churchill tanks from driving off the beach during the abortive landing on 17 August 1942, and so they built bigger versions as anti-tank obstacles. In the case of the west coast of Jersey, there were some 5 miles of open beach backed by dunes and farmland to defend, and here the forced and slave workers built five distinct sections of *Panzermauern*, PzM 1–PzM 5. The walls were covered with barbed wire, and at points where they offered clear fields of fire, embrasures for anti-tank guns were incorporated.

Staggering numbers of mines were laid. In April 1944, there were 54,000 on Guernsey, Jersey had 39,000 and even little Sark had 4,500, while Alderney – which had been cleared of most of its civilian population – had over 30,000 mines. It was these minefields that would be the undoing of two commando raids on the Channel Islands.

Perhaps the most sinister part of this programme was on the now almost depopulated island of Alderney. Here, four camps were built to house the labourers. They were satellite camps of the Neuengamme concentration camp outside Hamburg and were named after the Frisian Islands, becoming *Lager* (camps) Nordeney, Borkum, Sylt and Helgoland. The camps commenced operating in January 1942 and had a total inmate population of about 6,000.

Borkum and and Helgoland were for 'volunteer' workers, a misnomer since most of these were men who had been conscripted from occupied countries and sent to work in Germany or occupied Europe. Sylt was a true concentration camp that held a mix of German political prisoners, some arrested as early as 1933 and including a few leading communists, homosexuals, artists and those opposed to the regime, along with a relatively large number of Jehovah's Witnesses and Freemasons and several former Gestapo officials arrested for 'anti-social behaviour'. The remainder was made up of a sprinkling of German Jews and Russian prisoners of war, and according to some sources about fifty *Wehrmacht* officers arrested for black marketeering. Little remains of *Lager* Sylt today except some concrete sentry posts, the tunnel that ran from the commandant's house to the outside of the camp and the camp gateposts, on which a plaque has been fixed that reads: 'These gate posts mark the entrance to the former German Concentration Camp "S.S. Lager Sylt". Some 400 prisoners died here between March 1943 and June 1944. This plaque was placed here by ex-prisoners and their families 2008.'

The islands had a total of sixteen coastal defence batteries, as well as heavy and light flak positions. The most powerful guns were at the *Batterie Mirus* on Guernsey, which consisted of four Russian 30.5cm guns located at La Frie Baton on the west of the island. The construction of the battery position had consumed 45,000m³ of concrete. With Wurzburg radar target location, the guns could engage ships at ranges up to 32km (26 miles) and before D-Day ships of the Royal Navy would test the reaction times of the crew in a high-risk game of 'cat and mouse'. The battery had originally been named *Batterie Nina*; however, it was later renamed Mirus after *Kapitän-zur-See* Rolf Mirus, who was killed in action on 3 November 1941 aboard *Flugsicherunggsboot* 502 travelling to Alderney from Guernsey.

The guns were protected by bunkers, field fortifications and nine flak towers with 2cm anti-aircraft guns. While parts of the battery – like the fire control centre, ammunition stores and accommodation – were concealed underground beneath thick layers of reinforced concrete, the guns themselves were given a camouflaged protection that made them look like farm buildings or holiday bungalows.

How the 30.5cm guns came to be in Guernsey is a convoluted tale. They were designed by Schneider-Carnet of Le Creusot, France, and cast at the Putilov Arsenal in Reval (Tallinn), Estonia, in 1914 to become the main armament for a dreadnought of the Imperial Russian Black Sea Fleet, the *Imperator Aleksandr III*. The ship had been laid down at the Nikolaieff yard in August 1911, launched on 15 April 1914 and completed in June 1917. She was renamed the *Volya* after the Russian Revolution, and by September 1918 – with a German crew – was part of the defence of the Dardanelles.

She was returned to the Russians in November of that year, only to fall into Allied hands during the war with the Bolsheviks. *Volya* then became the flagship of the White Fleet, being renamed *General Alexeiev*. After several voyages, the fleet reached French-administered Bizerta in North Africa in mid-February 1921, where the ships were abandoned. Despite the Soviets demanding the return of the dreadnought, the French government decided to offset costs of new armaments by selling the greater part of the fleet.

Eventually the *General Alexeiev* was sold for scrap to the Kliaguine Company in 1928, laying up for three more years before finally being broken up for scrap. The twelve 30.5cm and eighteen 13cm guns were then placed in storage in Sidi-Abdullah in 1935, with the aim to return them to Russia. Kliaguine expressed an interest in selling the guns to Finland in September 1939, at the outbreak of the Russo-Finnish War. On 4 January, with an agreement reached with Helsinki, three Finnish cargo boats arrived at Bizerta, each to take on four of the twelve 30.5cm guns. The first eight arrived in Finland, but the remaining four never reached their intended destination at Petsamo. The last cargo vessel, the *Nina*, after which the Guernsey battery would be named, sailed for Genoa on 26 February and reached Norwegian waters on 11 March. The guns were still on board the *Nina* when the German Army overran Norway the following month. They were unloaded at Bergen and shipped to Friedrich Krupp A.G. at Essen, where extensive work was undertaken to refurbish and overhaul them. New ammunition was manufactured by Krupp and then the guns began their journey to Guernsey.

The other large-calibre guns on the islands, 15cm (6in), were mounted in either armoured turrets or open-topped reinforced concrete pits. This gave them a 360° traverse and meant that that fire from guns on Guernsey interlocked with those on Jersey and Alderney. Those on Jersey could engage shipping running along the west coast of the Cotentin Peninsula as it passed Carteret, while the guns on Alderney could actually hit mainland France around Cap de la Hague.

At the other end of the calibre scale, the defences had the unusual M19 *Maschinengranatwerfer*, or automatic mortar. The weapon was sited in an R-633 bunker that had six rooms, three for the M19 equipment and three for the fourteen men who made up the weapon crew and local defence. What made the M19 lethally effective was its rate of fire; manually, the crew could fire sixty grenades a minute – with the electrically powered loading system in operation, this rate jumped to 120 a minute, though this was only to be used in an emergency. Standard ammunition storage inside an R-633 was 3,944 rounds. Four M19 mortars were sited on Guernsey, one on Jersey and two on Alderney.

The Channel Islands were a tri-service command, and while the role of the *Luftwaffe* diminished as the tide of war moved against Nazi Germany, shipping – both commercial and armed ships of the *Kriegsmarine* – would play a significant role in the supply and defence of the islands until the end of the war.

Headquarters of the German Naval Commander Channel Islands (*Seeko-Ki*) were originally established in Guernsey in the summer of 1942 at the neighbouring La Collinette and La Porte Hotels. Radio communications were a vital part of operations at *Seeko-Ki* headquarters, and the powerful radio transmitters and receivers were first housed in the loft of La Collinette Hotel before the decision was taken to build the permanent bunkers in the hotel grounds. Work began in the autumn of 1943 and the signals headquarters, under the command of the Naval Signals Officer (MNO), *Oberleutnant* Willi Hagedorn, was operative on 1 February 1944. The adjoining *Seeko-Ki* bunker, linked by a short tunnel, and detached generator bunker were completed at a later date. The MNO headquarters handled all the important radio signals traffic for the German forces in the Channel Islands, especially after the Allied landings in Normandy. Messages were transmitted and received by naval codes using the Enigma enciphering machines on a variety of frequencies, operating under the station call sign 'Flu'. The bulk of traffic passed through Naval Headquarters in Paris and, during the final months of the war, linked directly with Berlin.[2]

This ability to talk to Berlin in the last months of the war would mean a shift in the balance of power on this islands, as Graf von Schmettow was replaced in February 1945 by 47-year-old Vice-Admiral Friedrich Hüffmeier, a former captain of the battle cruiser KMS *Scharnhorst* and, unusually for the *Kriegsmarine*, a fanatical Nazi.

Notes

1 The state construction organisation established in 1938 and named after its dynamic director, Fritz Todt. OT built military facilities in Germany and occupied Europe. Much of the work was of a very high standard, and motorways, air raid shelters and fortifications remain as mute tributes to German engineers and their enslaved labour force. Major OT projects included the *Reichsautobahn* motorways, the *Westwall* fortifications on Germany's border with France and later the Atlantic Wall, the coastal fortifications that stretched from the North Cape of Norway to the Bay of Biscay.

2 The Enigma was a highly sophisticated mechanical encryption system that had a keyboard and looked superficially like a typewriter. The German engineer Arthur Scherbius developed it in 1923 from a design by a Dutchman H.A. Koch, the German Army and Navy saw its potential and bought it in 1929. The Germans firmly believed that it was completely secure. In its simplest form for every letter it sent there were hundreds of millions of possible solutions. However, the Germans forgot that there are a finite number of letters in the alphabet; that no letter could stand for itself; and that the machine had no number keys so that figures had to be spelled out. The Polish intelligence services began reading some signals in 1932, the French in 1938 and the British in February 1940. For the British, the secrecy of the project was at such a high level – beyond 'top secret' – that they classified it as 'ultra secret', and so the operation became simply Ultra.

4

COMMANDOS AND RAIDERS, 1940–45

On 4 June 1940, immediately after the Fall of France and the evacuation of the BEF from Dunkirk, the newly appointed British Prime Minister, Winston Churchill, demanded that a volunteer raiding force should be formed to take the war back to newly occupied Europe.

For many British servicemen, the withdrawal from France and evacuation at Dunkirk had been a humiliation that was compounded by the subsequent *Luftwaffe* air attacks on Britain in 1940 and 1941 that hit civilian as well as military and industrial targets, and there was a real desire among the armed forces to take some kind of offensive action.

In a memo written on Tuesday 4 June 1940, Churchill proposed that these raiding forces be formed. They were initially called 'striking companies' but Churchill said they should be called 'commandos', a name he took from his experiences in the South African (Boer) War.

In the South African War of 1899–1902 between Afrikaans-speaking Boers and British and Imperial forces, both sides used cavalry and mounted infantry for patrolling and raids. Boer militia forces were grouped into 'commandos', a word taken from the Portuguese, and as the weight of numbers and improved British tactics forced the Boers onto the defensive, their commandos adopted guerrilla tactics. The tough Boers, who were excellent shots and good horsemen, sustained the war despite terrible hardships. The Boer civilian population, who had provided support, were moved into concentration camps by the British, who used a system of block houses and barbed-wire fences along railway tracks to restrict the movement of the commandos. By May 1902, these ruthless tactics had worked and the Boers sued for peace.

The young Winston Churchill, working as a war correspondent, had been captured by the Boers in 1899 and subsequently escaped. His admiration for his tough adversaries would include a lasting friendship with a former Boer commando leader, soldier and South African statesman, General Jan Smuts.

The Director of Military Operations and Plans, Maj. General R.H. Dewing, drafted the memorandum that would set the style for the new commandos. They would be largely based on Commands – the military regional administrative areas in the UK. The memo read: 'One or two officers in each Command will be selected as commando Leaders. They will be instructed to select from their own Commands a number of Troop Leaders to serve under them. The Troop Leaders will in turn select the officers and men to form their own Troop.'

Though many men in the pre-war Regular Army had lived by the adage 'Keep your eyes open, mouth shut and never volunteer for anything', they were among the first volunteers for the new force. Clifford Leach, who would later serve with F Troop No. 4 Commando, admitted that after volunteering, 'I didn't quite know what I had let myself in for.' Ken Phillott, a soldier with the Gloucestershire Regiment (Glosters), saw on battalion orders that 'volunteers were wanted for Special Duties'. He recalled: 'This seemed to offer something different, although I had no idea what these Special Duties would be. I informed my Company Commander that I wished to volunteer.'

Brigadier John Durnford-Slater, who was tasked with raising No. 3 Commando, recalled that while it was hard to judge a man in the course of a short interview:

On the whole the type I looked for was the quiet, modest type of Englishman, who knew how to laugh and how to work … What I was seeking and what I obtained were men of character beyond the normal. I considered that morale was the most important single factor making for success in war; that is the spirit that makes men strive and endure.

Training was initially undertaken at unit level, but at this stage in the war resources were limited and so in February 1942 the Commando Training

Centre (CTC) was established at Achnacarry castle in the Scottish Highlands. Under the command of Lieutenant Colonel Charles 'Charlie' Vaughan, it was responsible for training complete units and individual replacements. The training regime was, for the time, innovative and physically demanding, and far in advance of normal British Army training. Vaughan, a veteran of the First World War, remembered how men arriving in the front-line trenches of the Western Front sometimes quickly became casualties simply because they had not been properly trained at depots in Britain.

As soon as an intake of commando volunteers had de-trained at Spean Bridge railway station, they went straight off on an 8-mile (13km) speed march, carrying their weapons and kit to Achnacarry. When they arrived they were met by Vaughan, who stressed the physical demands of the course and that any man who failed to live up to the requirements would be 'returned to unit' (RTU). For anyone volunteering for Special Forces, to be RTU'd was then, and still is, the ultimate punishment

Exercises at CTC were conducted using live ammunition and explosives to make training as realistic as possible. There were inevitably injuries and deaths, but this was accepted as a price worth paying in wartime. Physical fitness was a prerequisite, with cross-country speed marching and close combat training including knife fighting techniques. Crossing the assault course with toggle rope bridges,[1] aerial ropeways, tunnels and walls was made more realistic with explosives charges being detonated close to the soldiers. Training was conducted by day and night in all weathers, and included river crossings, mountain climbing, weapons training, map reading and assault boat handling. Each course ended with the 'opposed landing' exercise, a simulated night beach landing using live ammunition, in which the instructors fired tracer ammunition close to the soldiers as they paddled their assault boats towards the shore.

On 12 October 1942, in a speech in Edinburgh about occupied Europe, Churchill gave the commandos a powerful endorsement:

The British commando raids at different points along this enormous coast, although so far only the forerunner of what is to come, inspire the author of so many crimes and miseries with a lively anxiety. His soldiers dwell among populations who would kill them with their hands if they got the chance, and will kill them one at a time when they do get the chance. In addition there comes out from the sea from time to time a hand of steel which plucks the German sentries from their posts with growing efficiency, amid the joy of the whole countryside.

At the same time that commandos were being raised, there was a drive to break down the long-standing barriers between the Royal Navy, Army and RAF and to conduct combined operations (combined ops). A combined operations headquarters was established under the dynamic leadership of 69-year-old Admiral of the Fleet Sir Roger Keyes, the hero of the Zeebrugge raid of the First World War. He held the post from July 1940 to October 1941, when, following a disagreement with the British Chiefs of Staff, he was replaced by Admiral Lord Louis Mountbatten.

Sir Roger Keyes stands out as the champion of the commandos in the face of War Office hostility at a very difficult period in the war, and so in effect can be described as the father of British Special Forces. 'Time spent in his company made one feel twice one's size; and that, of course is what leadership is all about,' wrote Lord Lovat, who would serve with distinction as a commando officer throughout the Second World War. 'He was, like most genuine people, a very uncomplicated man, with straightforward beliefs and simple views on life. Old Sir Roger had none of the devious ways which can pass for cleverness today. To let him down was unthinkable.'

Keyes' oldest son, Lieutenant Colonel (Lt Col) Geoffrey Keyes, would be awarded a posthumous VC for his part in Operation Flipper, a commando raid on 18 November 1941 in Libya that was intended to kill the commander of the *Africa Korps*, General Erwin Rommel. The raid failed in part because of poor intelligence – the building identified as the general's HQ was in fact a base for logistic troops.

Admiral Keyes' successor, the urbane, ambitious and well-connected 41-year-old Mountbatten, had served in the Royal Navy in the First World War and was the great-grandson of Queen Victoria.

At the outbreak of the war, Mountbatten had commanded the 5th Destroyer Flotilla and took part in the evacuation of Norway in 1940. As captain of the destroyer HMS *Kelly*, he had brought the severely damaged ship back to England at the end of the campaign. In April 1941, he was sent to Malta and saw action off Crete. HMS *Kelly* was finally sunk in air attacks on 23 May 1941 to the south of the island. Churchill then appointed him adviser on combined operations and he undertook the preliminary planning of the invasion of Europe. In March 1942, Churchill made him a member of the Chiefs of Staff Committee. The historian in Churchill loved the idea of an aristocratic fighting sailor, and with his good looks and flair for self-publicity Mountbatten enjoyed a very high public profile.

Mountbatten's exploits as skipper of the *Kelly* would be the basis of Noël Coward's film *In Which We Serve*, which was in production in England in the summer of 1942. Royal connections and his exploits had helped to make Mountbatten a familiar name in the USA, a country that had entered the war following the Japanese attack on Pearl Harbor on 7 December 1941. Though he had charm and diplomatic skills, and General Dwight Eisenhower was among his admirers, he also had his critics during the war amongst senior officers and afterwards amongst historians.

Nigel Hamilton, in his authorised biography of Field Marshal Montgomery, would write of Mountbatten:

> As Chief of Combined Operations he was a master of intrigue, jealousy, and ineptitude. Like a spoilt child he toyed with men's lives with an indifference to casualties that can only be explained by his insatiable, even psychopathic ambition … a man whose mind was an abundance of brilliant and insane ideas often without coherence or consistent 'doctrine'. Allied to the equally undisciplined, wildly imaginative Churchill – with whom Mountbatten would often stay for weekends – the two made a formidable and dangerous pair.

Between them, Churchill and Mountbatten would hatch plans for operations against the Channel Islands that, had they been realised, would almost certainly have seen a huge loss of military and civilian lives for no tactical or strategic gain, and the islands would have been bombed and blasted almost into extinction.

Writing when Mountbatten was still alive, Lord Lovat said of the chief of combined operations: 'Mountbatten was the cheerful extrovert who had been lucky at sea.' With hindsight, this reads very much like 'damning with faint praise'.

However, before Mountbatten took command to reinforce the spirit of co-operation between the services in combined operations, a distinctive red and dark blue flash had been designed. It featured the anchor for the Royal Navy, the recently introduced Thompson sub-machine gun (SMG) for the army and the RAF eagle. With small modifications, this insignia lives on today.

In 1943, with the combined operations philosophy well-established and several successful commando raids accomplished, His Majesty's Stationery Office (HMSO) published *Combined Operations*, a heavily illustrated paperback. Written by Hilary St George Saunders, who was serving as a recorder on Mounbatten's staff, it detailed the exploits under the combined operations command, including the formation of Independent Companies, Special Service Battalions and commandos, their training and use on operations including the Channel Islands, Bruneval, Lofoten Islands, Saint-Nazaire, North Africa (Layforce) and Dieppe. It was and remains a masterful example of wartime propaganda, designed to raise morale and show to the British that there was an élite force that was taking the war to the enemy.

Both the army and later the Royal Marines formed commandos, which were the permanent ground forces of combined operations. The commando units that were initially raised were numbered Nos 1 to 9, 11 and 12. Perhaps unsurprisingly, a No. 13 Commando was never formed.

They were later joined by a unique force with the same title. No. 10 Inter-Allied (IA) Commando was a formation that included anti-Nazi German personnel and other troops drawn from German-occupied countries. It had a British-staffed HQ and of the eight troops, Nos 1 and 8 were French, No. 2 Dutch, No. 3 German, Austrian, Hungarian and Czech – mostly Jews who had been given Anglicised names – No. 6 was Polish and No. 7 Yugoslav.

The origins of No. 10 Commando are shrouded in some mystery. It was officially formed in January 1942 and its first Commanding Officer (CO), fresh from commanding No. 4 Commando, was the colourful Lt Col Dudley Lister.

The French troops in No. 10 Commando were under the command of Alsace-born Marine Captain Philippe Kieffer and made up Nos 1 and 8 troops and a K-gun (.303 gas-operated light machine gun) Section of No. 9 troop. Fifteen French marines and officers, all originally from *1er Bataillon Fusilier Marine*, from the original soldiers of No. 10 Commando would play a significant part in the Dieppe operation, and four would provide invaluable assistance for No. 4 Commando.

No. 30 Commando was an inter-service intelligence-gathering formation. In 1942, the three Royal Marine Commandos were formed, numbering 40, 41 and 48. All army and Marine commandos were part of four Special Service Brigades that were in turn controlled by a Special Service Group. The title Special Service would be changed to Commando in 1944, in part because the letters 'SS' were associated with the *Schutzstaffel* – the Nazi political and military organisation – but also because in the US Army the Special Services were an entertainment and recreational organisation similar to the British Entertainments National Service Association (ENSA).

In the British Army today, the Parachute Regiment and SAS (Special Air Service), and in the Royal Marines the SBS (Special Boat Service), can all trace their origins back to the formation of the army commandos. Of the Western nations represented in No. 10 (Inter-Allied) Commando, only Norway did not develop a commando force. The French troops are the predecessors of the *Commandos Marine*, the Dutch troops of the *Korps Commandotroepen* and the Belgian troops of the *Paracommando Brigade*.

By 1942, the commandos were a force of between 460 and 500 men (about the size of a modern British Army infantry battalion), commanded by a lieutenant colonel and divided into six troops. Five were fighting troops of about sixty men, backed by a headquarters troop with attached heavy weapons. Weapons were largely those found within a British infantry battalion, though there was a wider distribution of automatic and specialised weapons and equipment was issued for specific operations.

The size and structure of the commandos and their role was not the only thing that set them apart from the army. George Cook, who served in F Troop of No. 4 Commando, recalled the different style of discipline and leadership:

> You'd volunteered for the commandos, they realised that you were human beings and you had a bit of sense, that you didn't need to be roared at and shouted at, screamed at all the time. Not only that, if you did anything, even in training, everything was explained to you. If you'd a different idea, even as a lowly Private, you could say 'Well, sir, don't you think if we went that way

instead of this way it would be easier?' If you were right that was the method that was adopted.

John Price from No. 4 Commando recalled: 'What I liked about the commandos after the ordinary infantry, we were allowed to have some common sense. We were allowed to show initiative. We were briefed before we went into action, not herded like sheep.'

In 1942, No. 62 Commando was established. It would be better known as the Small-Scale Raiding Force (SSRF) and consisted of a small group of fifty-five commando-trained personnel working under the Special Operations Executive (SOE),[2] but under operational control of Combined Operations Headquarters. No. 62 Commando itself was under the command of Maj. Gustavus 'Gus' March-Phillipps DSO, OBE. The driving force behind the SSRF was three remarkable men: 34-year-old March-Phillips, Maj. J. Geoffrey Appleyard DSO, MC, and Captain Graham Hayes MC.

Appleyard, or 'Apple', the son of a Yorkshire motor engineer, was an extraordinary man with a deep religious faith, strong convictions and dedication to winning the war. He said to a friend: 'It is not enough to do our duty. We must do more than our duty – everything we can, to the absolute limit.' Writing to his father, he said:

> I think we set out on these excursions very much in the spirit of Cromwell's injunction – 'Put your trust in God, and keep your powder dry.' We'll do everything humanly possible to make them successful, and after that, we'll put our trust in God, and in our belief in the righteousness of what we are striving for and in our cause.

He had been a champion skier and oarsman, and had earned a First in engineering at Cambridge. The nationals of many countries were recruited into the SSRF, including French, Poles, Dutch and Czechs. Some with German-sounding names were given new identities, or 'war names'. Many had initially been obliged to enlist in the Pioneer Corps as their only route into the British Army, and with it a chance to strike back at Nazi Germany.

In its short career, the SSRF enjoyed some significant triumphs, but a raid on Sark would be the trigger for Hitler's notorious 'Commando Order'.

On 20 March 1942, having driven down to Dorset, Appleyard and March-Phillips chose as their headquarters the secluded Anderson Manor, near Blandford Forum, since it was close to the ports of Poole, Portsmouth and Portland. The elegant Elizabethan house was large enough to accommodate thirty officers and men, but its rural tranquillity would change almost overnight with the building of:

> a pistol and tommy-gun range in the rear garden and a grenade range in a pit to the north of the house. An assault course was built among the trees in the drive and across the river. The cherub that used to adorn the fountain in the courtyard was an obvious target for pistols and other weapons and suffered as a result. Poole Harbour, the Dorset coast, the hills, heaths and forests of Purbeck became the training grounds for the Commandos. (www.andersonmanor.co.uk)

The SSRF now teamed up with Coastal Command, whose Motor Torpedo Boats (MTBs) were very fast and relatively quiet when running on auxiliary engine power only. This helped to minimise detection at sea and when close to hostile shores.[3]

Success depended on competence in the use of small boats inshore, particularly the dory – often the boat of preference. The dory is a small lightweight, shallow-draft boat, about 5–7m (16½–23ft) long, with high sides, a flat bottom and sharp bows. They are easy to build because of their simple lines. A typical SSRF raiding party was around eight to ten in strength, sometimes fewer.

In 1941, what would become the SSRF was called 'Maid Honor Force', after a Brixham trawler requisitioned by March-Phillips. It was converted for the clandestine transportation of weaponry. *Maid Honor* took five men to West Africa in August 1941, where they monitored enemy U-boat and surface ship movements. Other members of the group, which numbered thirteen in total, came by commercial liner in two parties. The climax was Operation Postmaster in January 1942, in which the Italian liner *Duchessa d'Aosta* and the German tug *Likomba* were boarded and towed from the neutral Spanish island of Fernando Po and taken to Nigeria. The success of Postmaster led to the expansion of the force and its redesignation as the Small-Scale Raiding Force.

The SSRF had mixed fortunes in its raids. Barricade and Dryad were complete successes. Aquatint on 12/13 September 1942, at Saint-Honorine on the Normandy coast, an area that would later be known as Omaha Beach, resulted in the loss of all the men involved, including March-Phillipps. The Germans, alert following the disastrous raid on Dieppe in August that year, intercepted the group and also opened fire on the MTB waiting offshore with Appleyard aboard. The men on the boat were obliged to move away and the outcome of the raid was that of the eleven men who landed, none returned. Three were dead, two were seriously wounded and four escaped. Two were captured unhurt. At the time, all the party offshore could hear was gunfire. It was devastating for Appleyard, who had lost many close friends. Following Aquatint, he took command of the SSRF.

On 15 December 1942, Appleyard was awarded the Distinguished Service Order (DSO). On meeting the now Temporary Maj. Appleyard at his third investiture in eleven months (he had been awarded the Military Cross (MC) for Operation Postmaster and a bar to the MC), King George VI was both amused and impressed, greeting him with: 'What, you again?' Most of the SSRF was sent to Algeria at the end of 1942, where it made up an important part of David Stirling's new formation, 2 SAS. Appleyard himself was reported missing in action (MIA) while returning in an aircraft that had dropped men of 2 SAS in Operation Chestnut in 1943. He was 27. His care for the men under his command was typical. Veteran special forces leader Maj. (later Col) Vladimir Peniakov, commander of Popski's Private Army (No. 1 Demolition Squadron PPA), said of Appleyard: 'He was one of the few officers who had developed the technique of the small-scale raid: the care he took of his men made him stand out among brother officers who were too excited by the prospect of adventure to think of anybody but their own selves.'

One member of the Aquatint raid, Captain Graham Hayes MC, managed to travel through France and made his way towards Spain. He was betrayed by a French double agent and handed to the Germans. After nine months' solitary confinement in Fresnes Prison, he was executed on 13 July 1943. On the same day that Hayes was executed, his great friend and co-founder of the SSRF, Geoffrey Appleyard, was lost over Sicily.

In many ways, commando operations could be characterised as the amphibious equivalent of the trench raids and fighting patrols of the First

World War. They kept the enemy on edge, gathered low-level intelligence and sustained British and Allied morale. While some commando raids were on a small scale, many were quite large-scale conventional attacks – albeit by élite troops – and some of the intelligence relating to Ultra that they gathered on the raids was literally 'war winning'.

Army commandos – like other Special Forces formations – would be disbanded at the end of the Second World War. However, the Royal Marines would continue the tradition and keep alive the challenge of winning the commando green beret.

Notes

1 A toggle rope was part of the standard equipment of Allied commandos during the Second World War. It was a thick cord 6ft (1.8 m) long, with a wooden toggle at one end in a tightly fitting eye splice, with a larger eye at the other end. This allowed them to be looped together to make a simple bridge or ladder or to secure around a bundle for hauling.

2 The SOE was created in 1940 when British military fortunes were at their lowest. Hugh Dalton, Minister of Economic Warfare, proposed in a paper, 'A new organization shall be formed forthwith to co-ordinate all action, by way of subversion and sabotage, against the enemy overseas.'

   The SOE was divided into three branches: SO1 (propaganda), SO2 (active operations) and SO3 (planning). The character of SOE operations largely reflected the conditions of the German occupation. It was seriously hazardous work, requiring a special breed of men and women. For example, 'F' section (France) of SOE is estimated to have lost about 25 per cent of the some 480 agents parachuted into France in the latter part of the Second World War. These were men and women selected for their linguistic skills and possible contacts in the area in which they might be operating. Like many other Allied special forces or covert organisations, it was disbanded in 1946.

3 In 1989, a service of remembrance was held in the St Michael's Chapel, Anderson, and a plaque unveiled. The service was attended by surviving members of the SSRF and family representatives of those who were killed in action or who had subsequently died.

5

OPERATIONS ANGER AND AMBASSADOR, 15 JULY 1940

On 2 July 1940, Churchill sent a memo to General Hastings 'Pug' Ismay, head of the military wing of the War Cabinet Secretariat, asking him to begin planning a raid on the Channel Islands as soon as possible:

> If it be true that a few hundred German troops have been landed on Jersey or Guernsey by troop-carriers, plans should be studied to land secretly by night on the Islands and kill or capture the invaders. This is exactly one of the exploits for which the Commandos would be suited. There ought to be no difficulty getting all the necessary information from the inhabitants and from those evacuated. The only possible reinforcements which could reach the enemy during the fighting would be by aircraft-carriers, and here would be a good opportunity for the Air Force fighting machines. Pray let me have a plan.

In the aftermath of Dunkirk there was a new urgency, and the War Office approved the proposal for the raid later that day; shortly after that, planning began in earnest. The operation, code-named Ambassador, would in many ways be a tipping point beloved of military theorists. The future of commandos and with it the role of Special Forces was under test – and on the day it nearly failed.

It was decided that a raid by 140 men would be made on the island of Guernsey, attacking the airfield, destroying aircraft and buildings, as well as capturing or killing German troops. The units that were chosen for the raid were H Troop from No. 3 Commando and No. 11 Independent Company.[1] No. 3 Commando, under Lt Col John Durnford-Slater, had only just been raised in Plymouth, having completed its recruitment on 5 July, and had not yet begun training, while No. 11 Independent Company, under the command of Maj. Ronnie Tod, had been raised earlier in June. No.11 Company was responsible for the first British commando raid, Operation Collar, launched near Boulogne on the night of 24/25 June 1940. The raid met with mixed success: two German sentries were killed and the only casualty was Lt Col Dudley Clark, along as an observer, who received a slight wound. The British Ministry of Information issued a brief but upbeat communiqué about the very modest raid:

> Naval and military raiders, in co-operation with the RAF, carried out successful reconnaissances of the enemy coastline: landings were effected at a number of points and contacts made with German troops. Casualties were inflicted on the enemy, but no British casualties occurred and much useful information was obtained.

The German propaganda machine would soon be calling commandos 'murderous thugs and cut throats' who killed soldiers and civilians indiscriminately, preferring to murder their enemies rather than take them prisoner. Following Operation Basalt on Sark on 3/4 October 1942, this idea would take root in Hitler's mind, with tragic consequences for captured Allied special forces.

During the planning stage of Ambassador, Durnford-Slater went to London, where he worked out most of the details with the actor David Niven, who had returned to Britain from Hollywood and was then serving as a staff officer in the combined operations headquarters.[2] Durnford-Slater would write of Niven: 'I found him a model of what a staff officer should be, lucid, keen, able and helpful.'

The operation began promisingly, and in many ways fitted a pattern that would be favoured by Special Forces today. The first phase of Operation Anger (named, it was said, as a reflection of Churchill's anger at the surrender and occupation of the Channel Islands) began on the night of 7/8 July and was a reconnaissance by 20-year-old Lt Hubert Nicolle, an officer in the Hampshire Regiment who was originally from Guernsey and had served in the Royal Guernsey Militia. He was transported across the Channel by submarine H 43, commanded by Lt G.R. Colvin, and a naval officer, Sub-Lt J.L.E. Leitch, rowed him in a two-seater canoe 2 miles from the submarine and landed him at Le Jaonnet Bay on the south coast. The canoe had been bought from Gamages, a London department store. 'So well equipped was the navy at this stage of the war,' comments Charles Cruikshank in *The German Occupation of the Channel Islands*, the official history published in 1975. There was some concern when the flat pack canoe had been assembled inside the submarine and it emerged that it would not fit through the hatch.

Once ashore, Nicolle was able to make contact with friends and family and, on a borrowed bicycle and wearing sunglasses as disguise, made his way around the island. Based on the information that he provided, it was determined that the garrison on Guernsey consisted of 469 soldiers, concentrated mainly around St Peter Port. Although there were machine-gun posts all along the coast, they were sited in a manner that meant that it would take about twenty minutes after an alarm being raised for reinforcements to be dispatched. The strength of the garrison had been provided to Nicolle by a grocer who supplied the troops. Once again in the history of the islands, 'Humint' was proving valuable.[3]

The next phase of Anger came when, after three days, Nicolle was exfiltrated from the island and his place taken by two more soldiers from the Royal Guernsey Militia – Second Lts Philip Martel of the Hampshire Regiment and Desmond Mulholland of the Duke of Cornwall's Light Infantry. At 1.30 a.m. on 9 July, a collapsible Berthon boat was launched from H 43, the submarine that had carried the two officers from England. Navigated by Sub-Lt Leitch, it nearly made landfall before breakers swamped the craft. Nicolle, waiting on the shore, waded in to help in the recovery, and as he and Leitch started the return trip the boat sank in 3.5m of water – fortunately, Martel and Mulholland, starting inland, saw what had happened and returned to help the two men.

So far so good.

The original plan had been for Ambassador to be carried out on the night of 12/13 July, but at the last moment it was moved to 14/15 July. Even then, shortly before embarkation, Durnford-Slater received intelligence that the Germans had reinforced a number of the places where it had been planned to land some of the parties, and so the plan had to be changed. After the details were worked out, final battle preparations were undertaken in the gymnasium at the Royal Naval College, Dartmouth, where some of the cadets, who had just had their prize-giving and were leaving on 15 July, helped the commandos with loading magazines and helping prepare the Bren light machine guns (LMGs) and the limited number of Thompson SMGs that had been brought down from London specifically for the operation.

At 5.45 p.m. the raiding force embarked aboard the destroyers HMS *Scimitar* and HMS *Saladin*, and, escorted by six RAF air-sea rescue launches, or crash boats, which would take them from the destroyers to the landing beaches, they set out for Guernsey.

Under the plan that Durnford-Slater had worked out, troops from No. 11 Independent Company would attack the airfield, while the commandos created a diversion. Durnford-Slater selected H Troop, since it was formed of Regular soldiers who had served in the BEF in France and would therefore be well trained. His part in the operation was relatively straightforward. When they had landed at the Jerbourg peninsula, they were to attack a machine gun position on the peninsula and destroy the telegraph cable to Jersey, located in a hut at the base of the peninsula. Meanwhile, Captain V.T.G. De Crespigny, the troop commander, with the main body of H Troop, would attack the barracks that were part of the now disused Jerbourg Battery. Lt Peter Young reluctantly accepted his mission to secure the beach. However, Durnford-Slater told the action-hungry Young that if it was quiet he could come forward. The password would be 'Desmond'.

Recalling the briefing they received in Dartmouth, Young wrote in *Storm from the Sea* that they were told that the enemy 'were young soldiers, and rather to our surprise we were told that they were not badly behaved – in 1940 it was difficult to imagine that any German was not a monster.' A shrewd part of the plan was for a twin-engined RAF Avro Anson multi-role aircraft to fly over the island to drown out the sound of the commandos landing and moving around.

There is a much-quoted axiom of war that 'No plan survives contact with the enemy'. However, Anger began to unravel very early on. During the passage across the Channel, two of the crash boats that were carrying No. 11 Independent Company dropped out with engine trouble, so now the company had only two launches. After the troops had boarded the remaining launches in calm waters, Boat 302 set off on a course to the little island of Sark as a result of a faulty compass. By the time the launch had returned to *Saladin* in preparation to sail the correct course, it was 2.35 a.m. and therefore too late to complete the mission. The problem was identified as having been caused by the destroyer's degaussing equipment that had reversed the compass, or because weapons had been stacked too close to the compass. In an attempt to land as many men as possible, Boat 313 was towing the *Saladin's* whaler, but this slowed down the crash boat and when the whaler began to take on water Todd realised they would not make Guernsey on time. Turning back, they were unable to locate the *Saladin* and made their own way back to England, picking up an RAF fighter escort at dawn.

The launches carrying No. 3 Commando had the same compass trouble, but while the skipper was taking his course off the compass bearing, Durnford-Slater was studying the coast line and realised that they were making course towards Brittany, not Guernsey. Fast thinking and a quick decision set them on the right course, and so in the end only the force from No. 3 Commando, consisting of just forty men, landed at a beach in Telegraph Bay just west of the Jerbourg peninsula at 12.50 a.m. on 15 July. It was now that they discovered that the launches had a deep keel designed for cutting through the open sea, and not the flat bottom of infantry landing craft. The change in the date of *Ambassador* by forty-eight hours meant that the tide was high rather than low and the launches were not grounding on sand at low tide.

The commandos managed to get ashore – albeit soaking wet after wading armpit-deep in the sea. Leading from the front, Durnford-Slater dashed up the long steep flight of concrete steps that led from the rocky beach 250ft up the cliff to the Jerbourg peninsula. With Sgt Knight close behind him, Durnford-Slater recalled that, 'By the time I reached the top I was absolutely done, but Knight was even worse, gasping for breath like an untrained miler at the tape.' The party from No. 3 Commando failed to find any of the 469-man German garrison. An enemy barracks and a machine-gun nest were located, but both were unmanned. The coil of barbed wire that was intended for the roadblock proved too heavy to bring up the steep steps from the bay, so Privates Fred and Pat Drain, two brothers on the raid who had been tasked with building a block, took rocks from a local garden and built a modest barrier across the road close to the distinctive Doyle Monument. When it was found in the morning by the Germans, they initially assumed that it had been constructed by islanders as an act of defiance.

The rendezvous (RV) with the destroyer that was picking them up was set for 3 a.m., and if they were late the captain of the destroyer was under orders to leave them behind, so the party subsequently made good time as they returned to the beach, stopping only to allow Lance Corporal Rann to cut a couple of telephone lines on the way – an act that inconvenienced no one except the islanders. De Crespigny broke into a cottage and questioned an old man, but to the officer's annoyance the man knew nothing. Peter Young recalled that, 'The whole incident caused a useless and noisy delay.' Durnford-Slater's memory of the encounters was that, 'the man we found was so terrified that he had entirely lost the power of speech; all he could do was let out a series of shrieks.'

The return trip to the beach was not an orderly withdrawal. With time pressing, Durnford-Slater recalled that the officers, 'got their men going on the run. In short order, I herded them like a sheepdog down the concrete steps.' In the rush down the steps, however, he tripped and fell and his cocked revolver went off. Young noted that, 'It seemed to me that for an unopposed landing this was proving unduly hazardous.' Upon arriving back at the beach, the raiders were greeted by the crew of a dinghy from one of the crash boats, who explained that there was a risk that the sea swell could drive the boats onto the rocks. The dinghy was used to ferry the weapons out to the crash boats, but, recalled Durnford-Slater, 'It was a tiny craft, no more than nine feet in length. With each load of weapons went two or three men. As it came in for the fifth run, a high sea picked it up and smashed it against a rock. The dinghy was a total loss, and one trooper was reported drowned.' In fact the soldier – Gunner J. McGoldrick – struggled to the shore, where he was taken prisoner. The commandos were going to have to swim for it.

Durnford-Slater recalled:

Three men came out of the darkness. I recognised Corporal D. Dumper of Lieutenant Smales' road-block party. 'Could we have a word with you, please sir?' Dumper said. He seemed a little nervous. 'What is it?' 'I know we should haver reported this in Plymouth, sir,' he said apologetically, 'but three of us are non-swimmers.' I was ready to explode. The original letter calling for Commando volunteers had specifically mentioned that they must be able to swim. Then I calmed down. 'I'm afraid there's nothing we can do for you except try to send a submarine to pick you up tomorrow night,' I said. 'You chaps hide up. Come back on the beach at two o'clock tomorrow morning and flash a torch.' I removed my tunic and struck out in the water.

The non-swimmers were left on the beach with additional French currency and the promise that, as in the orders they had received, a submarine would be off La Creux Mahle beach from midnight onwards on the following Wednesday 17 July. They were to make their way along the south coast to be in position at the RV.

The men reached the crash boats, some of whose crews dived into the sea to help the exhausted Commandos aboard. The next task was to locate the *Scimitar*, and at this juncture the engine of one of the crash boats broke down. The boat was taken in tow and the crew and commandos braced themselves for a very hazardous journey home. Happily, the captain of the *Scimitar* decided to make a final sweep, and the boats and destroyer linked up. It was decided to scuttle the broken-down crash boat, charges were placed on it and the *Scimitar* set course for England.

Aboard the destroyer on the return journey, de Crespigny saw that the colonel was shivering and generously put his battledress over the officer's bare shoulders. As they approached Dartmouth at dawn, de Crespigny said to his commanding officer, 'Oh, by the way, colonel, I do hope everything will be all right.' 'What do you mean?' 'I forgot to tell you that I've been suffering from scabies.'

The raid was a failure, as none of the objectives were achieved by the British. No casualties were inflicted upon the enemy, no prisoners were taken and the only damage done was a cut telephone line. Additionally, the quality of the planning and conduct of the operation has been called into question. Much of the equipment used was either unserviceable – faulty compasses, motor launches that broke down – or inadequate for the job – launches that were unable to come all the way into the beach due to their draught. Some of the tasks that had been assigned were impractical or had not been rehearsed – the coil of barbed wire intended for use as a roadblock was too heavy to carry from the beach – and intelligence relating to enemy dispositions upon the island was at best outdated or completely wrong. Young, who would go on to serve with distinction in Europe and Burma, had a more sanguine recollection of the operation:

> The raid was rather a fiasco, but it was an experience. The planning and improvisation was of a high order and gave us all confidence. We in H Troop certainly paid lip-service to the idea of lightness and mobility, but on this occasion we went loaded like donkeys. That was a lesson learned. It was at this time that we began to suspect that steel helmets were not much use for this sort of work. And we also held swimming tests.

In later operations in Norway and at Dieppe, commandos would go ashore in 'raiding order' – with load-carrying webbing that consisted of ammunition pouches, a small pack with extra ammunition and little else.

Young remembered ruefully what he was carrying in Operation Ambassador:

> We wore battle-dress, steel helmets, canvas shoes and gaiters. In an old-style officer's haversack I had three Mills grenades, a drum magazine for a tommy gun and a clasp knife. In my breast pockets were more magazines of the clip type. My armament included a .38 pistol, and I had almost some five feet of cord with which I intended to secure my numerous prisoners; maps, saws, compasses and other impedimenta were sewn into various parts of my costume. For some obscure reason I was carrying an additional fifty rounds of .303 rifle ammunition – we took our soldiering seriously in 1940!

In Berlin on 16 July, the *Führer* Adolf Hitler submitted to the commanders of three services of the OKW his directive for *Unternehmen SEELÖWE* – Operation Sealion – German forces were to invade Britain.

Notes

1 The Independent Companies, of which there were ten, were raised from volunteers in the 55th (West Lancs) Division. At the time, the 55th was a two-brigade Motor Division, consisting of 164 Bde: 9th Btn Kings Regt, 1/4th Btn The South Lancs Regt and 2/4th Btn South Lancs. Regt; 165 Bde: 5th Btn Kings Regt, 1st Btn Liverpool Scottish QOCH and 2nd Btn Liverpool Scottish QOCH. In many ways the Independent Companies were the origins of the commandos, since they were intended for guerrilla-style covert operations in Norway following the German invasion, Operation Weserübung.

   Each of the companies initially consisted of twenty-one officers and 268 other ranks. Number 11 Company, raised by Major Ronnie Tod on 14 June 1940, was formed from volunteers from the existing companies, and had an establishment of twenty-five officers and 350 other ranks.

2 Niven had served in the British Army before the war, but resigned to follow a career in acting in the United States. Despite public interest in celebrities in combat, and a reputation for storytelling, he remained discreet about his wartime career. He once said, 'I will, however, tell you just one thing about the war, my first story and my last. I was asked by some American friends to search out the grave of their son near Bastogne. I found it where they told me I would, but it was among 27,000 others, and I told myself that here, Niven, were 27,000 reasons why you should keep your mouth shut after the war.'

3 A stone commemorating the seventieth anniversary of the raid was unveiled on Thursday 9 July 2010 by Bailiff Sir Geoffrey Rowland, who called Lt Nicolle 'one of Guernsey's greatest heroes'. About 100 islanders attended the ceremony remembering the reconnaissance mission by Hubert Nicolle. The stone was placed above the site of his first raid on the island at Icart above Le Jaonnet Bay, where he came ashore and where he was picked up by the Royal Navy three days later. Nicolle returned in September 1940, but on this trip was forced to give himself up to the German authorities. He managed to escape from Spangenberg POW camp through a tunnel, only to be recaptured, and was held for the rest of the war until he was liberated by American forces in 1945. He died in 1998.

6

THE AFTERMATH OF OPERATIONS TOMATO AND AMBASSADOR, 15 JULY–21 OCTOBER 1940

The failure of Operation Ambassador was largely due to the haste with which it had been conceived and put together, but it was also indicative of the embryonic status of raiding and the commando concept.

On the political side, the raid was also a disaster. Churchill was furious regarding the 'comical' way in which the operation was undertaken. He minuted the Secretary of State for War on 23 July:

> It would be most unwise to disturb the coasts of any of these countries by the kind of silly fiascos which were perpetrated at Boulogne and Guernsey. The idea of working all these coasts against us by pin-prick raids and fulsome communiqué is one strictly to be avoided.

While acknowledging the failure, Durnford-Slater noted:

> We had gained a little experience and had learned some of the things *not* to do. It was very clear that we urgently needed good and reliable landing craft for such an operation. It was equally clear that two hours on shore was not long enough to accomplish any worthwhile aim.

For some months, the whole commando concept was in jeopardy; the force had many enemies amongst the more establishment officers in the British

Army. Many felt that a well-trained infantry battalion could do the work of a commando unit, and moreover by calling for volunteers the commandos were siphoning off the good soldiers from their regiments and battalions. As a concept, the commandos went on to perform with considerable success later in the war. Indeed, it has been argued that their future success in operations such as Overlord, the D-Day landings, was in part due to the early failures such as Ambassador, as many lessons were learned that proved vital in the planning and conduct of later commando operations.

Nevertheless, there were widespread changes. The Independent Companies were disbanded and their personnel used to raise the first twelve commando units. Much work also went into the planning side of raiding, and for the next eight months the commandos did little except train. To this end, formalised training schemes and schools were established and Churchill sought to invigorate the concept by replacing General Bourne, who had previously been the director of combined operations, with the veteran naval officer Admiral Sir Roger Keyes.

The raids may have been a failure, but for islander Frank Stroobant they are remembered with pride:

> The arrival and hiding of two British military agents, Lt J.M. Symes and Lt F.H. Nicolle, both Guernseymen, was merely the culmination of a series of acts of resistance which brought down on us the wrath of the Germans. But this incident seemed to convince the Germans that we should never learn to accept them as they hoped and had set themselves [sic] out to achieve. So they merely gave up trying to win us over; instead, they adopted a programme which would give us real cause to hate.

The bulk of the Ambassador raiders might be home, but there was still the small group of stranded non-swimmers as well as the officers-turned-agents Lts Martel and Mulholland on the island. While the former were dressed in British Army battledress, the latter were in civilian clothes and in war if captured could therefore be shot as spies.

Today, 'prone to capture' personnel like air crew or Special Forces are taught combat survival skills, conduct after capture and escape and evasion – but in 1940 these were unknown black arts. Winston Ramsey, who interviewed Fred Drain in *The War in the Channel Islands*, said that the men had a silk escape map[1] and compass collar studs; however, their sole armament was a .38 Webley & Scott revolver that, as a military policeman, Corporal Dumper had as his personal weapon.

Morale was good because they were confident that they would be rescued. They climbed back up the steps and then, as they were walking on a course parallel to the road, they discovered an overgrown shed that contained tins of tangerines and some tasty cheese. Some night-time foraging produced some tomatoes, so the men were happy to lay up and wait until 10 p.m. on Wednesday. They took up position at the bay and used their torch to signal out to sea until 2 a.m., when the batteries faded.

In England, Commander-in-Chief Plymouth did not back up Lt Col Durnford-Slater's request for a submarine for the rescue operation, and the record bleakly states, 'for naval reasons the attempt to take the men off later was not possible'.

With no rescue, the commandos were hidden by Mr and Mrs Bourgaize, proprietors of a village store in Pleinmont Road. However, after attempting to secure a fishing boat for an escape, they realised that there was now little chance of a rescue and so walked in broad daylight to the airport and surrendered. Interrogated by the Germans, they gave away little. Significantly, they did not describe the proposed larger objectives of Ambassador, but if they had, writes Charles Cruikshank, the Germans 'would have formed an even lower opinion of the enemy's efficiency'.

Evidence of the raid had already been discovered by the Germans before the surrender, and had caused considerable excitement. Though Durnford-Slater says the non-swimmers who had remained behind had buried abandoned kit, it was discovered along with the colonel's battledress blouse with his name sewn into the collar. 'Durnford is a well-known name in the Channel islands and some of the Durnfords there were harried a good deal by the Gestapo [sic] who thought that I might still be lying up in the Island, harboured by namesakes.'

The Germans ordered Ambrose Sherwill, the Attorney General in Guernsey, to authorise a thorough search. In his briefing to the police, he observed, 'I can foresee all sorts of trouble if people land here clandestinely … however detestable the duty of reporting the presence in our midst of such strangers may be, in the present circumstances I can see no way of avoiding it.' The police report of 15 July 1940 states that they found abandoned equipment and sighted a waterlogged boat drifting out to sea. This was probably the crash boat and indicates that the attempt to scuttle her had failed. Significantly, Sherwill said that the police had found rifles, machine guns, steel helmets, uniforms and equipment. In later operations, commandos and SOE operatives would leave small items of equipment like insignia or headgear to indicate that the raid had been the work of British forces, thus hopefully diverting German attention away from the local population and all the repression that might follow. On Guernsey, the kit and the soldiers left behind following Ambassador simply pointed to poor preparation and implementation of a flawed plan.

However, the fact that there were uniformed British soldiers still at large on the island would be the saving of Lts Martel and Mulholland. Since they knew the island, and many properties had been left empty following the evacuation in 1940, they were able to hide up in an empty house in St Martins. The house adjoining a barn they hid up in proved to be owned by the Dame of Sark's daughter. The Dame learned of this through the island grapevine and, on the pretext of visiting Guernsey to check on her daughter's property, brought the two young officers some tinned food. The Dame explained to them that there was no chance of getting a fishing boat and escaping to England because the craft were closely guarded and fuel rationed.

Time and opportunities for escape were running out, and after Martel had stayed with his sister and Mulholland with his mother, both men knew that following Ambassador their presence on the island would become more widely known, which would put their relatives and friends at risk. They contacted the resourceful Sherwill, who realised that the officers could be shot as spies since they were not in uniform. Ingeniously, two sets of uniforms from a stock of Guernsey Militia uniforms were obtained and some alterations made to make them resemble battledress. When they surrendered they were treated as soldiers and, as prisoners of war, were sent to France. Those who helped them were, however, arrested and also found themselves sent to prison in France, though they were allowed to return to Guernsey in January 1941.

The director of the newly formed Combined Operations Executive (COE), Sir Roger Keyes, had no radio contact with the soldiers on Guernsey, so on 3 August an islander serving in the British Army, Sgt Stanley Ferbrache, was landed at Le Jaonnet Bay. He discovered that he was too late to exfiltrate the two officers and then, after gathering some low-level intelligence, he wondered if he too was going to be abandoned when a pick-up failed. On the second night, the boat arrived and the sergeant made it back to Plymouth. It looked as if a viable system was in place.

The courageous Hubert Nicolle was asked if he would once more put his life and that of his friends and family at risk and land on Guernsey. Good soldier that he was, he said 'yes' and so, on 4 September, along with Guernseyman James Symes, a fellow officer from the Hampshire Regiment, he was landed from an MTB at Petit Port. Once ashore, Nicolle found refuge with his uncle, Frank Nicolle, the assistant harbour master, while Symes was concealed by the father of his girlfriend Mary Bird. The two men spent three days gathering what intelligence they could, and then made their way to the RV at Petit Port. Bad weather prevented the MTB from making the RV, and this would be repeated for two more nights.

At this stage in the war, the COE seemed hell bent on reinforcing failure when it sent Captain John Parker to Guernsey. Parker was a Regular soldier with the South Lancashire Fusiliers who had spent his childhood in Guernsey, where his father still lived. According to Barry Turner in *Outpost of Occupation*, Parker had one mission to land under cover of darkness, contact Symes and Nicolle on the following day and then on the third night the three of them would be picked up and brought back to England. However, in their books Peter King and Charles Cruikshank say that Parker had an additional mission – to gather intelligence for Operation Tomato.

Churchill was convinced that the Channel Islands were still thinly garrisoned and that an amphibious assault, code-named Tomato, was feasible. Its objective was simply 'to destroy or make prisoner all the enemy in the Channel Islands'. Churchill saw it as an operation that would boost morale at home and show the Germans that they were not invincible. The plan called for a twenty-four-hour occupation to achieve this – however, it was felt that the islanders would feel doubly abandoned when the raiders left and they faced the wrath of the German forces. It was also soon realised that this was too ambitious, so the proposed operation was scaled down.

The objective would now be to capture the aerodromes on Jersey and Guernsey, and cause as much damage as possible to the German military and civilian staff on the islands. The plan called for two forces, each 750 strong, to attack Jersey and Guernsey, while 250 men were to be divided between Sark and Alderney. Tomato was therefore four operations, and therefore potentially four times as complex. To add to the complexity, the plans for Jersey and Guernsey called for landings at two points on each island. On Guernsey these would be between Point de la Moye and the Jerbourg peninsula. A small advanced party would be put ashore from a submarine to create a diversion to the rear of the German positions covering the beaches. The same tactics would be employed on Jersey, with landings on the north coast at Grève de Lecq and another on the west coast.

One of the many problems thrown up in the planning phase of Tomato was the lack of dedicated landing craft. Air-sea rescue crash boats had demonstrated their deficiencies in Ambassador, and with the Battle of Britain now at its height were fully committed. Water taxis and Scottish salmon fishing cobles were suggested. The latter could carry a platoon and had a speed of 6 knots. They could be brought to the Channel Islands slung from the davits of six small converted merchant ships. While this was seriously impractical in the proposed time frame, by 1942 the idea had become reality with vessels like HMS *Prince Albert*, a converted Belgian cross-Channel ferry that was fitted out to carry Landing Craft Assault (LCA) and would convey No. 4 Commando to a position off the French coast during Operation Jubilee.

Two years before Jubilee, Captain Parker, burdened with both a rescue mission and a reconnaissance role, was landed from an MTB near La Corbière on what turned out to be the wrong beach, and after shredding his elbows on the coastal gorse decided that walking was easier than crawling. When he reached the top of the cliffs, his career as an agent came to an abrupt halt when he fell into a trench adjoining a German flak position and was made prisoner by an alert sergeant. Fortunately he was in uniform and so was treated as a POW, and though subject to an intense interrogation he did not reveal the purpose of his mission.

Details of his interrogation survived and are quoted at length in *The German Occupation of the Channel Islands*. His equipment included an issue revolver, torch, collar stud compass, silk escape map of Europe and a small file sewn into his pullover. He also had a vacuum flask of coffee, some concentrated meat and white bread, and a bottle of whisky. His uniform and

equipment indicated that he was a soldier, not an agent, and he was transferred to a POW camp. There was, however, more to Parker than being a bluff
infantry officer. Prior to his departure, he had memorised a code that was to
be passed to fellow POWs if he was captured. One of the first to be informed
of it was Lt The Hon Terence Prittie – who subsequently escaped. The code
was circulated widely among POWs and was used to send information back
to Britain and facilitate escapes.

On Guernsey, the Germans now suspected that there were other British
soldiers on the island. Maj. Von Bandelow, the Guernsey commandant, was
told by von Schmettow to propose to Sherwill that if any British soldiers at
large gave themselves up, they would be treated as prisoners of war. It was
a diplomatic way of ensuring that island life was not disrupted by house-
to-house searches and the population antagonised. Von Bandelow, however,
chose as his adjutant a less diplomatic emissary. This officer passed the message about the amnesty but added that if, following the date set, 'members of
the Armed Forces were discovered later, the Germans would select twenty
prominent citizens and shoot them'.

The amnesty date had been delayed from 19 to 21 October, and on that
day Nicolle and Symes presented themselves at St Peter Port police station
in their 'uniforms' five minutes before the amnesty expired at 6 p.m. and
were taken into custody. Thirteen of their friends and family were rounded
up, and it emerged under questioning that Nicolle was on his second visit to
the island. The German authorities on the islands were keen to suggest that
the surrendered officers were men who had remained under cover from the
invasion in June 1940 rather than reconnaissance troops or raiders.

For Symes and Nicolle, there were nerve-racking days as they were treated
not as British soldiers but as enemy agents, whose punishment if captured
in war was death. It was the personal intervention of von Schmettow that
saved them from this fate – though as Cruikshank points out, the motive may
have been less humane but rather to ensure that German rule on the islands
continued to be accepted with comparative docility. The execution by firing
squad, which was what the judges wanted, of two local boys would at the
very least have created tension and friction.

Arrests followed the surrender of Symes and Nicolle, and among them
was Ambrose Sherwill, whom the Germans had correctly assumed knew a

great deal more than he was saying. He was held in the grim Cherche-Midi Prison in Paris.[2] This cold, lonely and intimidating place was too much for James Symes' father, Louis, who had been held by the Germans as a POW in the First World War.

He was found dead in his cell, kneeling with an open Bible in front of him – he had slashed his wrists.

Back on Guernsey, the German after-action analysis of Operation Ambassador is telling. They concluded that the objective had been to take prisoners, preferably officers, and between twenty-five and thirty 'long service volunteers' under the command of a lieutenant had been given special training. Details of the voyage and landing were accurately collated, though the names of the destroyers were not known.

Had Churchill seen the German analysis, his anger and disappointment at the outcome of Ambassador would have been even greater. Since the raiding party had only two hours ashore to complete its mission under cover of darkness, detailed preparations were essential, the Germans stated. However, the men had only been told of their mission when the ships were under way, and moreover had practised landings on a flat coast with no opposition. They had not been issued with the necessary equipment, a notable deficiency being climbing irons to allow them to cut telephone lines. With soldiers drawn from different units, there was no cohesion, and finally 'they had been mad to include non-swimmers in the party'.

There were some plaudits. The narrowest part of the Jerbourg peninsula was a shrewdly selected objective, since it was a likely position for an observation post. The beachhead was remote and concealed. Had the roadblock been covered by fire, it would have been difficult to pass. The commandos were given credit for cutting telephone lines, but it was assumed that the dumped barbed wire was to cover the withdrawal, not for the roadblock.

Analysis was also going on in London. The lack of any intelligence about Guernsey led Sir Roger Keyes to minute the Prime Minister on 21 September, 'I understand from my conversation with you today that in present circumstances you do not wish me to proceed with the project against the Channel islands, especially in view of the lack of guns required if the islands are to be held for a period.' He added that agents had not been recovered from the islands due to bad weather.

Churchill, one suspects reluctantly, replied, 'Hold up the project for the present.'

The main lesson that the Germans drew from their analysis of Ambassador was that outposts and promontories were vulnerable, particularly at night. Operation Dryad would prove them right.

On the night of 21 October, *Luftwaffe* bombers hit Liverpool for the 200th time. The threat of invasion might be receding, but the Blitz was in full swing across the British Isles.

Notes

1 The maps and miniature compasses were the products of MI9, the escape and evasion branch of Military Intelligence that officially came into being on 23 December 1939. The maps themselves were mainly small-scale, covering large areas; many were copied from maps then available from Bartholomew's in traditional paper form. (Bartholomew's had waived all royalties as part of the war effort.) The printers were Waddingtons, who, having produced board games, had considerable expertise in this field. One of the most talented designers at MI9 was Christopher Hutton, who, besides developing the maps, produced what was the world's first multi-tool, an escaper's knife that had a strong blade, a screwdriver, three saws, a lockpick, a forcing tool and a wire-cutter.

2 Sherwill was a First World War veteran who had been commissioned into The Buffs in 1916 and a year later had won the Military Cross and been promoted lieutenant. During the early part of the German occupation of the Channel Islands, he was president of the Controlling Committee. Imprisoned in 1940 but released on 30 December 1940, as a former British Army officer he was later deported to Laufen detention centre, returning to Guernsey after the war. Here he served as Bailiff between 1946 and 1959, and was knighted in 1949. In 1960, he retired to Alderney, where he died in 1968.

7

OPERATION DRYAD, 3 SEPTEMBER 1942

Operation Dryad was Geoffrey Appleyard's brainchild, and even after seventy years it stands out as a classic of its kind, involving small numbers of men, stealth and an operation that gathered valuable intelligence and prisoners for minimal casualties – a couple of sprained ankles (see Appendix II).

The objective, the Casquet Lighthouse, had been built in 1724 on a rocky outcrop, about 5 miles west of Alderney. Alderney is in the middle of the two fastest currents in the English Channel, 'The Race' and 'The Swinge'. The Race is a notorious strait of water between Alderney and Cap de la Hague in France. At high tide, water flows through the channel at a high rate and is sucked back down as the tides recede. Hazardous rocks within a few miles of the island and an uneven seabed add to the turbulence, so the area is always treated with respect by even experienced sailors. The Casquets and neighbouring rocks have been the site of many shipping disasters, among them the SS *Stella*, which foundered in 1899 with a loss of 112 lives, and the British man o'war *Victory* in 1744, lost with a complement of 1,100. Mariners were therefore delighted when the lighthouse began operating.

The Casquet Lighthouse complex consists of an 89ft conical tower and two shorter towers, with a walled courtyard and accommodation for the lighthouse staff. It is sited on the highest point of a cluster of steep barren rocks. A diaphone – foghorn – was installed in one of the towers in 1921, and a radio in the other tower in 1926. For the Trinity House crew on the Casquets, this was a challenging posting since all food and fresh water had to be brought to them by boat from Alderney. The lighthouse was converted to automatic operation in November 1990 and is now monitored from the Trinity House Operations and Planning Centre in Harwich.[1]

In 1940, the Germans took over the lighthouse and buildings, which they nicknamed the *Huetchen*, and installed a transmitter station to support naval operations. The small garrison consisted of a *Kriegsmarine* petty officer, *Obermaat* Mundt of *3 Batterie, Marine Flak Regiment 20*; three *Kriegsmarine* radio operators, *Funkgefreitters* Dembowy, Kraemer and Reineck; and an army guard force of an NCO, *Gefreiter* Abel, and two soldiers, Kepp and Klatwitter. Mundt had been in command of this isolated post for only thirty days in September 1942.

Its very isolation made it a perfect objective for a commando raid, but the rocky shore and fierce currents around the lighthouse may have given the German garrison a false sense of security. Until the raid, the only event of any interest was on 28 August, when an exhausted and off-course carrier pigeon had landed on the outcrop. Examination of its message container revealed that it had been sent by an agent in France and had a list of towns, with details of the adjoining German-controlled airfields. This barely legible message was sent on to the *Hafenkommandantur* in Cherbourg.

March-Phillips' orders for the raid are concise and clear.

The officers of the raiding party consisted of Maj. Gus March-Phillips DSO, OBE, in command; Anders Lassen, who in 1945 would become the first foreigner to win the VC; Captain Graham Hayes MC; and Appleyard. Also in the group was Private Orr, a German speaker who March-Phillips mentioned in his after-action report 'marshalled the prisoners and did much to make the search successful'. Adam Orr was in fact Abraham Opoczynski from Poland.

Having spent holidays in the Channel Islands as a schoolboy, Appleyard was quite familiar with the dangerous tide rushes that could smash a small boat against the rocks. Lt Freddy Bourne was the skipper of a powerful MTB that would used for the mission. The 60ft MTB 344 had affectionately been dubbed 'The Little Pisser' because of her high top speed of 33 to 40 knots – which made her difficult to handle. She was one of the experimental MTBs built in 1942. As a raiding craft she was ideal, since when she was close to the enemy coast she could run fairly silently on an auxiliary engine with an underwater exhaust. She was armed with two 18in torpedoes (though these were stripped out to reduce weight), two Vickers machine guns and Lewis guns. A normal crew was six or seven.

The MTB sailed from Portland Bill at 9 p.m., but, March-Phillips wrote in his report:

> In spite of a very careful overhaul, the port engine again gave trouble and the passage had to be made at a reduced speed of some 25 knots for the first 25 miles. It was then possible to increase the engine revolutions and the normal cruising speed of 33 knots was maintained until within 5 miles of the objective.

It was Bourne's first command and Appleyard acted as navigator.[2] Appleyard wrote, 'After innumerable fruitless attempts, this operation took place in spite of what has come to be called Dryad weather, wind force 3 rising to 4 and sometimes 5 … It was pretty nerve-racking as it's a notoriously evil place and you get a tremendous tide race round the rocks.'

There were a total of twelve men on the mission. All went well and Appleyard was the first to leap ashore with the bowline. Hayes was in control of the stern-line, which had been attached to the kedge-anchor that had been dropped on approach to prevent the boat from being smashed against the rocks. Although several large swells surged against the rocks, the landing party, in a Goatley[3] boat, paddled quietly to the island and made it safely ashore without any damage to the boat. Appleyard handed the bowline to another and Hayes remained in control of the sternline as the raiding party departed. They had deliberately chosen a point below the engine house tower on the lighthouse complex that was not an obvious landing place. Though they then had to scramble up 80ft of rocks, any noise they made was drowned by the sound of the waves.

Shortly after midnight on 3 September – the third anniversary of the outbreak of the Second World War – the party made its way unchallenged through coiled barbed wire up the steep rocky surface to the courtyard wall. They found that a 'knife rest' barbed-wire barrier blocked the entrance to the courtyard, but were able to climb over the wall.

'At this point,' writes March-Phillips, 'the order was given for independent action and the party was split up and rushed the buildings and towers according to a pre-arranged plan.'

Appleyard and Sgt Winter dashed up the 75ft spiral staircase to the tower light, only to find it unoccupied. The garrison had been taken totally by surprise. Appleyard said, 'I have never seen men so amazed and terrified at the same time.' Three were sleeping, two were just turning in and two others were on duty. Even though an open box of hand grenades and a weapon described as an Oerlikon, but probably a 2cm flak 30, were found, the seven Germans were taken prisoner without a shot being fired. The commandos considered blowing up the weapons, but reckoned that since they had achieved their mission in silence they would ensure that it remained that way. March–Phillips noted that, 'If a good watch had been kept, or if any loud noises had been made on the approach or on landing, the rock could have been rendered pretty well impregnable by seven determined men.'

One German, who was in charge of the lighthouse, fainted at the sight of the commandos. Another who was in bed was initially thought to be a woman because he was wearing a hairnet.

March–Phillips wrote:

> The prisoners were re-embarked immediately and taken down over the rocks by the way the raiding party had come up, some of them still in their pyjamas, as time was getting short and it was expected that the operation of embarkation would take some time. Re-embarkation commenced at 0100 hours. The wireless was then broken with axes and the buildings and offices searched for papers, documents and code books. The light and the engine room were left intact.

Though the raiders were obliged to dump the weapons they had captured, what they did bring back to England was more valuable: a codebook for harbour defence vessels F.O. i/c France, signal books, records, W/T diary, procedure signals, personal letters and photographs, identity books and passes, ration cards, station log, ration log, light log and gas mask.

Some of this material would probably have been forwarded for analysis to the Government Code and Cypher School at Bletchley Park. While capturing the lighthouse crew was undoubtedly a coup, the codebooks would have been of significant value in the effort to crack the German Enigma mechanical encryption system. Commando operations in Norway also targeted the German Enigma codes and encoding machines, and their capture was a vital weapon in winning the war against the U-boats operating in the North Atlantic.

By good luck, the raid on the Casquets took place a short time after the duty signaller had sent a routine situation report to the German naval HQ in Cherbourg, and this ensured that the raid would remain undiscovered until dawn.

March-Phillips wrote:

> Meanwhile the embarkation of the prisoners was proceeding under the direc-
> tion of Captain Burton and Captain Hayes. This was a particularly difficult and
> hazardous operation as the slope of the rock at this point was at least 45 degrees
> and the prisoners had to slide down and be hauled into the boat by Mr Warren,
> the bowman, as she rose on the swell. Great credit is due to all concerned that
> this operation was successful for one mistake might have meant the swamping
> of the boat which would have brought disaster on the party.

Jumping back onto the Goatley, Appleyard broke a bone in his foot and Peter Kemp was accidentally stabbed in the upper thigh as they boarded, and so the two officers became the only casualties in the operation. It was this injury that put Appleyard in plaster and would prevent him joining the ill-fated landing party in Operation Aquatint on the night of 12/13 September 1942.

'When the search party was finally embarked at 0110 hours there were nineteen men in the Goatley, which rode the swell admirably, though danger-ously low in the water,' added March-Phillips.

The following day, the supply boat from Alderney set out to the Casquets and among the crew was George Pope, the pilot on Alderney. As they approached the Casquets, they noted that there was no smoke coming from the chimneys and that none of the crew and guard force had come down to the little jetty to help with the stores delivery. Pope joked that 'perhaps they have all gone to England'. It was a joke that backfired – his wife and young family were terrified when, suspected of passing information on to the raiders, he was questioned for several hours.[4] The crew of the supply boat boarded an inflatable dinghy and rowed to the rocky outcrop. Here they found the empty lighthouse and wreckage, and realised that it had been raided – the discovery of a khaki woollen cap comforter, something of a commando trademark, confirmed that the lighthouse had been raided by the British.

The Senior Naval Officer Channel Islands, *Seekommandant Kanalinseln*, who happened to be visiting Alderney that day, ordered the immediate reoccupation of the lighthouse by a relief crew of eleven petty officers and ratings from Alderney harbour.

Four weeks after Dryad, in a conference with his senior officers, Hitler mentioned the raid, saying:

> Above all, I am grateful to the English for proving me right by their various landing attempts. It shows up those who think I am always seeing phantoms, who say 'Well, when are the English coming? There is absolutely nothing happening on the coast – we swim every day, and we haven't seen a single Englishman.'

There was some dispute between the *Kriegsmarine* and the *Heer* (Army) as to whether the Casquets should continue to be manned since it was so vulnerable; in the end the garrison on the Casquets was increased to platoon strength. The armament went up with the installation of a 2.5cm Pak anti-tank gun, five machine guns and, curiously, an anti-tank rifle. There were additional wire entanglements, three static AFm W 42 flame-throwers were dug in and thirty landmines were also laid – however, finding where on the rocky feature they could be sited must have been a challenge.[5]

The Casquets were supplied by two of the harbour vessels from Alderney about every ten days, and the men rotated. In the latter part of the war the light was not lit, but the position was used as an observation post for the *Westbatterie* on Alderney, using radio and heliograph to report sightings

The garrison fluctuated but normally it was thirty-three, composed of one officer, three NCOs and twenty-one soldiers from the army, and one petty officer and seven sailors from the *Kriegsmarine*. For some months it was reported that this group included a junior officer who volunteered for the post to escape the consequences of an unfortunate *affaire* in France – it seemed as if the fictional characters of Victor Hugo and Swinburne who had populated the remote location had become reality.

Thousands of miles to the east, 3 September 1942 would be a momentous day. In the Soviet Union, men of the German 6th Army had begun to penetrate the suburbs of the industrial city of Stalingrad. They would become bogged down in vicious street fighting that would climax in a defining battle of the Second World War.

Notes

1 The rocks have a place in literature as well as marine and military history. A.C. Swinburne's poem, 'Les Casquets', is based on the true story of the Houguez family, who lived on the island for eighteen years. The Houguez were originally from Alderney, and the poem describes how their daughter falls in love with a carpenter from Alderney, but moving to his island, she finds the 'small bright streets of serene St Anne' and 'the sight of the works of men' too much, and returns to Les Casquets. The French writer Victor Hugo, who lived in exile on Guernsey, wrote, 'To be wrecked on the Casquets is to be cut into ribbons; to strike on the Ortac is to be crushed into powder … On a straight frontage, such of that of the Ortac, neither the wave nor the cannon ball can ricochet … if the wave carries the vessel on the rock she breaks on it, and is lost.'

2 In all, Bourne and the crew of MTB 344 took part in seventeen raids off the north coast of France and the Channel Islands. When the SSRF was disbanded, Bourne was awarded the DSC for his role in their operations. Bourne died in 2002 aged 82.

3 Designed by, and named after, Fred Goatley of Saunders-Roe, the Goatley boat was a collapsible boat with a wooden bottom and canvas sides that measured 3.5m (11ft 6in) overall, 1.3m (4ft 6in) beam and 0.5m (1ft 9in) deep, and only 200mm (8in) when collapsed, could carry ten men yet it weighed only around 150kg. Two men could assemble the boat in two minutes.

4 George Pope is one of the more intriguing characters thrown up by the occupation. In *Channel Islands at War: A German Perspective*, George Forty describes how Pope had sailed into Alderney on his yacht with his family a day or so after the Germans arrived on the island. He worked for them during the occupation 'then mysteriously sailed away again after the liberation. Was he a secret agent?' asks Forty.

5 A further raid on the lighthouse was reported in 1943. Included in the raiding party was the anglophile Hollywood actor Douglas Fairbanks Junior, who had joined the staff of the combined operations HQ in London. It is unclear what the outcome was or whether this was essentially a publicity exercise – or if it was simply one of the Second World War's myths.

8

OPERATION BRANFORD, 7 SEPTEMBER 1942

The little island of Burhou was the objective for Operation Branford. The raiding force supplied by the SSRF was commanded by Captain Colin Ogden-Smith, with 2nd Lt Anders Lassen, and consisted of six men. The aim was to establish whether the half-mile-long and 300yd-wide island could be used as a base for artillery to support larger-scale amphibious attacks against Alderney to the south. As such, Branford was a product of Mountbatten's obsession with the islands.

The plan was to travel across from England in MTB 344 and then row to the rocky island by Goatley boat. However, it seemed that the operation would have to be aborted at the outset when, after about an hour at sea, the port engine of the MTB cut out. Since German E Boats were known to be operating in the Channel, it was decided that it would be prudent to return home to Portland. The MTB mechanic worked hard on the engine and it roared back into life, with fuel pressure returning to normal. Ogden-Smith decided the operation should go ahead, with the proviso that if the engine cut out again they would call off the raid.

Safe navigation past the islet of Ortac, the Danger and Dasher rocks and the Burhou reef was helped by a powerful searchlight that was believed to be located on Guernsey and a light on Alderney that flashed every four or five seconds, and then by a red navigation light on Sark.

Ogden-Smith wrote in his report:

Shore was reached at 0028 hours and the landing made on the reef at a place 60 yards west of the southernmost point of the island. The rock here is steep and in steps. The boat was held off by kedge anchor. There was no noticeable tidal set and the sea was absolutely calm. The party, less cox and bow who remained with the Goatley, made its way for 60yd over broken rock which was wet and slippery with seaweed to the rockline above high water. The only building on the island was a house about 400yd NE of the landing place.

In his report Ogden-Smith also stated that:

Pack artillery or mortars or loads requiring two or three men are practical. Wheeled or track guns would present great difficulties as there are no sand beaches and all landings would have to be made over rock. There are a number of places where high-angle guns [could] be placed though the ground is very soft where the grass grows. There is sufficient crest clearance except immediately behind the rough ridge rocks.

Rather ominously, they found that the single house in the centre of Burhou had been partially destroyed by shellfire and there were shell craters around it. They were not to know that the little island had been used as a target for the German *Batterie Annes* on the Giffoine on neighbouring Alderney. Armed with four 15cm SK C/28, which elevate to a maximum of 47° 30', and gave it a range of 23,500m, *Batterie Annes* had the most modern armament of the island's batteries and was well protected by heavy and light flak batteries.

The party split into two groups, Corporal Edgar taking two men to examine the western side and Ogden-Smith covering the central and eastern side. While they were on the island, they saw that a new crew had taken over the Casquets lighthouse and were signalling to Alderney by lamp using three Morse As as their call sign. The reason why they were using a signal lamp was probably because the radio smashed in Operation Dryad was still out of commission.

The uneventful operation ended at 1.30 a.m. when, after an hour ashore, the party returned to the Goatley and made their way to the MTB. By 4.30 a.m. they were safely back in Portland. Mountbatten noted that the raid had been successful and had provided useful information.

Today, Burhou is a listed bird sanctuary famous for its puffin colony. It has a hut that will house eight people but cannot be visited between March and July, which is the breeding season.

Ogden-Smith would serve with distinction in Special Forces and with the SOE, with the code name Dorset, and as a member of a Jedburgh[1] team parachuted into France as part of the wider D-Day operations. Trapped by German troops, he was killed in a firefight along with two French comrades, Gerard de Carville and Maurice Miodon, at Querrien, Quimperle, Finistere, on 29 July 1944. They are buried together at Guiscriff Communal Cemetery.

Notes

1　In Operation Jedburgh, agents from the British SOE, the US Office of Strategic Services (OSS), the *Free French Bureau Central de Renseignements d'Action* (Intelligence and Operations Central Bureau) and the Dutch and Belgian Armies were dropped by parachute into occupied France, Holland, and Belgium to conduct sabotage and guerrilla warfare, and to lead the local resistance forces in actions against the Germans. The operatives were nicknamed 'Jeds'.

9

OPERATION BASALT, 3–4 OCTOBER 1942

Among the probes by commando forces against the Channel Islands, Operation Basalt against the little island of Sark, undertaken by seven men of the SSRF and four from No. 12 Commando,[1] led by Captain Geoffrey Appleyard, would have tragic consequences that no one could have foreseen.

At the time of the raid, the island had a small garrison drawn from 6 *Kompanie, Infantereiregiment* 583, 319th Division. It was made up of one heavy machine-gun section, one light mortar group and one anti-tank platoon. Engineers had laid twenty-two separate minefields containing a total of 939 S-mines, and a five-man detachment who were working on the harbour were billeted at the Dixcart Hotel. The *Inselkommandant* was *Oberleutnant* Herdt.

Before the war, the Appleyard family had taken holidays on the island and so, on leave at home in Yorkshire, Appleyard had run through old films of these holidays to refresh his memory – somewhat to the surprise of his parents.

The commandos left Portland in MTB 344 at about 7 p.m. on Sunday 3 October 1942, rowed ashore in a dory and landed at 11.30 p.m. near a cave. In bright moonlight, they scrambled 120ft up the cliffs and made their way inland from Point Château, which juts out into the sea between Dixcart Bay and Derrible Bay – rocks on which the young Appleyard had sunbathed in the 1930s – and moved along a track on a feature known as the Hog's Back.

Moving inland in the autumn darkness, they spotted what appeared to be a hut with a radio mast and figures grouped around it. Appleyard crawled cautiously towards it and then, as the patrol was about to open fire, he realised that the 'figures' had not moved because they were rifle range targets, the radio mast a flagpole and the hut a target store. As they moved past some apple trees, Bruce Ogden-Smith grabbed some of the fruit and was told off by his brother, who whispered that he was 'was on a commando raid and not a scrumping expedition'. The commandos chuckled but were silenced by Appleyard.

Moving on, the raiders took cover as a German patrol crunched past them, and the commandos were amused to hear a sleepy soldier swearing and his comrades chuckling. They reached a small cottage called Petit Dixcart that was unoccupied, and then crossed the stream in the wooded Dixcart valley. Pushing through thick gorse and bracken, they reached an isolated house named La Jaspellerie. Breaking a pane of glass, they let themselves in through the French windows.

The house was in darkness and the occupant, Mrs Frances Pittard, the recently widowed wife of the local GP, frightened the commandos. Seeing the group with their faces blackened with camouflage cream, she assumed that the house was on fire. However, reassured, dressed and returned, she proved very informative. Spotting a loaf of bread on the kitchen table, one of the commandos asked if they could take it back to Britain to be analysed. Mrs Pittard explained that this was her bread ration for the week, so they cut off one corner. Sitting in the kitchen, she said that there were about twenty Germans in the nearby Dixcart Hotel, which was only a few hundred yards away. As the daughter of a former Royal Navy commander, she commented that the German garrison were poor physical specimens, but they were polite and respectful. She added that the islanders regretted that the king had not mentioned them in his last Christmas message. The commandos shook hands with Mrs Pittard and slipped out into the night. Appleyard realised that if they were to extend their time on Sark to capture prisoners at the Dixcart Hotel, they would risk missing the rendezvous with MTB 344, so a corporal was sent back to the beach with instructions for the skipper to wait for thirty minutes beyond the allotted time.

Mrs Pittard had provided the raiders with a map and a copy of the *Guernsey Evening Press*, which had the deportation order signed by *Oberst* Knackfuss. She declined an offer by the raiders to take her with them back to England. It was an offer that she would come to regret.

When the raiders returned to Britain, the deportation order would be copied and widely circulated, producing dramatic newspaper headlines such as 'Nazis Send Captured Britons as Slaves, Island Raid Reveals' and 'Islanders Starve as Nazis Grab Food' in popular papers like the *Daily Sketch* and *Mirror,* and even the august *Times.* The *Sunday Chronicle* declared that *Oberst* Knackfuss 'should go down on the black list alongside the murders of Lidice and those who stole the food from the Greeks and left them to starve! … the real truth has emerged of deportations and forced labour'.

In *Islands in Danger,* Alan and Mary Wood describe how after the commandos had left La Jaspellerie, they passed a yew tree where Appleyard recalled that in a pre-war summer holiday his younger brother had found a half crown (a coin that today would be worth about £15).

When they reached the little hotel, they saw that there was a single sentry patrolling outside. Before the hotel could be entered, the sentry would need to be silenced. According to the Woods, the sentry was:

> obviously very tired and sleepy. Anders [Lassen] drew his knife[2] from its sheath – it was the first time he had used it, and he did not like it. He waited until, from the sound of the German's steps, he knew he had reached the end of his beat and was turning round.
>
> The others, listening behind, heard nothing but a sudden gasp. Anders dragged the German behind a bush.

King, in *The Channel islands War 1940–1945,* makes the observation that neither Appleyard's nor the German official report make mention of the sentry being knifed by Lassen.

The commandos now approached the annex to the little Dixcart Hotel.[3] It was a prefabricated building linked to the main hotel by a covered passageway. There was some trouble opening the door and the party were sure that the Germans would be alerted. According to the Woods, the commandos found that the inmates had stacked their rifles in an outer room – this was probably the passageway. The door at the end was opened to reveal a passage with doors on either side. Appleyard gave the order that the doors should be opened simultaneously. Sleeping men were dragged from their beds. By now, five men had been captured and were in the crowded corridor outside the rooms.

With their trousers around their ankles, the prisoners were bound with a lightweight cord. Some accounts report that they were tied with toggle ropes, but Bruce Ogden-Smith, interviewed by Winston Ramsey, said, 'We had taken a grey-coloured cord with us specifically to tie the Germans up as the purpose of the raid was to bring back prisoners.' Despite these restraints, once outside the Germans realised that the raiding party was comparatively small and attempted to escape. A running fight developed. Two men got away, though one of them was wounded, and two soldiers, 30-year-old *Gefreiter* Heinrich Esslinger and 28-year-old *Unteroffizier* August Bleyer, were killed. It is unclear whether they were caught in crossfire or killed by Anders Lassen. Ramsey, researching *The War in the Channel Islands Then and Now*, located the graves of Esslinger and Bleyer in the military cemetery at Fort George, St Peter Port, Guernsey. In addition there was the grave of *Obergefreiter* Peter Oswald, whose death is listed as 4 October 1942 – was he, as Peter King believes, the sentry knifed by Lassen before the attack on the hotel?

One of the two men held by Lassen managed to escape as Germans poured out of the main hotel building. Incredibly, in the chaos and violence in the hotel, Bruce Ogden-Smith grabbed a glass ashtray produced by the Guernsey Brewery Company to promote their milk stout, stuffed it down his battledress jacket and took it back to Britain.

German sources stated that the prisoners' mouths had been stuffed with grass to prevent them from shouting, and that they had been *Fesselung*, a word that translates as fettered or bound, and it was this that would trigger the retribution against Canadian prisoners.

Moving fast, the raiders retraced their route back to the beach. They escaped with a prisoner, who was interrogated on returning to Britain at the naval base at Portland, but most importantly they had brought back with them written evidence that islanders were being deported.

The Woods include a rather unrealistic episode in *Islands in Danger*, where they assert that:

> On their way back in the MTB, comparing notes on what had happened, they realised that the binding of prisoners might be represented as technically against the rules of war. Anders Lassen was so upset at the possibilities for

German propaganda that he volunteered to go back alone, find the bodies, and remove any ties round their wrists.

The Woods say that Appleyard overruled him on the grounds that the risks were too high and that they had a prisoner and useful intelligence to be brought back to Britain. By now, the German soldier was so terrified that he was virtually carried by Lassen as they made their way along wooded paths, onto the Hog's Back and down to where they had left their boat. They were just in time – the MTB was about to leave when the crew spotted the commandos, who boarded it at 3.45 a.m.

About two months prior to Operation Basalt, on 19 August, the Canadian 2nd Infantry Division had been committed to Operation Jubilee, the large-scale amphibious raid against the French port of Dieppe. It was a very costly operation; of the 6,086 men who made it ashore, a total of 3,623 were either killed, wounded or captured and the raid achieved few of its objectives. Against explicit orders, a Canadian brigadier took a copy of the operational order ashore. This was subsequently discovered by the Germans among the wrecked vehicles and bodies on the beach, and found its way to Hitler. Among the dozens of pages was an instruction to 'bind prisoners'. The orders explained that this was to prevent them from destroying documents of intelligence value. However, the Germans asserted that bound prisoners had drowned on landing craft that had sunk or had been shot by the Canadians.

When Basalt was combined with Jubilee, it produced an act of retribution that even today shames both the Allies and the Germans. A few days after the Sark raid, Radio Berlin reported:

> Sixteen British fell upon a German working party consisting of one NCO and four men, whom they tied up in their shirts with a thin but strong cord. The men were not allowed to put on more clothes, but were led off to the beach, and when they resisted this improper treatment the NCO and one man were killed by bullets and bayonets, and another soldier was wounded.

German communiqué stated at least one prisoner had escaped and two were shot while resisting having their hands tied, and claimed this 'hand-tying' practice was used at Dieppe. Subsequently, on 9 October, Berlin announced

that 1,376 Allied prisoners (mainly Canadians from Dieppe) would henceforth be shackled.[4] The Canadian government responded with a similar
shackling of German prisoners held in Canada.

On Guernsey, *The Star* quoted the German Anglo-Irish propaganda broad-
caster William Joyce – known to British listeners as Lord Haw Haw because
of his distinctive aristocratic drawl. In the piece, Joyce said:

> The British Government takes refuge in flimsy excuses, and the argument that
> humanity varies according to circumstances. The German Supreme Command
> have never deemed it necessary to resort to such a distinction. They have
> observed a standard of chivalry in which the British Government evidently
> does not believe.

This tit-for-tat shackling continued until 12 December, when the Swiss
Red Cross achieved agreement with the Canadians to desist, and with the
Germans some time later after they received further assurances from the
British. However, before the Canadians ended the policy, an outbreak of seri-
ous violence by German prisoners had occurred at Bowmanville POW Camp.
By this time, many German camps had abandoned the practice or reduced it
to a token gesture, simply leaving a pile of shackles in a prison billet.

Back in Britain, the Woods describe how Appleyard was summoned to
see the Prime Minister in his room in the House of Commons. Churchill's
opening words were a growled, 'What have you been up to, my boy?', before
he put his arm round the shoulder of the young officer and congratulated
him on the intelligence he had gathered. Interviewed in the 1980s, Bruce
Ogden-Smith corroborated this, saying, 'I believe "Apple" reported direct to
the Prime Minister himself who was not in the least worried.'

The shackling was public retribution, and it was reported on and commen-
tated on in the world's electronic and print media. However, unknown to the
Allies, Basalt would have a lasting and fatal impact on subsequent commando
and Special Forces operations during the war.

Enraged by the raid and the humiliating death of the soldiers, Hitler issued
the Commando Order on 18 October 1942, which in effect gave German
commanders licence to execute captured Special Forces soldiers. Like so many
of Hitler's more notorious instructions, the Commando Order does not actually

directly sanction murder, but states that if captured they were to be handed over to the *Sicherheitsdienst* (SD), which by the unwritten rules of the period implied that they would be brutally interrogated and then shot (see Appendix III).

For what was in effect a fighting patrol, the impact of Basalt was already being felt as the raiders were still making their way home. At 3.50 a.m. the German divisional HQ had been informed of the raid; LXXXIV *Armeekorps* learned of it by 4.30 a.m., Seventh Army HQ at 6.10 a.m. and thirty minutes later Army Group D in Paris and the Chief of the General Staff had been informed. It took three hours for the staff at the HQ to digest the news and draft an eleven-point questionnaire with the covering note that answers were required by telephone by 11 a.m.

The questions were:

1) Who is the responsible *Inselkommandant* or Commander for Sark?
2) What was the state of the weather at the time of the attack?
3) How was the landing or climbing site protected?
4) Was the billet inside or outside a strongpoint?
5) Was the engineers' billet protected?
6) Was the engineer unit and its accommodation known to the *Inselkommandant* to whom it was designated?
7) Had an alert been raised?
8) At the time of the attack had combat noises been heard and by whom?
9) What communications does the island possess and what is the chain of communication?
10) What is the reason for the lapse in time between the attack at 4.10 and the report to Seventh Army HQ at 7.45 [Berlin Central European Summer Time]?
11) What is the current strength of the Sark garrison (unit, troops and whether reinforced)?

The fear that these questions produced is hard to imagine today – every German soldier knew that a transfer from the comfort of garrison duty in France to a punishment battalion and the grim winters and ruthless enemy on the Eastern Front was tantamount to a death sentence. The questions about the failures of command and control on Sark required answers fast – and convincing answers at that.

At 11.45 a.m. – forty-five minutes after the deadline had elapsed – the replies were phoned back. The timings are the original Berlin times:

1) Oblt Herd [*sic*] Kp. Chef. 6/IR 583.
2) Misty, starlight at higher level, heavy ground fog, consequently poor visibility.
3) Landing place not precisely established yet, probably Dixcart Bay defended by single S-minefield.
4) To be clarified in due course by personal investigation by Division's Kommandeur.
5) Engineers' billet lay about 500 metres from the coast and 400 metres from the company reserve strongpoint.
6) The *Inselkommandant* knew of the presence of the engineers unit. The question of command and billeting is being clarified at the moment.
7) The alarm was given by the Company Commander at 4.10 after rifle fire and calls for help.
8) No battle noise was heard during the attack on the billet.
9) Telephone cable from *Inselkommandant* on Sark to Regimental Command Post IR 583 on Guernsey. All strongpoints on Sark are linked to one another.
10) 4.47 Report from Company to Regiment. 4.50 Report from Regiment to Division. 5.30 Report from Division to Corps HQ which only referred to cries for help, shots from a house in the centre of the island, wounded, confused, in the course of further investigation, a possible attack considered. Chief of Staff ordered fuller investigation to establish whether it was an enemy attack, sabotage or a drunken disturbance. 6.40 Second message from Division. 6.45 Corps HQ advised (with consultation). 6.55 Message relayed to Commanding General. 7.00 Call from Commanding General to Operations Section re details of report and presentation. 7.10 Message to Seventh Army HQ.
11) Garrison on Sark: 6/IR 583 reinforced by one platoon 14/583; one heavy MG platoon; one heavy mortar section; three anti-tank guns, three flame-throwers (as fixed weapons) and one light machine-gun.

A more detailed report on the raid was sent to HQ LXXXIV *Armeekorps* by HQ 319 *Infanterie Division* under the personal signature of the divisional commander, *GeneralMajor* Müller. The account explained that a *Pionier* detachment of 2./Pi Bd 319 consisting of one *Obergefreiter* and four *Schutzen* had been sent to Sark to repair defences in the harbour. They were billeted in Dixcart House, which was about 600m away from the island's reserve troops.

That they were billeted away from the company reserve was contrary to orders issued by General Müller, and for this *Oberleutnant* Herdt, the former company commander of 6./IR 583, was court-martialled. It was the same fate for the company orderly corporal senior *Gefreiter* Schubert, who had failed to pass on to the company commander that at 2.10 a.m. Auxiliary Customs Assistant Marburger, the guard on the pier, had heard engine noises out to sea. He telephoned this information to the orderly corporal. 'It was his (Schubert's) duty to contact the strongpoints concerning the report of engine noises, and not wait for them to contact him.' It is easy to imagine that the corporal thought that the customs officer was 'hearing things'.

The report described how, at 3.55 a.m., the guard of the reserve troops heard the sound of the fight at the Dixcart Hotel and alerted Schubert, who in turn passed the report on to Herdt. The officer then led a patrol from the reserve troops towards the hotel. It was here that they found *Gefreiter* Klotz naked, hiding in the garden. He described what had happened. It stated that between 3.30 and 3.50 a.m. the soldiers of the *Pionier* detachment were awakened, handcuffed and marched off:

> *Gefreiter* Klotz was able to shed his handcuffs; knocked down the British soldier guarding him and escaped into the darkness. Seeing this, the other soldiers also tried to escape, but only *Gefreiter* Just, who was wounded, succeeded. *Obergefreiter* Bleyer and *Gefreiter* Esslinger were shot down and stabbed. Senior *Gefreiter* Weinrich remained as a prisoner of war.
>
> Engine noises were heard at 04.25 hours and Herdt ordered the Customs boat with five soldiers and an MG34 to patrol the coast off Derrible and Dixcart Bays. The officer then joined *Oblt* Balga in a sweep of the area. The raiders had gone but the Germans recovered 2 daggers (Commando knives), 1 sub machine-gun magazine, 1 pistol magazine, 1 pair of wire cutters, 1 hand-spike, 3 torches, 1 woollen cap, 1 muffler, several pieces of rope (toggle ropes).

In February 1944, *Obergefreiter* Klotz would be presented with a watch in recognition of his bravery in escaping after he had been 'cold-bloodedly tied up by the English'.

Probably the best analysis of what happened at the Dixcart Hotel annexe appears in *Islands in Danger*:

> The truth seems to be that each man secured his own prisoner in his own way; and that in the confusion, with men shooting and shouting in the dark, nobody could know exactly what happened. Appleyard's own official report, for instance, shows he believed four of the Germans had been shot.

For the population of Sark, who had enjoyed a relatively untroubled occupation, there were now new restrictions. Throughout the island, guards were doubled and armed. The arrival of the *Geheime Feldpolizei*, who spent weeks questioning islanders, raised the level of fear and tension to a new high. Mrs Tremayne noted:

> We used to hear about the 'Gestapo' in Germany taking people off in the middle of their dinner and putting them into concentrations camps, but to enter your house and march you off at a moment's notice, without any explanation, is a ghastly thing to do. No one knows whose turn will be next.

For the owners of the Dixcart Hotel, Miss Duckett and Miss Page, the early hours of 4 October and the days that followed would be a nightmare. At 4 a.m., they were awakened by thunderous knocking on the front door and a German officer pushed his way in, shouting, 'You have the British here!' The officer and his men then searched all the rooms in the buildings while the two spinsters stayed up for the rest of the night in a state of confusion and suspense, consoling themselves with cups of mint tea. When the *Geheime Feldpolizei* arrived at the hotel, they could not believe that, as they asserted, the two ladies had slept through the raid and had no idea what had happened. It was only then that they saw Mrs Hathaway's horse-drawn van arrive and German soldiers carrying two coffins out to the vehicle. 'Then,' Miss Page said later, 'we were thrilled to bits to think our boys had been here.'

It was almost a month later that the *Geheime Feldpolizei* questioned Mrs Pittard. The doctor's widow had spent sleepless nights wondering if there would be another raid or when the Germans would come to question her. According to the Woods, she was 'given away by the window pane which the commandos had broken to get into her house'. However, Cruikshank says that German plans to evacuate the entire population of Sark following the raid were halted when 'a helpless and somewhat simple-minded woman' (the widow who had directed the raiders to the Dixcart Hotel) appeared at the island headquarters and volunteered the information that she had been awakened by the commandos and had given them a map. When the Germans examined her – and gave her a rough time – they promised that she would not be deported to Germany for more detailed questioning. Mrs Pittard may have appeared 'simple-minded' to the Germans, but in voluntarily presenting herself at the headquarters she probably hoped that this honourable gesture would bring an end to the searches and interrogations that were making life insufferable for the population of the island.

In Berlin, the *Oberkommando des Heeres* (OKH), the Army High Command, had proposed that the island should be completely evacuated, in part as a punishment and also to remove any risk that assistance might be given to commandos on subsequent raids. *Generalfeldmarschall* Gerd von Rundstedt, *OB West*, Commander in Chief in the West, concurred with *Generaloberst* Jodl, the *Oberkommando der Wehrmacht* (OKW), Armed Forces High Command Chief of Operations, that the extent to which the troops relied on the civil population was such that if they were removed the garrison would have a desert on their hands. Von Rundstedt pointed out angrily that the raid had succeeded only because orders had been disobeyed.

By now the German command on the Channel Islands had established that it was only Mrs Pittard who had offered assistance to the commandos, though a number of people like Issac Carré and George Hammon, who had been arrested as he inspected his rabbit snares, were taken to Guernsey for questioning. At one stage the apparent detailed knowledge of the raiders of the disposition of the troops and the location of the minefield near Point Château led to the wild idea that the RAF had dropped carrier pigeons on Sark and these had been used to send intelligence back to Britain.

The toughest time would be endured by Mrs Pittard, who was arrested, transported to Sark harbour in the horse-drawn butcher's van and taken to Guernsey, where she was held in prison for eleven weeks – with the first week in solitary confinement. The lonely, frightened woman spent the first days sobbing in her cell, wondering what was in store for her. She was the only woman in her section of the prison and would later be treated with sympathy, given privacy and even allowed to dry her hair in front of the governor's sitting room fire. After eleven weeks, she was released and allowed to return home – but this would only be a short respite.

Mrs Pittard had been promised that if she co-operated in the investigation she would not be deported to Germany. However, what seemed reasonable in the Channel Islands was not acceptable in Berlin. A formula had to be worked out that ensured that the word of a German officer – the promise to Mrs Pittard – could be honoured, but that in the end she could be deported.

The rather tortuous solution was to include her in another batch of deportees. The deportees from the Channel Islands included former officers and reserve officers, and people with previous convictions, politically suspect persons, those who refused to work, young men without useful employment, clergy, leading public figures and wealthy people who might exert an anti-German influence, and those inhabitants of Sark not engaged in agriculture. Among those who left the islands were Ambrose Sherwill and the American husband of the Dame of Sark – who, though not in good health, was selected because he had served in the Royal Flying Corps in the First World War.

These deportations were in part a punishment, but in fact retired British Army officers were gathering intelligence. On Jersey, Maj. Crawford-Morrison, who was the air raids controller and used this as cover, was assisted by two other retired officers, Majors Manley and L'Amy. Along with other helpers who were nominally working for the Germans, they built up a picture of the German fortifications on the island. The maps made from this information were then filmed by Stanley Green, a projectionist at a cinema in St Helier. When Crawford-Morrison was deported to Germany in 1942, he concealed the films with him and they were eventually sent to Britain. L'Amy, who had managed to remain on the island, gathered information until the liberation and passed it on to men and women escaping from the island.

This time, if the person to be deported was the head of a family, then the whole family was also to be deported. Intended deportees were interviewed at the *Feldkommandantur*, as a result of which a number were given exemption from deportation, mostly based on medical grounds.

On 5 February 1943, the German authorities sent out the final deportation notices by mail, warning that transportation would take place on Tuesday 9 February. However, bad weather and problems with the boat delayed the transportation, and on 13 February the deportees finally left for St Malo.

Researching *Islands in Danger*, the Woods recalled a conversation: 'Many years later a Sark lady still had an aggrieved tone in her voice as she remarked to the present authors: "We were all getting on all right during the Occupation, until the Commandos spoilt everything by coming and murdering two German soldiers."'

Hitler was obsessed with the Channel Islands, the only part of Great Britain to be controlled by Nazi Germany, and the humiliating death of the soldiers on Sark, as well as the incompetence of the garrison, prompted him to order stronger defences as well as issuing the Commando Order.

The paths to the beaches were mined and put off limits, and new minefields were laid. The numbers are staggering: from a mere 939 mines on the island, the figures jumped to 2,339 and eventually would stand at 4,000 on the beaches, cliffs and bays. This inevitably led to tragic accidents, and in October 1944 4-year-old Nanette Carré, playing near her home, would be killed by a mine. Other measures were enforced that were designed as part of a collective punishment – the curfew was reduced to even shorter hours, fishing was banned and houses along parts of the shoreline were deliberately destroyed. Throughout the island, guards were doubled and armed.

What added to the German discomfort was that in North Africa, the 8th Army had just won a clear victory at El Alamein, one that Churchill had accurately described as 'the end of the beginning'. In the Soviet Union, the defeat of the 6th Army at Stalingrad would follow a few months later – Nazi Germany was now on the back foot.

Recalling Operation Basalt, Bruce Ogden-Smith would later say, 'We never thought about the significance of what we had done until the press took it up.'[5]

The date 3 October would be significant in the wider history of not only the Second World War but also in the exploration of space. At the top secret German research establishment of Peenemünde on the Baltic, the first A4 rocket (later known as the V2) was successfully launched. It flew for 147km and reached a height of 84.5km, becoming the first man-made object to reach space.

Notes

1 The complete force was Appleyard, Pinckney, Colin Ogden-Smith, Lassen, Dudgeon, Bruce Ogden-Smith, Flint, Robinson, Edgar, Forster and Stokes. Sergeant Bruce Ogden-Smith, brother of Colin, had elected to remain an NCO even though his background and education made him an obvious choice for a commission. For nearly 200 years, the Ogden-Smith family had made fishing tackle that had been sold through a shop in St James that sold hand-made boots and quality hats. A pre-war Territorial soldier at a time when there were many gentlemen NCOs – particularly in the London Territorial Army (TA) – he had stuck to his principles, even flunking a War Office Selection Board course for potential officers by writing rude words on an intelligence test paper which he said was 'a waste of time'.

2 This was almost certainly a Fairburn Sykes fighting knife designed by two close combat instructors at the Special Training Centre at Loch Ailort, William Ewart Fairbarn and Eric Anthony Sykes. The knife was 11½in (29cm) long with a double-edged tapered blade 7in (18cm) long. While it could be used in a slashing attack, the method taught to British and Allied special forces was a stabbing action directed at one of the key arteries. The silence and speed of Lassen's attack suggest that he cut the sentry's carotid or subclavian; the latter, according to Fairbarn, 'is not an easy artery to cut with a knife, but, once cut, your opponent will drop, and no tourniquet or any help of man can save him.'

3 The Dixcart is Sark's oldest hotel and today has nine bedrooms that are en-suite with TV, telephone and tea-making facilities. The comfortable lounges have ancient fireplaces with wood-burning stoves. There are extensive gardens which lead down through the orchard to Dixcart Bay. The hotel is open throughout the year, offering bed and breakfast accommodation.

4 Tom Winter and other members of the SSRF captured on Aquatint were among the British prisoners fettered.

5 The Ogden-Smith brothers were a formidable pair. Bruce next joined the commandos' fledgling Special Boat Section, now the Special Boat Squadron (SBS). According to his Commando Certificate of Service, this transfer would have taken place in January 1943, so he saw service in the Middle East prior to winning his DCM and Military Medal (MM) in the space of three weeks in January 1944. The former decoration was for Operation Postage Able, a protracted beach reconnaissance of St Laurent on 17–21 January, and the latter for Operation KFH, a similar reconnaissance of La Riviere on the night of 31 December 1943 to 1 January 1944. On both operations he worked with Major Logan Scott-Bowden, RE, who would win the DSO and MC.

Beach reconnaissance was the brainchild of a naval navigator, Lt-Commander Nigel Clogstoun-Willmott, who believed that charts and aerial photographs provided insufficient information for a major amphibious operation. They did not, for example, show the hardness of the sand, a matter of obvious interest in landing tanks and trucks. Experience gained in landings in North Africa in Operation Torch and earlier at Dieppe in 1942 validated Willmott's concern. Combined Operations Pilotage Parties (COPPs) were formed, and in the winter of 1944, based in the sailing club at Hayling Island on the south coast of England, beach reconnaissance of the French coast began in earnest. By this stage in the war, Clogstoun-Willmott was a sick man and not fit for winter swimming, but he had trained other swimmers, including Scott-Bowden and Ogden-Smith.

10

ATTABOY, BLAZING, CONSTELLATION, CONCERTINA, COVERLET AND CONDOR: THE RAIDS THAT NEVER WERE

Churchill's anger at the capture of the Channel Islands, as well as his demand for offensive action, led to more ambitious projects than commando raids. He wanted the islands either recaptured or at least held for a significant time – such as twenty-four hours. This produced plans for Operation Attaboy, a raid by 5,000 men against Alderney.

Sir Roger Keyes, the director of combined operations and the Joint Planning Staff, put forward numerous well-reasoned objections. Surprise could not be guaranteed in light of the speed at which agents who had landed had been captured and the reception given to Royal Navy vessels that had ventured too close to the Channel Islands. Fighter cover would be at a disadvantage, with a limited loiter time, while the *Luftwaffe* would be operating from bases in mainland France. The only beaches that were suitable for landings were on the north and north-west coasts, but to land here required a spell of calm weather over three or four days, owing to the swell. The outlying navigational dangers also meant that ships would have to make a long, slow approach across strong tides. Finally, the capture of Alderney would bring no strategic gain and long-term maintenance would be a problem.

Churchill stated that even twenty-four hours on the island would be worth the heavy casualties that were anticipated. He minuted General Ismay on 8 March:

I thought it would have been possible to take it one night, hold it the next day under strong Air patrol, and leave the following night. I understood that the Air Force might be able to give the Air support during the single day, and that this would bring about many fruitful engagements with the Germans such as are now sought over the Pas de Calais.

I do not know why it should be supposed that the French coastline is not so well defended as ATTABOY. There is this difference also, whereas the numbers in ATTABOY can be outmatched by us, those available on the mainland have measureless superiority.

Happily, the plan was abandoned – but not the idea.

In 1942, Mountbatten, now the director of combined operations, argued in favour of Operation Blazing, the capture of Alderney. The advantages of holding the island he asserted were:

a) A small craft base for cutting the enemy coastal convoy route.
b) An advance RDF (radar) station to extend the Fighter Command Coverage.
c) An emergency landing ground.
d) A diversion which may cause withdrawal of enemy air forces from other fronts, including the withdrawal of bombers from Norway.
e) A diversion which may cause the withdrawal of military forces from other fronts.
f) An opportunity for bringing enemy air forces to battle under reasonably favourable circumstances.
g) A springboard for further combined operations.

The force required for this operation would be:

Naval:
Six *Hunt*-class destroyers
Five Infantry Assault Ships (4 LSC, 36 ALC)

Eight Motor Gun Boats (MGB)

Four shore-based ALC

Eighteen TLC

Thirty 'R' Craft

Four Schuyts

Military:

Four infantry battalions

One parachute battalion

One commando and two troops

One squadron and one or two troops of tanks

Thirteen Bren carriers

One light battery

One field company RE

One MG company

Signal, RAMC and RASC detachments

Ten Pioneer sections

Three light AA batteries

Four bulldozers

Some transport to follow

RAF:

330 bomber sorties, including four squadrons for low-level bombing

40 parachute dropping aircraft

Eight smoke aircraft

Fighter wings for protection of returning aircraft

Fighter wings for cover over shipping in the harbour

Fighter wings to cover the withdrawal of the shipping on D1

Four Intruder sorties against enemy aerodromes on the night of the assault

One anti-flak squadron

One close support fighter squadron

Fighter sweep to anticipate the first enemy reaction

Offensive sweeps to meet the air situation which develops

One close support fighter squadron at call

RAF servicing commando

Mountbatten stated that the attack would begin with ninety commando soldiers landing at the foot of the cliffs at the western end of the island. The main defences were then to be bombed for sixty-five minutes, from twenty-five minutes before nautical twilight. These attacks would then be followed by a low-level bombing attack with high explosive and smoke on Fort Albert – the Victorian fort that commanded the entrance to St Anne's. Five minutes later, the parachute battalion would drop to the rear of the harbour defences and launch an immediate attack. Meanwhile, the destroyers would shell the harbour defences to cover the approach of the main assault force east of Fort Albert. Smaller forces would land near Fort Albert and in the old harbour. The second wave of troops would bring with them the light anti-aircraft (AA) batteries, and at this stage the troops not required as a permanent garrison would withdraw. The operation, Mountbatten confidently asserted, would be completed by early afternoon. The garrison would then remain on the island until further notice, supplied each week with 400 tons of rations, ammunition and stores.

'All very simple,' Cruikshank observes dryly in *The German Occupation of the Channel Islands*, 'as seen by the Chief of Combined Operations.'

'To win over the Chiefs of Staff to allocate such generous resources to what was clearly a limited objective, Mountbatten needed powers of persuasion he simply did not possess,' writes Barry Turner in *Outpost of Occupation*. 'As Chief of the Imperial General Staff, General Sir Alan Brooke admired Mountbatten's energy but had no faith in his "wild proposals" which had more to do with personal aggrandisement than winning the war. No one trusted Mountbatten.'

After further deliberation with the Air Officer Commanding on 5 May 1942, Operation Blazing was reduced to a large-scale raid, to take and hold the island for twenty-four hours, or longer if the situation and enemy reactions allowed. It was now under the optimistic title of Operation Aimwell.

The forces required for this new operation were reckoned to be:

Naval:
Six *Hunt*-class destroyers
Five Infantry Assault Ships (5 LSC, 33 ALC and 2 MLC)
Eight MGBs
Seventeen TLC

Thirty 'R' Craft

One Hospital Carrier

Military:

Six Troops SS. Brigade (550 all ranks)

Fourteen Churchill tanks

Thirteen Bren carriers

Four 3.7in howitzers

One field company RE

One troop (four guns) Bofors AA

One field ambulance

RC of Signals

Services

Total military force: 3,000 all ranks

RAF:

200 to 250 medium and heavy bomber aircraft

Twenty-four Blenheim bombers – 500lb HE and 250lb smoke bombs

Fourteen smoke-laying (army co-operation) Blenheims

Eighteen long-range coastal fighters

Eight Spitfire wings (24 squadrons)

Twelve Intruder fighter aircraft

Twenty-four night fighters

The 1st Guards Brigade was put on standby to move to the Isle of Wight for training, but in the end the whole operation was abandoned, in part because the newly appointed head of the Airborne Division objected to the use of this valuable asset in the anticipated parachute assault, and because Operation Jubilee, the raid on Dieppe in August 1942, had now taken precedence.

Interestingly, in June 1942 the German high command produced a study that was almost an echo of the objections raised by the British Chiefs of Staff to an attack on Alderney. The analysis by *Armeeoberkommando* 7 stated that an enemy fleet could not survive the Alderney Race. Their bases were hundreds of miles away, and a large naval force would inevitably be spotted, especially in the short summer nights. Large ships could not reach the beaches. Treacherous currents would make it difficult for small boats to land troops. The batteries on Alderney controlled the Race, at least when visibility was good; the four huge guns of the Mirus battery on Guernsey would play their part; and the guns on Jersey were effective to within 5 miles of the French coast.

The tragic losses suffered by the Canadians at Dieppe give an indication of the sort of casualties that might have been incurred in Attaboy or Blazing. However, this does not seem to have deterred Mountbatten, who in 1943 proposed Operation Constellation, a series of landings on the Channel Islands that were composed of Concertina, an assault landing on Alderney, Coverlet on Guernsey and Condor on Jersey. He argued that, 'There is no doubt that the enemy has fully appreciated the value of the Channel Islands, and the potential threat those islands would offer if re-occupied by our forces.' Under the code name Concubine, an effort was made to collect intelligence about the islands. Concubine I focussed on Jersey and Concubine II on Guernsey. It was reconnaissance for the Concubines that would be the reason for some of the small-scale commando raids on the neighbouring islands to Jersey, Guernsey and Alderney.

Of all the proposed attacks, it was Concertina that was seen as the most viable. However, for it to have any chance of success it would require forty-eight hours of good weather, sea states that were no greater than a low swell and a cloud ceiling of 8,000ft. While the good weather and cloud ceiling might ensure a greater level of accuracy for air attacks, they would also be ideal conditions for the numerous enemy flak batteries on the island.

Assuming that the air attacks had gone according to plan, the next phase would be amphibious and/or airborne landings. Longy and Saline Bays had been selected for landing infantry and vehicles, but there would also be subsidiary landings at Telegraph and Hannaine Bays. Following the air and sea bombardment it might be possible for airborne troops to be parachuted or airlifted. However, as Cruikshank writes, 'The first would not succeed because of the very strong defences; the second was not feasible because the dust and wreckage caused by the bombing would produce too many casualties among the airborne troops.'[1]

Of the other proposed Constellation operations, Cruikshank writes:

'Condor', perhaps the most terrifying operation against the Channel Islands conceived while Mountbatten was Chief of Combined Operations, could have been a second Dieppe. It was to begin with naval bombardment of the east and west coast of Jersey, followed by paratroop and infantry landings, and by scramble landings by commandos in the south-west. The paratroops were to drop on the race-course, on the airfield and at St Peter's Mill from 192 aircraft. On the second day artillery would land and more infantry would extend the eastern beachhead to the high ground overlooking Grouville Bay. The troops on the west coast would link up with the commandos who had landed at Noirmont Point in the south-west.

Next day tanks would be landed on the east coast, the western beachhead extended to the high ground north of St Aubin's Bay, and La Moye peninsula 'pinched out'. The climax, at least on paper, came on the fourth day, with a three-pronged attack on St Helier.

As Cruikshank notes, 'The plan gives no estimate of the invaders' losses, nor of civilian casualties, nor of destruction of property in St Helier, where the final battle was programmed to take place.'

Planning notes and maps held in The National Archives at Kew show how the attack would have developed – the fact that some of the open beaches that were proposed as beachheads had been identified by the Germans as likely landing sites and were already well defended seems to have been ignored by the chief of combined operations.

In *Outpost of Occupation*, Barry Turner spells out the relationship between Churchill and Mountbatten. They 'had one thing in common, it was their love of Boy's Own adventures. Goaded by the Prime Minister, Mountbatten came up with ever more fanciful schemes for sending Hitler into one of his tantrums.'

As early as 1941, air reconnaissance photographs showed that the Channel Islands were being fortified. Mountbatten commented, 'Each island is a veritable fortress, the assault against which cannot be contemplated unless the defences are neutralised, or reduced to a very considerable extent by prior action.'

This was the problem, as 'prior action' meant either naval or aerial bombardment. Although most defences were on or near the coast, the inaccuracies of bombing or shelling had the potential to pulverise two-thirds of Guernsey's land surface, and at least half of Jersey's. Because of the likely substantial civilian casualties, the operations were shelved. Alderney was almost unpopulated, so civilian casualties were not an issue – however, accuracy was. Professor Solly Zuckerman, the British government's operational analysis expert, estimated that for Concertina to have any hope of success the little island would need to be bombed for three nights by 1,500 medium and heavy bombers, delivering a total 4,600 tons of bombs. There would be three aiming points: one dead centre of the long axis of the island; the second a mile to the east of that point; and the third a mile to the west. Zuckermann estimated that 3,650 tons would be on target.

In *The Channel Islands War 1940–1945*, Peter King makes the observation, 'Fortunately these plans were stillborn, and after D-Day, massive German fortifications, and the fate of French coastal towns subject to air attack, were convincing arguments against attempting any such invasion.'

As part of wider operations in Europe, there would be one final discussion of an attack on the Channel Islands – strictly there were three, under the code names Rankin Case A, B and C. By the end of 1943, at Supreme Headquarters Allied Expeditionary Force (SHAEF), Lt Gen Frederick Morgan, Chief of Staff to the Supreme Allied Commander (designate), or COSSAC, addressed the idea. Rankin Case A was predicated on the idea that the strength and morale of German forces in Western Europe was so low that it was feasible and desirable to launch a smaller assault than that envisaged for D-Day, and that the islands could be recaptured as part of this operation. Case B was the optimistic idea of German withdrawal from occupied countries, most likely Norway and western France. 'In this case, it was necessary, for political as well as strategic reasons, to occupy the areas vacated, but it was important that the main forces of the Allies should not thereby be tied down far from the eventual centre of action,' said Morgan. Rankin Case C applied in the case of an unconditional surrender, where organised resistance had ceased in Europe and the island garrisons would be disarmed. Rankin Case C would become Operation Nestegg in 1945.

Prior to D-Day, under political pressure, a study was made to see if the Channel Islands could be recaptured as part of the larger Overlord operation. The case for their recapture was that this would deny the Germans a radar outpost and powerful coastal artillery. However, since the operation would require three or four divisions as well as considerable naval and air support, this was deemed an unacceptable diversion of resources from the main effort of D–Day. Finally, it was pointed out, and would later be demonstrated, that shipping running close to the Cotentin peninsula would be out of range of the guns on the islands.

The Channel Islands would have to wait until Nestegg hatched.

Notes

1 On 16 February 1945, in the campaign to liberate the Philippines, men of the US 503rd Parachute Combat Team and US 24th Infantry Division landed on Corregidor Island in Manila Bay, the heavily fortified island 4 miles long and 1¼ miles wide which was held by 6,700 Japanese troops. The preliminary bombardment that started on 24 January included 2,028 effective sorties, with 3,163 short tonnes (2,869 tons) of bombs dropped on Corregidor. At 3 miles long and 1½ miles wide, Alderney is not dissimilar in size to Corregidor, and the proposed weight of bombs for Alderney is about the same as that expended on Corregidor. However, to this should be added close-range naval bombardment by cruisers and destroyers of the US Navy. Of the 7,000 US troops committed to the capture of Corregidor, 207 were killed and 684 wounded. The Americans had complete control of the air and sea around the island, which would not have applied to the British in 1943, and the cost in lives would have been far greater.

11

OPERATION HUCKABACK, 27–28 FEBRUARY 1943

The objective of Operation Huckaback was the little island of Herm. Herm is only 1½ miles long and less than half a mile wide. It is oriented so that its greatest length runs north–south. The northern half of the coastline is surrounded by sandy beaches, the southern half is rocky. Historically, the island had been home to monks and smugglers, while before the war the white sandy beaches had made it a holiday paradise that also had a modest fishing and farming community. Efforts had been made before the war to ensure that it was not developed, and it was a nature reserve with a unique white shell beach to the north-east. The island had a golf course, a small combined post office and general store, and in 1931 a population of forty-eight, but with the exception of a caretaker and his wife, who looked after Belvoir House, the main residence on the island, they had all been evacuated in 1940. Today, the island remains an unspoilt haven.

The raid was carried out by No. 62 Commando (SSRF) over the night of 27/28 February 1943. It was originally planned for the night of 9/10 February, as part of several simultaneous raids on the smaller islands of Herm, Jethou and Brecqhou. The objective of the raids was to take prisoners and gain information about the situation in the Channel Islands. It was to be carried out by forty-two men from the SSRF and No. 4 Commando, but was cancelled because of bad weather.

Huckaback was reinvented as a raid on Herm alone. Among the party were two men from No. 3 (Jewish) Troop/X Troop, No. 10 Commando:

Lt Patrick Miles, whose real name was Hubertus Levine, and Sgt Frederick Bentley, whose real name was Frederic Bierer. Both men were almost certainly German speakers but whose Jewish identity was concealed behind a very English *nom de guerre*.

The objective of the new raid was to establish if the little island could be used as a fire base for artillery to support a larger operation against Guernsey.

Ten men of the SSRF, under command of Captain Patrick (Pat) Porteous VC[1] and Lt Thompson, were brought to a point to the south of the island by MTB 344, and then rowed a dory to the shingle beach of Rosaire. After three unsuccessful attempts to scale the soft clay cliff, Porteous finally managed to climb up the bed of a stream and pulled the others up using toggle ropes.

On reaching Belvoir House, they reported that it had been broken into and left abandoned. Further reconnaissance found that the Old Tower of Herm and the château were also deserted. The party spent three hours on the island, finding no evidence of German troops or civilians, though they were unable to check the houses clustered around the small quay on the western side of Herm.

In fact the caretaker of Belvoir House, Mr F.M. Dickson, had heard the commandos moving around and had taken the wise precaution of dousing all lights and locking the door.

Sheep were seen grazing and some notices in German were also reported; one near the château indicated that the building and surroundings were out of bounds to troops. The commandos left propaganda leaflets in various conspicuous places. A little like today's gang tag, to indicate that commandos had made the raid they also chalked the letter 'C' on various walls. However, the most important part of the operation was that the gently shelving shell beach would be viable for landing artillery. Interestingly, German troops had used the beach for disembarkation drills during their training for Operation Sealion. It was reported that a *Propaganda Kompanie* (PK) camera team had joined the exercise to make a dramatic film showing how Britain would be invaded.

Three years after their training exercise, the Germans were unaware that the island had been visited and happily did nothing to improve its defences, so today it retains much of its pre-war character. A flak battery was later sited on the island, and on 24 August 1943 it engaged and shot down an aircraft that crashed into the sea off the east coast. The gunners' victory was short-lived when they learned that they had downed a *Luftwaffe* aircraft.

A further raid on the island was proposed in the Hardtack series of operations. Hardtack 22 would have been carried out by No. 2 US Ranger Battalion in January 1944, but like other Hardtack operations in early 1944 in north-west France it was seen as too close to the Normandy area that would be the location for the D-Day landings, and so to prevent the Germans from reinforcing the area it was cancelled. Moreover, by now, with the nights becoming shorter, small cross-Channel raids were seen to be impracticable as the time ashore would be limited.

During the occupation, German officers would periodically visit Herm to shoot rabbits for the pot and chat to Dickson, the caretaker, whom they nick-named Robinson Crusoe, impressed by the length of his enormous beard. On 28 April 1945, Dickson and his wife were joined by *Obersleutnant* Hans von Helldorf, who had been banished to Herm by *Vizeadmiral* Friedrich Hüffmeier. The admiral feared that, as in the July 1944 plot against Hitler, the aristocratic army officers on the Channel Islands were plotting against him. Von Helldorf had been under surveillance ever since his removal as chief of staff at the end of February 1945, when the ardent Nazi Hüffmeier had edged out von Schmettow as commander of the Channel Islands.

Vizeadmiral Hüffmeier would have his brief moment of glory in the Granville raid in 1945 before the humiliation of surrender a few weeks later.

At the same time that the men of Huckaback were moving stealthily around Herm, in Norway a remarkable commando operation was under way. Operation Gunnerside would be evaluated by the SOE as the most successful sabotage operation of the Second World War. A team of SOE-trained Norwegian soldiers penetrated the heavily guarded Norsk Hydro at Telemark in Norway. Their target was the production facilities and stock of a liquid called 'heavy water' that was a by-product of the production of fertiliser. Physicists realised that it could have a critical role in the development of an atomic bomb, which it was believed was under way in Germany.

The Norwegian saboteurs destroyed the entire inventory of heavy water produced during the German occupation, over 500kg (1,102lb), along with equipment critical to operation of the electrolysis chambers. Small items of British equipment were left to show the Germans that it had been a British operation, to ensure that the local population did not suffer retribution. Although 3,000 German soldiers were dispatched to search the area for the commandos, all of them escaped; five of them skied 400km to neutral Sweden, two proceeded to Oslo – where they assisted Milorg, the Norwegian secret army – and four remained in the region for further work with the resistance.

It remains one of the terrifying 'what ifs' of the Second World War – what would have been the outcome of the conflict if a German atomic weapon had been the warhead of an A4/V2 rocket, and London the target?

Notes

1 Captain Porteous had been awarded the VC for his part in the successful attack by No. 4 Commando on the German coastal battery code-named 'Hess' as part of the larger Operation Jubilee, the attack on Dieppe in August 1942.

12

OPERATION HARDTACK 7, 25–26 DECEMBER, AND HARDTACK 28, 29–30 DECEMBER 1943

There were nine Hardtack raids at points along the northern French coast and Channel Islands. Probably the most useful was Hardtack 21 on 26–27 December 1943 by No. 1 French Troop, No. 10 Commando, which gathered intelligence on the defences of what would later be Utah beach. The most tragic was Hardtack 36 on 24–25 December 1943 against the Dutch coastal town of Wassenaar, in which all the men from No. 8 French Troop, No. 10 Commando, were killed. Tragedy would also strike the two Hardtack operations against the Channel Islands.

Operation Hardtack 28, which had been planned as a simultaneous raid with Hardtack 7, was launched against Jersey and would be the only commando raid on the island during the war. It was a raid that would end in tragedy and show that some of the residents of Jersey had adopted a 'live and let live' relationship with the occupying forces.

The party of nine men was commanded by 22-year-old Captain Phillip Ayton of No. 12 Commando, an officer in the Argyll and Sutherland Highlanders. It included three French commandos from No. 10 Commando with their officer, Lt Hurlot. Their motor gunboat reached Petit Port on the northern coast of Jersey and the commandos landed in a small rocky cove at 10.45 p.m.

After crossing a wire fence, they found two buildings – one a corrugated iron shed and the other stone-built – both of which were deserted and appeared in the past to have been used by fishermen. After travelling for 200yd up the valley from the cove, they came to a 1m-high fence to which were attached red and white signs with the wording *MINEN* and *STOP MINES* . It was then that they realised that the first fence they had encountered had been the forward edge of a minefield, and miraculously they had crossed it without triggering a mine.

Pushing uphill, they reached the cluster of buildings variously described as a farm or a hamlet that had the quaint name of Egypt. It was deserted and showed what appeared to be shell damage. In fact Egypt had been abandoned, it was said by its Jewish owner, and consequently the Germans had turned the locality into an infantry training area as well as a target for the big 21cm guns of 3 *Herres Küsten Artillerie Regiment* 1265 at *Batterie Mackensen*, located to the north of St Martin's Church about 3 miles away. As the commandos skirted the area, they came across a notice in English and German that confirmed its function: 'Military Zone – Civilians Strictly Forbidden'.

The raiders then made their way across country to an observation post that was well camouflaged, but to their disappointment unmanned. There were other concrete emplacements, but the poor state of the trenches suggested that the position was no longer in use.

The commandos decided that they would move on the roads, marching in the open as if they were a German patrol. Arriving at La Geonniere, they knocked on the front door of the farm and, after twenty minutes, a very nervous Miss Le Feuvre opened a window.

They asked her whether there were any Germans or German positions in the locality, but she said she did not know and directed them to a neighbouring farm owned by two brothers, John and Hedley Le Breton. When Ramsey interviewed the brothers for *The Channel Islands Then and Now*, he learned that Miss Le Feuvre believed that she had been visited by a German, 'but that she was surprised that they all spoke good English!'.

When the commandos knocked on the door of the Le Breton farm, a man appeared who stood speechless with his mouth open. This was Hedley Le Breton who, they were not to know, had mild learning difficulties – which explained his confused silence.

Once John Le Breton had established that the men with blackened faces were indeed British soldiers, they were invited in – though a guard was posted outside the farm. Inside, Captain Atterbury learned that there were no Germans billeted in farms or houses in the area. They did not know if the observation post that the commandos had reconnoitred was occupied, but they knew that there were a few Germans at the hamlet of Porteret.

They said the strongpoint at Les Platons was manned by about fifteen Germans and ten Russians. The official summary continues:

They told us that the Russians were prisoners compelled to work for the Germans; they thought they were armed and did patrolling duties the same as the Germans. The sentry at this strongpoint usually stays very near the centre and does not patrol or go near the perimeter of the strongpoint. They told us that the strongpoint was quite well armed but did not know the actual strength.

Les Platons, on the north coast, at 136m (446ft), is the highest part of the island.

The report based on the conversation with the Le Bretons stated that the estimated strength of the German garrison of the island was 1,000. Most of the transport was horse-drawn due to fuel shortages, though motor vehicles operated in St Helier. The beach at Petit Port was mined, but unsurprisingly the Le Bretons did not know the exact position of the mines. Similarly, they knew that there were mines around the Les Platons strongpoint but did not know their exact position.

The after-action report noted that neither farmer had seen any German patrols in the area, though a patrol of armed Russian troops had arrested them for being out after curfew. After they had explained that they had permission to be out, they were released. They explained that the wintertime curfew was from 9 p.m. to 7 a.m.

Perhaps disappointedly to senior military and political leaders in Britain, they said that there was no resistance movement on the island and the population:

is generally not hostile to the Germans. The farmers explained that the island is so small that it would be difficult to get up a movement of resistance without German reprisals. The population is very frightened of the Russians who are ill fed by the Germans and they had to forage around the farms for food; but they were sorry for them as they were suppressed by the Germans.

Though there was no organised resistance, there was a good deal of resentment towards the Germans for having removed half the available medical supplies on the island, which the report states had been sent by the Red Cross. The garrison also took half of the food produced or imported to the island. Feeding on farms was not a problem; however, in the town and villages, where the Germans had greater control, 'conditions were quite bad'.

The brothers gave the commandos copies of the local paper and also a German paper, a glass of milk to all of the patrol and offered to guide them to the strongpoint at Les Platons. This they did, taking the patrol to the outer eastern perimeter of Les Platons.

The assistance given to Captain Ayton by the Le Breton brothers is at odds with the version of events described by Madeleine Bunting in *The Model Occupation*, who writes that the Hardtack 28 team:

> returned to Britain with the disconcerting information that residents of Jersey had not been co-operative; one woman refused to tell them where there were Germans, and told them to ask at another farmhouse. They did so, and found two petrified brothers who told them there was no resistance movement and people were getting on well with the Germans.

On the perimeter of Les Platons, Captain Ayton and Lt Hulot conducted a close reconnaissance of the position and located what looked suspiciously like a minefield. What appeared to be sticks about 10in high were visible at regular intervals – one of these was carefully moved, but there was no reaction. The two officers may have been messing with the notorious S-Mine or *Schrapnellmine* 36, a bounding anti-personnel mine that contained about 360 steel balls that blasted in a 360° arc when the mine exploded about a metre above the ground. They found no sentry, but also no entrance to the strongpoint.[1]

Up to this point, Hardtack 28 had been very lucky – but the patrol's luck was soon going to run out.

Captain Ayton realised that there were now only forty-five minutes to make it back from Les Platons to their landing point at Petit Port and the crew of the dory who would take them out to the MGB waiting offshore. They reached Petit Port at 4.45 a.m. to discover that the dory was not there. They moved along the coast, flashing a torch at fifteen-minute intervals in an attempt to attract the dory crew's attention. Lt Hulot reported that they reached a three-strand cattle fence that extended down the cliff and crawled underneath it, and were about 5yd on the other side when the French officer reached the fence:

> Suddenly, there was a vivid flash which lit up the whole area and a loud explosion which sounded like the explosion of two No. 82 grenades. I first thought that a German patrol had found us and proceeded cautiously forward but saw no one and presumed Captain Ayton had trodden on a mine.

The young captain was found, badly wounded and trapped in brambles, on the edge of the cliff. The patrol then heard the engines of the MGB that was just visible about 400yd offshore. The dory had in fact returned to the MGB but was ordered back to shore. The patrol flashed their torch and the dory reached the shore, and with great difficulty Captain Ayton was put onto the little boat at 5.20 a.m. Hulot noted that despite the explosion of the mine, which in the silence of the winter darkness must have been overwhelming, there was no response from the troops in Les Platons.

Incredibly, Captain Ayton survived the journey back to Britain and was rushed to the Royal Naval Auxiliary Hospital at Dartmouth, where despite intense efforts to keep him alive he died on Boxing Day 1943. He is buried in the military plot at Longcross, beyond Townstall churchyard on the Totnes road.[2]

If Hardtack 28 had been dogged with bad luck, their ill-fortune would pale besides that of Hardtack 7 (the numbering was out of sequence), a reconnaissance raid against Sark aimed at capturing prisoners and gathering intelligence.

The five-man team from No. 8 French Troop, No. 10 Commando and No. 12 Commando was led by Lt A.J. McGonigal, and on the night of 25/26 December they attempted to climb the cliffs at Derrible Bay. They found the going too challenging and aborted the operation. In his report, McGonigal baldly describes what went wrong. They had rowed from the MGB in a dory and arrived at the bay at 11.45 p.m., and after a difficult climb worked their way along Pointe Derrible, a hazardous, steep-sided, rutted promontory that jutted into the sea. 'It was not until 0100 hours that the last ridge connecting the point to the mainland was reached; this consisted of a knife ledge,' McGonigal reported. 'On one side there was a sheer drop to Petite Derrible Bay, and on the other side a similar drop to Derrible Bay. An attempt to cross this ridge proved unsuccessful. The ridge itself was about thirty feet in length with no footholds, and [the] ledge itself was too sharp to provide a hand grip.'

The men then climbed down off the ridge using their toggle ropes, only to be confronted by a climb up a sheer cliff as their route onto mainland Sark. It was now 2 a.m. and the men made their way back to the dory. They re-embarked and rowed to Derrible Bay, where McGonigal and Sgt Boccador of No. 10 Commando landed and examined the beach. To both men the cliffs appeared unscaleable. The two men returned to the dory and the complete force made their way to the MGB by 4.25 a.m.

McGonigal noted, 'although the patrol made a certain amount of noise through loose stones falling over the edge, no signs of any enemy sentries or patrols were seen'.

However, the German garrison appears to have been aware that they had had visitors. In the early hours of Boxing Day, Mrs Julia Tremayne was awakened by hammering at the door and shouts of 'Open the door at once!'.

The day before, she had enjoyed two modest Christmas gifts of candles from Mrs Hathaway and a piece of chocolate from the vicar of St Peter's, who was now in a deportation camp. Now she opened her window to ask who was there, and saw a German officer with three fully armed soldiers. They demanded to search the house and, with her daughter Norah, Mrs Tremayne followed them around the house and outbuildings as cupboards and doors were thrown open and torches flashed over the inside. Mrs Tremayne was terrified that her diary would be discovered, but the search party departed and, unable to sleep, the two women sat in the kitchen sipping hot drinks.

Two nights later, the commandos were back.

This time they landed to the west, at Pointe Château. It was a route that had been used by the Operation Basalt party on 3–4 October 1942, and it would prove a fatal decision. In the year following the raid by Appleyard and Lassen, the island had been heavily mined.

After climbing a 200ft cliff face, they were on to the Hog's Back. Here they encountered a wire fence that McGonigal noted consisted of three strands of very thick copper wire and two thinner strands of ordinary wire. The wire was cut and the party was on the track along the Hog's Back. Thick gorse gave them excellent cover as they moved northwards. The patrol commander was leading and checking the route for mines when two exploded behind him, fatally wounding Corporal Bellamy, who died a few minutes later, and severely wounding Private Dignac.

McGonigal's report states, 'The first mine had exploded about two feet behind Corporal Bellamy, the last member of the patrol, and the second mine about five feet left of it.(The empty container was taken from the first hole and brought back with the force).' All the indications are that they had entered a minefield containing *Schrapnellmine* 35 mines, rigged with ZZ.35 pull switches attached to trip wires. The injuries to the two French soldiers were from the steel balls in the inner container that had exploded above the ground.

Now came the grim process of extracting the wounded men and exiting the minefield, which they did initially by pulling them onto the track using toggle ropes. 'The force then started to carry Corporal Bellamy and Private Dignac out of the minefield,' wrote McGonigal, who was now in the lead – feeling for mines as they made their way back to the coast. As they moved cautiously they tripped two more S Mines, one exploding in front of them and one to the side. McGonigal was wounded and now the only unwounded man in the patrol was Sgt Boccador, the shrapnel having inflicted further injuries on Private Dignac that proved fatal.

But the nightmare was not yet over.

McGonigal writes:

In view of the fact that my force had sustained such casualties, I decided to leave the two bodies, retrace my steps and return to the boat. No sooner had we started to move, however, than more mines went up all around us. I cannot say how many there were but at the time we had the impression of being under fire from a heavy calibre machine gun. We continued our withdrawal to the dory.

He noted with regret that they had been unable to locate the No. 536 Radio set that had been hidden under a rock on the outward leg of the patrol, nor recover the rope that had been used to scale the Pointe Château.

In his patrol report, McGonigal wrote that though they searched carefully for mines, neither he nor Sgt Boccador felt or saw any indications of them. The injuries were sustained by men who were standing or kneeling – anyone who was lying flat was uninjured. As with Hardtack 28, he noted that the explosion of the mines produced no reaction from the German garrison.

In the morning, a German patrol recovered the bodies of the two dead French commandos and they were buried in a small military section of St Peter's Church. Mrs Tremayne noted, 'Two graves were dug in our little churchyard and they were thrown in at dawn one morning, with not one prayer said over them, poor dears. A wooden cross was erected, their names put on and Mrs Hathaway sent two wreaths of camellia.' After the war, André Dignac was exhumed and reburied in France. The grave of Corporal Bellamy has the rather austere French concrete cross with the words 'Bellamy R. Mort pour La France 28-12-1943'.

Other minor raids planned for 1943 but never carried out included Cats-Whiskers against Brecqhou. Pussyfoot against Herm was planned by the SSRF for the night of 3/4 April 1943. Its aim was to reconnoitre the western side of the island which the Huckaback raid had been unable to do. There was also a plan to capture a prisoner. Ten men from the SSRF set off in MTB 344. However, thick fog prevented a safe landing so the raid was cancelled. Sark would have been revisited in Operation Bunbury, a raid that was ambitiously intended to kill or capture the entire garrison of the island. Cats-Whiskers was timed to follow Pussyfoot, but again bad weather forced the cancellation of the raids.

In *The Model Occupation*, Madeleine Bunting writes:

The raids on the islands achieved nothing more than a few scraps of information, but they had very serious consequences for the islanders: Guernsey lost an able President of the Controlling Committee in Sherwill, and the raid on Sark led to more deportations. The raids provoked anxiety on the part of the islands' population, who believed they were futile. No doubt they felt that they could do without this sort of attention from Britain.

Peter King, in *The Channel Islands War 1940–1945*, says of the raids:

The balance sheet … is hard to draw. Brave men sacrificed their lives, and brave Islanders put their lives at risk to help them. Something at least was done to harass the Germans and make the Islanders feel they were not completely neglected. Information was obtained. A few Germans were captured or killed. But several were captured and killed in the ranks of the Commandos, and in the case of the two serious raids: Ambassador and Basalt, Islanders on Guernsey and Sark suffered a good deal through imprisonment or deportation, damage to property, fines, curfew, fishing restrictions, and the frightening presence of the *Feldpolizei* which they mistook for the Gestapo. Had the raids got worse there can be little doubt that the German response would have escalated, and so the taste of war the raids brought to the Islands was received with mixed feelings.

In *The War in the Channel Islands Then and Now*, Winston Ramsey writes:

> Altogether in three years' operations, three Commandos had been killed, two wounded and six men had been made prisoner; two or possibly three Germans had been killed, one wounded and another eight captured. On balance, therefore, the Commandos possibly won by a hair's breadth but against that one must set the considerable reprisals carried out against the populations – many of whom abhorred the very idea of the raids.

In *Islands in Danger*, the Woods quote General Walter Warlimont of the OKW, who wrote immediately after the last raid on the islands, 'Nowhere can be considered safe. The enemy may strike at any time and any place.'[3]

Less than a year after the Hardtack raids, the Allies landed on the relatively thinly defended Normandy coast on D-Day, 6 June 1944. In 1943, if Field Marshal Erwin Rommel had not been overruled by Hitler, the Channel Islands would have been evacuated and the men of the 319th Infantry Division would have left the islands to be deployed to man positions along the Normandy coast.

Though they would have had to leave behind a considerable number of fixed fortress weapons on the islands, they would have brought with them nearly 600 MG 34 machine guns, 108 8.1cm mortars, thirty 3.7cm, nine 5cm and fifteen 4.7cm anti-tank guns, and twelve 8cm FK 30 (t) and forty 10.5cm leFH field guns, in addition to personal weapons and nearly 9,000 infantry, along with supporting artillery, engineers, signals and trained tank crews. The commando raids on the islands, though modest but costly in human lives and disruptive to the islanders, had kept Hitler focussed on the defence of the islands and so ultimately had been proved worthwhile.

A few days before the Hardtack operations, there was a significant appointment in the Allied command structure. On 27 September, General Dwight D. Eisenhower was appointed Supreme Allied Commander in Europe – he would be in overall command of the Allied forces that would land on D-Day, an invasion that was only nine months away.

Notes

1 After the war, on 23 June 1963, a plaque was given to the brothers by the Free French and attached to the wall of the farmhouse, acknowledging their help given to the commandos, who are named as Capt. Ayton, Lt Hulot, Sgt Roberts and Cpls Houcourigary, La Stang and Roux.

2 Operation Petrify, a raid against St Peter Port, Guernsey, by the SSRF on 8/9 January 1943 was finally cancelled because of bad weather. The plan was for four men, Lts Anders Lassen and Ian Warren, with two NCOs, to make their way into the harbour in Folbots – two-man collapsible canoes also known as Cockle canoes – under cover of darkness and attach limpet mines to any ships that could be found. The four men had actually transferred from MTB 344 for the run-in when the operation was cancelled. 'Had it been carried out successfully,' writes Charles Cruikshank, 'there would almost certainly have been heavy reprisals against the people in Guernsey, and perhaps in the other Islands as well.'

3 Sark would suffer an 'invasion' in August 1990, when, armed with a semi-automatic pistol, André Gardes, an unemployed French nuclear physicist, attempted a single-handed invasion. The night Gardes arrived, he put up signs declaring his intention to take over the island at noon on the following day. His invasion plans were foiled when, while sitting on a bench, changing the gun's magazine and waiting for noon to arrive, he was arrested by the island's volunteer police constable.

13

BY AIR AND SEA, 1940–45

Before the Channel Islands were cut off by the D-Day landings and the subsequent liberation of northern France, air and sea interdiction attacks had been hitting the shipping plying between the mainland and the islands.

On 3 November 1941, SS *Batavier V*, a Dutch cargo/passenger ship that had been seized by the Germans in 1940 and operated between France and the islands, was sunk by a Royal Navy MTB west of Cap Gris Nez.

On 3 February 1943, Operation H.K. was launched by the Royal Navy, intended to intercept convoys between Cherbourg and Alderney that crossed each other off the Cap de la Hague, east of Alderney. At dusk on 3 February, a Polish and a British destroyer left Plymouth. As they sighted the Quesnard light at the north-east end of Alderney, the leading lights of Alderney harbour being lit seemed to be an indication that ships were in the area. Normally in wartime these lights would have been extinguished, since they would provide navigation and reference points to enemy ships and aircraft. There was a full moon and cloudless sky, so visual contact could be made over many miles. Then, as the two destroyers were 5 miles from Cap de la Hague, the Quesnard and Alderney harbour lights were extinguished, but moments later the light on Cap de la Hague came on. It was then that the Polish and British skippers saw a target, two 500-ton Dutch coasters.

In a brutal, one-sided action, the destroyers opened fire at 1,000yd, hitting both ships, and then closed in to sink them with depth charges. German shore batteries on Cap de la Hague added to the misery of the stricken coasters, firing a few rounds at one of the sinking vessels.

What had appeared to be a small-scale action to the British had a much wider impact than they had anticipated. The two vessels were the *Hermann* and the *Schleswig-Holstein*, and at the time the Germans were actually unsure whether the ships had been sunk or captured, and coastal gunners could add little light. That the ships were unescorted was the result of an administrative blunder. On board were men who were going on leave, some forty-two soldiers, forty-three flak gunners and forty-three OT workers, the latter German, Flemish and French. These men had actually been ordered off the ships at Alderney but had sneaked back on board. It is possible they were able to do so because they had been given the nod by the Alderney *Hafenkommandant* (harbour commandant), *Kapitän* Parsenow, who was one of the passengers. He would die that night in the bitter cold sea.

Following this attack, new convoy procedures were introduced, but these could not prevent losses due to weather and tidal conditions.

It has been stated that there were six or seven major convoy battles around the Channel Islands during the war. However, it was not all one-sided and in October, after the German blockade-runner *Münsterland*, carrying a cargo of latex, wolfram and tungsten – strategic metals vital for the German war effort – had successfully evaded the US and Royal Navies in both the Pacific and Atlantic, a series of hastily planned attacks were put together.

As *Münsterland* exited the flak cover of the port of Brest on 23 October, Operation Tunnel was hastily activated from Plymouth. HMS *Charybdis*, a *Dido*-class anti-aircraft cruiser, and six destroyers, including HMS *Limbourne*, were dispatched to intercept the ship and her escorts. The operation brought together a mixed bag of six destroyers, with *Charybdis* as command ship. None of the crews in this ad hoc formation had worked together before.

The Germans had the advantage with their excellent radar chain along the French coast, as well as good liaison between each vessel and a strong force of *Elbing*-class fleet torpedo boats[1] from the 4th Torpedo Boat flotilla to protect the convoy. The designation *Flottentorpedoboot* (fleet torpedo boats) is a little misleading, as these vessels were in effect medium-sized destroyers with an armament that allowed them to provide anti-aircraft defence, launch torpedo attacks and undertake escort duties. They were a very effective 'maid of all work'. T23, which would be the nemesis of the *Charybdis*, would escape from its base in northern France following the D-Day landings, and after the war served with the French Navy as the *Alsacien*, before being scrapped in 1955.

A pre-war postcard showing 'The Death of Major Peirson' by the American artist John Singleton Copeley and depicting the death of Peirson in the Royal Square on 6 January 1781. The caption to the postcard concludes, 'This was the last battle in which British troops were engaged on British soil.' The Second World War was yet to scar the shoreline of the islands. (Private collection)

King George V, with French President Raymond Poincaré and General Douglas Haig, inspects a guard of honour drawn from the Royal Guernsey Light Infantry on 7 August 1918. Channel Islanders fought in both world wars, and before they were occupied the islanders raised considerable sums of money to support the war effort in the Second World War. (WF Collection)

The iconic picture of a German military band marching along Le Pollet past the Lloyds Bank in St Peter Port, Guernsey. The juxtapostion of obviously British institutions and German soldiers delighted the occupiers. (Cody Collection)

In one of the nineteenth-century forts that circle the islands, a German sentry examines a cannon resplendent with a British royal cipher. Victorian and even older fortifications were incorporated into the German defences. (Cody Collection)

Standing on a seafront that only months before would have been a holiday venue for families from mainland Britain, a German sentry surveys an empty horizon. Until June 1944 the garrison on the Channel Islands enjoyed a very comfortable existence. (Cody Collection)

The image of a soldier guarding the coast on the Atlantic Wall was one that was heavily exploited by the *Propagandaministerium* of Dr Goebbels. It was both reassuring and rather romantic – the reality was that it was boring and tinged with the fear that the soldier and his unit might be sent to fight on the Eastern Front. (Cody Collection)

A German MG34 machine-gun post in an improvised coastal anti-aircraft position soon after the occupation of the Channel Islands. Temporary sandbagged emplacements would be replaced by reinforced concrete batteries around the islands. (WF Collection)

A *Luftwaffe* NCO receives directions from a Channel Island policeman. The police found themselves in a difficult situation where what in peacetime would be seen as petty criminality, under occupation became a form of resistance. (Cody Collection)

The Germans made innovative use of inflatable craft for river reconnaissance and to construct floating bridges. On the Channel Islands, when sea conditions permitted, they were used for local movement to offshore positions. (Bundesarchiv)

Crewed by *Luftwaffe* gunners, a 2cm Flak 30 anti-aircraft gun covers the approaches to a harbour as a fishing vessel in *Kriegsmarine* service sets off on patrol. (WF Collection)

With his Kar K98K rifle at the ready, a young NCO scans the shoreline. Until the Allied landings in June 1944, the Channel Islands were seen as a comfortable posting far away from the death and destruction of the Eastern Front. From 1944 onwards, the garrison starved. (WF Collection)

A range-taker with an EM34 *Entfernungsmesser* gives the crew of a 2cm Flak 30 the range of an approaching aircraft. Once the target aircraft was within range, the gunner would use the optical sights mounted on the gun. Flak cover over the Channel Islands made them a major threat to Allied aircraft. (WF Collection)

An anti-tank gun position sited at an angle on an anti-tank *Panzermauer* on Alderney. The overhang at the top of the wall would have made it an effective obstacle for infantry – in addition, the wall would have been festooned with barbed wire. (WF Collection)

A recruiting poster for the *Britisches Freikorps*, a formation of renegade British and Commonwealth servicemen that fought for the Germans. It was originally known as the Legion of St George. Efforts were made to recruit Channel Islanders held in internment camps in Germany. (WF Collection)

An Enigma electronic encoding machine. This high-speed solution to manual encoding of radio transmissions was believed by the Germans to be completely secure. Work by Polish, French and principally British experts cracked the codes, and because this intelligence was deamed to be above Top Secret it was given the classification Ultra Secret. (WF Collection)

The warning to telephone and radio operators 'Beware the enemy is listening' appeared on equipment, and is here stencilled on a bunker wall. The enemy was indeed listening and, perhaps more significantly, breaking the 'unbreakable' Enigma code. (WF Collection)

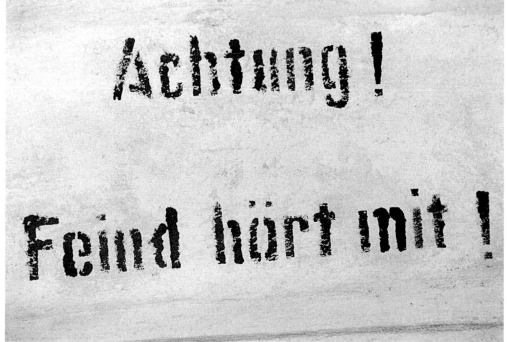

The MP3 fire control position at Mannez Garenne, Alderney, popularly known to the locals as the 'Odeon' after its resemblance to inter-war cinema architecture. In the foreground is the parapet of 88mm Flak battery '*Hoehe 145*'. (WF Collection)

The rear entrance to the 'Odeon' on Alderney – its full designation was *Marinepeilstände* 3. To the right of the embrasures can be seen the circular grills covering the gas filtration system. (WF Collection)

An *Abwehrflammenwerfer* 42 static flamethrower that consisted of a large fuel cylinder 53cm (21in) high and 30cm (12in) wide, with a capacity of 29.5 litres (6½ imperial gallons), containing a black viscous liquid, a mix of light, medium, and heavy oils. These mines could be command-operated or linked to a tripwire. Some were positioned to protect the Casquets lighthouse. (WF Collection)

Sited to fire to give interlocking fire along a likely landing beach, this position on Alderney has been camouflaged with local limestone and landscaped into the hillside – it would have been very hard to locate until the crew opened fire. (WF Collection)

Marine Peilstände und Meßstellen 1 (MP 1) at Noirmont Point, Jersey, was close to *Batterie Lothringen*. It was a naval direction and range-finding position that had four floors, each with an optical range-finder for one of the four 15cm L/45 naval guns of the battery. (WF Collection)

A haunting memorial on Alderney to the foreign labourers – either prisoners of war or political prisoners – who died in the construction of the defences on the island. Since Alderney was effectively depopulated, acts of terrible brutality were inflicted on these labourers of which the islanders had no knowledge. (WF Collection)

With a morale-boosting slogan painted above the embrasure, a machine-gun position covers the rear entrance to a bunker on Alderney. The quality of the construction work is still evident over seventy years later, with reinforced concrete, stonework and a massive steel beam. (WF Collection)

An S Mine with S.Mi.Z 35 (pressure) and Z.Z.35 (pull) switches. Bounding S mines (*Schrapnellmine*, *Springmine* or *Splittermine*) were extensively laid on all of the islands and would cause casualties to several of the commando raids. The S Mine contained 360 steel balls that were lethal at close range and could cause casualties up to 140m. (WF Collection)

Following British commando raids, the coastline of even the smallest islands was heavily mined. Here, a little cove has warning signs and wire fences indicating a minefield. (Cody Collection)

The Teller 42 anti-tank mine contained 5.5kg of TNT or a mix of TNT and *Amande und Meßtol*, and was activated by weights of between 100 and 180kg. The mine would wreck soft-skinned vehicles and cut the tracks of tanks and self-propelled guns. In addition to mines, the Germans used captured French artillery shells as demolition charges and mines. (WF Collection)

The grave of Lieutenant Lightoller DSC in the Bayeux Commonwealth War Graves Cemetery. Lightoller was killed in the German raid on Granville in March 1945. The war in Europe ended on 8 May 1945, almost exactly a month later. (WF Collection)

Generalmajor Heine with *Kapitänleutnant* Arnim Zimmerman at 7.14 a.m. on 9 May 1945, in the cramped wardroom of HMS *Bulldog*, off St Peter Port. VE Day, the end of war in Europe, had officially been over for twenty-four hours. (WF Collection)

Delighted crowds gather around British soldiers in 1945 as Operation Nestegg swings into action. If the Allies had been obliged to assault the islands, the cost in military and civilian lives would have been enormous. (Cody Collection)

The surrender formalities over, British soldiers mingle with the delighted islanders. The Channel Islands had endured a very long occupation, which had become particularly grim after they were cut off from the mainland after D-Day. (Cody Collection)

In October 1943, the German convoys were making the best use of the autumn light and weather conditions. The convoy with the *Münsterland* was to run close to shore, where the coastal batteries could engage targets out to 15 miles. At sea, the escorts' tactics were to draw the attacking force away from the high-value convoy.

The British force was a column of seven ships, three cables apart, sailing at 17 knots, that would pass through established points to sweep westward along the likely route of the convoy. *Charybdis* picked up vessels on its radar some 7 miles ahead, but it was not equipped to monitor the German radio traffic.

Meanwhile British *Hunt*-class destroyer HMS *Limbourne* had its radar masked on ahead bearings by the *Charybdis*, but picked up German radio transmissions indicating that at least six naval units were close by. This vital information was not exchanged between the two ships.

At 1.38 a.m., the German fleet torpedo boat T23 sighted *Charybdis* a few miles north of the Sept Isles off northern Brittany. *Charybdis* had picked it up and was swinging to port, but was hit by a full salvo of six torpedoes. The first torpedo struck her port side, flooding a boiler room and resulting in a 20° list to port. The second struck aft, wiping out electrical power and taking the list to some 50°. *Charybdis* took an angle by the stern until almost vertical, staying like that for about half an hour before the bulkheads gave way and she sank at 2.30 a.m.

The German force proceeded east, leaving the British in confusion. Both the senior officers' ships were sinking and had lost communications, while the rest of the force were manoeuvring at high speed.

The torpedo that struck HMS *Limbourne*'s forward magazine destroyed the forward section of the ship, but she would remain afloat because the bulkhead held. It was later decided to sink her, to keep her out of German hands.

Some 460 men on the *Charybdis* were killed; 107 were saved, but the ship sank, and with forty of HMS *Limbourne*'s men dead, the action had cost the Royal Navy 500 lives, making it the biggest single Allied loss of life in naval actions in the Channel in the war.

HMS *Charybdis* was lost because of an avoidable series of events. A well-trained and drilled enemy force had reduced a superior British task force to equality in minutes, and made its convoy safe, without firing a gun or taking any losses. The British had made so many errors, both ashore and afloat, that the disastrous operation was used as a lesson at the Royal Navy staff officers course.

Soon after the loss of the *Charybdis*, the bodies of twenty-one Royal Navy sailors and Royal Marines were washed up on Guernsey. The German occupation authorities decided to bury them with full military honours. Graf von Schmettow gave a funeral oration that included the memorable lines, 'In the death which follows and results from duty done, the heart knows no frontier lines, and mourning becomes international.'

The funeral was an opportunity for many of the islanders to demonstrate their respect for the men who had died, and their loyalty to their sovereign. Over 5,000 out of the 20,000 islanders who had remained in Guernsey during the war travelled on foot or bicycle to Le Foulon, St Peter Port, to attend the funerals. They brought with them more than a thousand wreaths, many with messages of support for the British forces. They completely outnumbered the German naval and military personnel who had come as a firing party and pall bearers, and their silent presence, looking down on the small German party at Foulon cemetery, was a powerful demonstration of anti-Nazi feeling. It would be a turning point in the German occupation of the island.

The funeral service strengthened the morale of the islanders, who by this time had endured over three years of German occupation with little chance to show their commitment to 'King and Country'. The Germans subsequently banned members of the public from attending the funerals for the additional twenty-nine sailors whose bodies were later washed up. On Jersey, where bodies from the two warships were washed ashore, the German authorities did not permit a public funeral (they had learned their lesson from a previous public demonstration at the funeral of some Allied airmen), and allowed only a brief mention in the *Jersey Evening Post*.

On Guernsey, a memorial brochure was published with photographs of the burials. The German news censor Horst Schmidt-Walkhoff restricted its size and circulation. He ordered that no more than 2,000 copies, 'and this only after continued pleading', were to be printed. But privately, defying these instructions and at great risk to the personnel of the company, the newspaper published 5,000 copies, which were eagerly sought-after and quite inadequate to meet the demand.

Writing in the *Evening Post* in September 1945, Frank Falla summed the emotion of that day:

> Did the Germans for one moment, following the outward expression of our innermost feelings, question which way after three and a half years of trial and tribulation under their misrule; did they question which direction our true feelings and steadfast allegiance lay?

Despite the British naval losses, the *Münsterland* was a valuable target and the RAF launched a series of low-level air strikes between 24 October and 26 November. Whirlwinds of 263 Squadron made several large-scale attacks against her in Cherbourg harbour. As many as twelve Whirlwinds participated at a time in dive-bombing attacks carried out from 12,000 to 5,000ft using 250lb bombs. The attacks were met by very heavy anti-aircraft fire, but virtually all bombs fell within 500yd of the target. Only one Whirlwind was lost during the attacks. The *Münsterland* was eventually sunk on 20 January 1944 by the radar-directed heavy coastal batteries sited near Dover. In all, the Dover guns fired forty-six salvoes, in part because the time of flight of the shells could be anticipated by the master of the *Münsterland*, who manoeuvred his ship in a zig-zag course. However, when she grounded at Cap Blank Nez the ship was doomed.

The British coastal batteries near Dover had earlier claimed a significant victory when, on 4 October 1943, they sank the SS *Livadia* off Boulogne. This modern cargo ship had been used to deliver some of the ex-French Char B1 bis tanks of Pz Abt 213, the armoured unit based in Jersey, Guernsey and Alderney.

The waters off the Channel Islands were not only hazardous for the Royal Navy but even more dangerous for the *Kriegsmarine*. There were six or seven major convoy battles in the area, some of these taking place in February and September 1943 and August 1944.

Tides,[2] currents and weather also took a toll of shipping around the islands, which saw at least 500 Germans a week moving between the Channel Islands and mainland France. On 12 March 1941, the SS *Staffa*, a Guernsey-based motor sailing boat that had been taken over by the Germans and operated around the islands, broke her stern moorings in Alderney and was driven onto rocks and badly holed. In January 1943, the *Shockland* hit a rock and sank off the south coast of Jersey; sheltering below deck were German military personnel and fifteen French prostitutes[3] from the military brothel. Their only exit was a single ladder that led to an 18in-square hatch – nearly 130 perished. In November 1942, in a 'friendly fire' incident, a *Kriegsmarine* torpedo boat fired on an unidentified vessel – there were seven killed aboard the vessel, including *Generalmajor* Christiani, the commander of supply troops for the 319th Division.

On 8 May 1944, Free French Navy MTBs sank the SS *Bison*, a Belgian-built, Danish-operated vessel that had been taken over by the Germans in 1940 and used to run supplies along the French coast to the islands.

On the night of 12/13 June 1944, two Royal Canadian Navy (RCN) destroyers, the *Haida* and *Huron*, launched Operation Accumulator, a deception plan in support of the D-Day landings.

Their missions were to make fake radio transmissions that indicated that a follow-up force was heading for Granville. It was hoped that they would be intercepted by monitoring stations on the Channel Islands, and on the mainland German forces would be diverted away from the Normandy beachhead. The beginning of the operation went smoothly, with the two ships signalling that the invasion fleet had been delayed by engine problems, and giving a revised plan. However, the radios on the *Haida* broke down, forcing the *Huron* to continue alone; the two ships were also spotted by an Allied reconnaissance plane, which radioed back that it had found 'unidentified warships'. Despite the hard work of the crew of the *Huron*, the operation provoked no reaction from the Germans.

MTBs of the RCN sank the MV *Hydra* near St Helier on 22 June 1944. She was a Dutch vessel that had been commandeered by the Germans and used to transport *Todt* workers and equipment, but had also made two trips in April and May 1944 with French Red Cross supplies.

RCN MTBs struck again on 5 July 1944, when the *Minotaur*, carrying Sylt prisoners and *Todt* workers from Alderney, was torpedoed and sank with two other ships not far from St Malo. About 250 were drowned, including a number of French Jews. On 4 July it had been part of a convoy of five small ships that left Jersey shortly before midnight and headed for St Malo. *Hinrich Hey* led the way, her sister patrol ship *Walter Darre* bringing up the rear.

Of the five boats, the *Minotaur* was carrying 468 slave labourers and also aboard were some children and a group of French prostitutes. At 1 a.m., when the convoy was some 8 miles from St Malo, it was ambushed by five MTBs of the RCN 65th (Canadian) MTB Flotilla, commanded by Lieutenant Commander J.R.H. Kirkpatrick, DSC, RCNVR, which fired flares to light up the convoy and then launched almost every torpedo they carried. The torpedo hits were followed by accurate gunfire.[4]

The *Hinrich Hey* sank immediately. Two minutes later, the *Walter Darre* went down only 350m away. The fire of the MTBs then concentrated on the *Minotaur,* which received three direct hits. Her bow was almost blown off, but her captain managed to keep her afloat by going full astern. Many of those aboard the *Minotaur* had been killed by the time the Canadians broke off the action and disappeared back into the darkness. In total, more than 250 had died in just four minutes of action.

Not all the naval actions around the islands were between ships. On 14 June 1944, there was an artillery duel between *Heeres-Küstenbatterie* HKB Roon and *Marine-Küstenbatterie* MKB Lothringen on the German side, and on the British side the destroyer HMS *Ashanti* (F51, commander John Richard Barnes) and the Polish destroyer ORP *Piorun* (G 65, ex–*Nerissa*, commander Tadeusz Gorazdowski). There were no hits on either side.

Though the islands had been demilitarised by the summer of 1940, they played a small but significant part in Operation Haddock, a long-range air attack on 11–12 June 1940 against Fascist Italy by RAF Armstrong Whitley bombers of Nos 10, 51, 58, 77 and 102 Squadrons Bomber Command, who refuelled on Jersey and Guernsey before flying on to attack targets in northern Italy.

The *Luftwaffe* raids on the islands in 1940 were not the last air attacks, and as the war swung in favour of the Allies the weight of air attacks increased. There were in total twenty-two raids on the islands, which resulted in ninety-three deaths and 250 injuries – many of them among *Todt* port workers or on transports to and from France. The first RAF raids began in August 1940, not long after the *Luftwaffe* attacks, and were aimed at Guernsey airport – now a *Luftwaffe* base. On the evening of Friday 9 August, the RAF raiders counted between forty and fifty enemy aircraft – fighters, twin-engined bombers and transports – and claimed a direct hit on a transport and one of the hangars. On the ground, the Germans reported that five bombers had attacked the airfield, killing one soldier and wounding four civilians. A barracks near the airfield and fuel stores were destroyed by fire. The second raid, on the following day, hit hangars, but the bomber crews reported that all the aircraft had disappeared. Coastal Command also hit the target area. On the third day there was 'accurate bombing from high altitude' by medium bombers, and *The Times* of 13 August reported that smoke from the fires that they started could be seen 'seven miles away'. In 1942, attacks switched to the port facilities, and in 1944, with the build-up to D-Day, the intensity increased as bombers hit both ports and military installations. The attacks prior to D-Day could have been part of the deception plan to ensure that German attention was focussed away from the Normandy area.

Throughout the war, the threat from the air was constant. Mrs Tremayne, whose diary gives a unique insight into life under German occupation, noted that air raids on Guernsey airport in August 1940 produced 'perfect Bedlam'. On 23 August, the first bomb fell on Sark.

In July 1941, Guernsey airport was the target for renewed attacks, and on 3 September Mrs Tremayne and her daughter, Norah, watched from Gouilot top on Sark as Allied aircraft attacked barges en route to Guernsey, later switching their attention to the airport. There were more attacks on Guernsey in 1942, directed at the harbour, that lasted several nights and produced fires that could be seen on Sark 8 miles away. Two ships were sunk and Polish *Todt* workers killed. Inevitably, damage was done to St Peter Port. The SS *Lafcomo*, an American-built bulk carrier that had been seized from her French owners in Bordeaux in August 1940, was hit in a strike by three RAF Beaufort fighter-bombers on 6 January 1942 while she was unloading cement in Guernsey. She was refloated a month later but was subsequently not operated around the islands.

As the war moved in favour of the Allies, so the tempo of air attacks on shipping off the Channel Islands increased. On 18 July 1942, in a typical shipping strike, RAF Spitfires attacked two HS transport boats and two *Vorpostenboot* (VP) boats, or outpost boats, known to the Allies as flak ships. As the fighters strafed the boats, one man jumped overboard, nine were killed and thirty-three wounded.

On 9 September, a small convoy consisting of the Dutch-built coasters MV *Henca* and MV *Tinda*, escorted by two armed trawlers, were attacked by RAF fighter-bombers north of Alderney. One of the trawlers was badly strafed, suffering two dead and seventeen wounded, and the *Henca* sank after being hit by a bomb.

Later that year, on 23 November, Sgt E.J. Singleton, the pilot of Lancaster bomber W4107 from No. 49 Squadron based at Scampton, Lincolnshire, achieved a remarkable feat of airmanship. The bomber crew was one of nine that had been tasked with an attack on the city centre of Stuttgart. On the return leg they were hit by flak that started a fire and punctured the fuel tanks. Singleton gave the crew the order to bail out. Now, with the rear gunner, Sgt L.W. Saunders, as his navigator, the pilot attempted to make it back to England. When they saw an island below them they guessed that it was the Isle of Wight. Singleton spotted a long open field and put the bomber down in a wheels-up emergency landing. As the two men staggered from the wrecked four-engined bomber, they discovered that they had actually landed on Sark. Today, the site is known as the aeroplane field. All the crew survived, albeit held in separate POW camps in Germany.

On 7 December, Westland Whirlwind fighter-bombers of No. 263 Squadron RAF attacked shipping in Jersey harbour. The planes flown by Squadron Leader Robert Sinckler and Warrant Officer (WO) Donald Burton McPhail of the Royal Canadian Air Force (RCAF) were hit by flak and crashed into the sea.

On 27 April 1943, the elegant German motor schooner MV *Helma* was sunk by Whirlwind fighter-bombers off Jersey. She had been built as a sailing ship in 1914, then modified as a motor schooner in 1936. She had carried stores between Granville, St Malo and the Channel Islands, but on the day she sank her cargo was a load of potatoes from the islands.

The RAF struck again on 23 May, when they caught a convoy of eight ships off St Peter Port. Bombs hit the Dutch-built MV *Ost Vlaanderen*, which was carrying a cargo of cement, before she could make it to the shelter of the harbour.

In June 1943, the bodies of two RAF sergeant pilots were washed ashore on Jersey. A military funeral was arranged by *Oberleutnant* Zepernick, adjutant to the *Inselkommandant*, and on 6 June hundreds gathered along the route to Mont l'Abbé Cemetery. The coffins were each draped with the Union Flag and had wreaths from the States of Jersey and the *Luftwaffe*. Men of the

Luftwaffe provided the pall bearers and the firing party. The Bailiff, Alexander Coutanche, dressed in his ceremonial robes, laid two wreaths, one in the name of the King and the other on behalf of the States. Journalist Leslie Sinel noted in his diary, 'A couple of ugly incidents were narrowly averted outside the cemetery during the day when some young men gave expression to their feelings to some women who were known to be friendly with the enemy.' The girls, dressed in their mourning finery, had attended the burial and were not welcome. Later, two truck-loads of wreaths were sent to the cemetery and hundreds of Jersey people filed past the graves.

On 27 May 1944, United States Army Air Force (USAAF) P-47 Thunderbolt fighter-bombers attacked the barracks at Fort George. The word that circulated around the islands was that several Germans playing football had been killed, though shrapnel from the flak batteries also killed one person and injured several others. A bomb exploded near the home of Mrs Cortvriend, fracturing her water pipes. She noted that from then on, 'scarcely a day passed without large formations of planes flying overhead'. On Sark, Mrs Tremayne recorded 15 June as 'another hellish night'. Attacks aimed at St Peter Port were recorded by Mrs Cortvreind, but she also saw the progress of the fighting in France following the D-Day landings. Fires could be seen and explosions shook their house by day and night.

At 5.15 p.m. on 14 June, rocket-firing USAAF Thunderbolts attacked the U275, a U-boat commanded by *Oblt* Helmut Bork and based in Brest. The submarine had entered St Peter Port and was berthed near the Dutch-registered MV *Karel*. The salvo of rockets missed the U-boat but hit the *Karel*, killing two crewmen and wounding two others. The U-boat later sank with all hands on 10 March 1945, when she hit a mine south of Newhaven.

On 27 July 1944, a Lancaster bomber crashed in the sea east of Essex Castle, Alderney, but *Kapitän* Massmann, who since 1943 had been the harbour commandant at Braye, did not order out any boats to assist the crew. Two of his staff later stated, 'all of us were surprised that nothing was done for their rescue'. After the war, Massmann was brought to London with a view to prosecution, but none took place.

Between May and August 1944, air attacks intensified and about twenty-five ships were either sunk or damaged. With the coast of northern France now liberated by the Allies, the Channel Islands were cut off – though, incredibly, a tenuous air link would be maintained with the shrinking Third Reich by long-range Heinkel He 111 bombers up to the last months of the war. The courageous pilots of these aircraft carried casualties who could not be treated on the islands, as well as post from the Reich and soldiers' letters from the islands.

There were at least twenty-two Allied air attacks on the Channel Islands, resulting in ninety-three deaths and 250 injuries, many of these being *Todt* workers in the docks or on transports. Ten RAF aircrew were killed in these attacks, the USAAF lost two men and the RCAF lost one, as did the Belgians serving in the RAF. Reminders of these air attacks can still occur. In 1993, a 500lb bomb was found on the sea bed 500yd from St Peter Port harbour signal station. It was exploded safely by a Royal Navy underwater ordnance clearance team.

For the garrison of the Channel Islands, the liberation of the Cotentin peninsula in July and August 1944 meant that they were now completely cut off. They would, however, still try to play a part in the war. The four 15cm Kanone 18 (K18) guns of *Batterie Blücher* on the eastern side of Alderney had a range of 24.5km, and this put the north-west corner of the Cotentin peninsula within range. With radar and optical range-finding, the guns were hitting targets on land as well as shipping in the area with their substantial 43kg shells. According to *Oberstleutnant* Günther Keil, CO of the 919th Grenadier-Regiment in the Cotentin peninsula (Normandy), then CO of the Jobourg/Cap de la Hague peninsula defence after the fall of Cherbourg, he received help from a battery on Alderney.

Interestingly, the men of *Heeres-Küstenbatterie* (HKB) 461 manning the guns were soldiers rather than naval gunners. The reason was that the guns had originally been designed as field artillery, but proved too cumbersome and consequently had been deployed in static locations, where they were very effective. They were commanded from Balmoral House in the Longis Road, in the garden of which was mounted a rangefinder on a wooden tower.

On 19 July, there was an artillery duel between HKB *Blücher* and the destroyers HMS *Onslaught* (G04, commander The Hon. Anthony Pleydell-Bouverie) and HMS *Saumarez* (G12, captain Peter Grenville Lyon Cazalet). HMS *Saumarez* had some casualties and sustained damage from the

German fire. The decision was taken by the Allies that the battery should be silenced. Bombing was ruled out, in part because of its inaccuracy and the risk to civilian lives but also because the flak coverage of the islands was formidable; there were twenty-two batteries, ranging from light, through medium to four which were 8.8cm flak guns, and consequently a daylight air raid would, it was feared, be very costly.

In order to silence the German battery, at 7.30 a.m. on 12 August, the battle-ship HMS *Rodney* (captain Robert Oliver Fitzroy), with its 16in guns, escorted by the destroyer HMS *Faulknor* (commander Charles Fraser Harrington Churchill) sailed from Portland to carry out a bombardment. The log of the bombardment details the one-sided but ultimately ineffective action:

> 12.15 hours *Rodney* arrived off Cherbourg and with the assistance of a US Navy tug from Cherbourg *Rodney* was manoeuvred into position at 90 degrees to the coast about 20 miles from and broadside to Alderney.
>
> 14.10 hours *Rodney* opened fire on the Blucher Battery of four guns on Alderney, spotting was carried out by a RAF Spitfire from 26 Sqdn. Great accuracy was required due to the nearby British civilian population.
>
> 16.42 hours after firing 75 x 16in shells, 40 of which fell very close to the battery, *Rodney* ceased fire. The spotting aircraft reported that the shoot[ing] had achieved the destruction of 3 of the 4 guns.
>
> 17.00 hours *Rodney* and *Faulknor* set sail for Portland arriving there at 22.30 hours.

Despite glowing contemporary Royal Navy reports of the bombard-ment, and the belief by the crew of *Rodney* that their fire had been effective, only one gun was put out of action for any length of time. The Germans transported it to Guernsey for repair and spare parts were flown from Germany.

A trench system around *Batterie Blücher* received heavy punishment and *Rodney*'s fall of shot was very accurate – forty shells out of seventy-five fired fell within a 200m radius of the battery's centre. However, overall, results were very disappointing, especially as *Batterie Blücher*'s guns were in open pits with no overhead protection. The bombardment by *Rodney* demonstrated that the effect of naval gunfire against hard targets could be considerably overestimated.

Three of the German guns were firing at Allied shipping again by 30 August, and by November all four were in commission, with plans afoot to resume bombardment of the Cotentin.

Since Alderney was practically devoid of civilians, there were no civilian casualties, although two German soldiers were killed, neither of them belonging to the gun crews, all of whom retreated into bunkers. The two dead men were buried in the military cemetery just north of the Longis Road, behind the Stranger's Cemetery. Though German soldiers were killed in accidents and committed suicide on Alderney, these two soldiers were the only battle casualties. The cemetery also had the grave of Private Leonard J. Cross of Company 'A', 35th Regiment US Army, whose body was washed ashore on 14 January 1945.

What makes this episode significant is that it was the first time since HMY *Helga* shelled Liberty Hall in the Easter Rising in Dublin in April 1916 that a Royal Navy warship had fired on Crown territory. It would not be repeated until 1982 during Operation Corporate, when naval gunfire support played a significant role in the campaign to liberate the Falkland Islands from Argentine occupation.

Notes

1 Construction of the fleet torpedo boat class craft took place in the Schichau shipyard in Elbing (now Elbląg), hence the Allied name for the class. The first examples were commissioned in late 1942 and the last in late 1944.

   Displacement: 1,295 long tons (1,316 short tonnes) (standard); 1,755 long tons (1,783 short tonnes) (maximum)
   Length: 97m (318ft 3in) (water line), 102.5m (336ft 3in) (overall)
   Beam: 10m (32ft 10in)
   Draught: 3.22m (10ft 7in)
   Installed power: 32,560 shp (24,280kW)
   Propulsion: 2 x Wagner geared steam turbines, 2 x shafts
   Speed: 32.5 knots (60.2km/h; 37.4mph)
   Range: 2,400 nautical miles (4,400km; 2,800 miles) at 19 knots (35km/h; 22 mph)
   Complement: 205
   Armament: 4 x 10.5cm (4.1in) guns, 4 x 3.7cm (1.46in) anti-aircraft guns, 9 x 2.0cm (0.79in) anti-aircraft cannons, 6 x 53.3cm (21in) torpedo tubes, 50 mines.

2 Jersey has a 10m (32ft) tidal rise and fall, Guernsey 8m (26ft) and Alderney 7m (22ft). In some locations around the islands there are currents of 8 knots (9mph).

3 Brothels – *Freudenhäuser* (houses of joy) – were established by the German authorities in St Helier and St Peter Port. The first Guernsey brothel was established in February 1942 and had a staff of two men and thirteen women. One for the OT staff was set up on Alderney. The women in the brothels were provided with civilian ration books on the orders of FK515, being classed as far as rations were concerned as 'heavy workers'.

4 The 65th Canadian Motor Torpedo Boat Flotilla operated Fairmile Type 'D' boats of 115ft. They were hard-chine pre-fabricated double mahogany vessels, the hull being sub-divided into nine watertight compartments. They were driven by Four Packard 12 cylinder 1,250 horsepower supercharged patrol engines with two underslung rudders and carried 5,200 gallons of 100 per cent octane gas, and had a range at maximum continuous speed of 506 nautical miles. Two Ford V-8 auxiliary engines provided electric power.
   Displacement:-
   Designed: 85 Tons
   Actual displacement: 105 tons
   Overall length: 115ft
   Waterline length: 110ft
   Beam: 21ft 3in
   Forward draught: 4ft 6in
   Aft draught: 5ft
   Full speed: 27 to 34.5 knots
   Armament:-
   4 x 18in high level torpedo tubes
   1 x 6pdr CWT MARK VII gun
   4 x .5in Vickers machine guns on two twin MK V (power operated) mountings
   4 x .303in Vickers gas-operated machine guns in two twins on bridge wings
   2 x 20mm Oelikons
   Crew:-
   three officers, twenty-seven men, varied according to operational requirements.

14

SIEGE AND SURVIVAL, 1944–45

On the day the Allies landed in France, Rommel was on his way to Germany to join his wife in birthday celebrations, and most senior officers in the Normandy and Brittany area were in Rennes for a map table exercise to rehearse their response to an Allied invasion. Among the officers was Graf von Schmettow, who had been invited to inspect a section of the Atlantic Wall on the Cotentin peninsula. It came as a shock to him to discover that it was well below the standard of his island fortifications. When news came through that the Allies had landed, von Schmettow immediately contacted the islands and was reassured to learn that no landings had taken place and that everything was in order. Dodging bombers and fighter ground attack aircraft, he made it back to his command by 7 June. On the islands, the news of the Allied landing was greeted with delight by the population, and one eyewitness reported, 'hundreds of people in Guernsey went nearly mad with joy and excitement singing "Roll Out the Barrel", and "There'll Always Be an England".'

On the islands, the garrison braced themselves for an Allied assault. An intelligence summary produced in July stated, 'According to intelligence reports from higher authorities, an attack on the Channel Islands by 40 to 50 commando groups approximating to a division, is daily expected.' On Jersey, the Bailiff, Coutance, was issued an *Ausweis Nr. 334*, a special pass to allow him to travel to and from the *Festungskommandant* and his home at Clos de Tour, St Aubin. Coutance needed it because he had been tasked with organising emergency accommodation at the Royal Court House. However, with his fuel rationed to 1 gallon a week, his driver would where possible let the car freewheel downhill or push it.

Following D–Day, a major priority for the Allies was to capture a port where men, ammunition and stores could be speedily and efficiently unloaded, and the faster this could be done, the greater their chance of breaking out from Normandy. The obvious objective was the port of Cherbourg at the northern end of the Cotentin peninsula. On 22 June, US VII Corps under General J. Lawton Collins – known to his men as Lightning Joe – began the assault on Cherbourg. After a hard fight, which included naval gunfire support and house-to-house fighting, the port was liberated on 26 June, when the US 79th Division secured Fort du Roule that overlooked the harbour. The German demolitions and mining in the harbour took time to repair and clear, but by mid-August Cherbourg was in limited use.

Between 24 and 31 July, in Operation Cobra, the US VII and VIII Corps rolled down the western edge of the Cotentin peninsula. Granville fell to 8th Corps on 30 July, and after a hard fight that began on 5 August St Malo was liberated on 17 August by 8th Corps, and particularly the 83rd Ohio Division under General Macon.

The defences of St Malo were concentrated in five strongpoints built by *Organisation Todt*: to the west of the city, the La Cité fort, a vast subterranean complex carved out of a peninsula between the Rance estuary and the Bay of St Servan; in the Bay of St Malo, two fortified islands, Cèzembre and the Grand Bey; and to the east, the Montaigne St Joseph and the La Varde fort, natural geographical features fortified with concrete, which were the first stubborn pockets of resistance encountered by US forces coming from that direction.

The Channel Islands would play a small but significant part in the battle for St Malo. On 7 August, von Schmettow sent the hospital ship *Bordeaux*[1] with two escorts to the port and evacuated 600 wounded and about ninety unwounded troops. About fifty men from the island garrison joined the defenders of St Malo to serve as anti-tank crews and the commander, *Oberst* Andreas von Aulock, ordered all German shipping in the harbour to make a run for the Channel Islands – nine ships made it safely. During the fighting for the city, the USAAF employed napalm for the first time. An inherently inaccurate weapon, the jellied petrol not only sticks to a target as it burns but also exhausts the oxygen in the surrounding area, causing suffocation.

When St Malo finally fell, *Oberst* von Aulock, a veteran of the First World War and the Eastern Front with a monocle, leather coat, German shepherd dog and a mistress with connections to Russian royalty, seemed to epitomise the arrogant German officer to his American captors. Von Aulock may not have realised his threat to turn St Malo into a second Stalingrad, but his engineers had been ruthlessly efficient in the destruction of the docks and harbour facilities. The demolition work was so thorough that when US Army engineers handed the port over to the French on 21 November it was still not operable. With ports like St Malo and Cherbourg still needing major reconstruction, it fell to the smaller ports in Britanny, like Granville, to handle shipping from Britain.

The defence of the little island of Cèzembre gives some idea of what an attack on the Channel Islands would have cost in life and ordnance. Cèzembre is a rocky island with a surface area of approximately 18 hectares (44 acres), is 750m long and 300m wide, and is almost 3 miles due north of Dinard and St Malo, and consequently covers the approaches to these ports. It had first been fortified at the end of the seventeenth century, but in 1944 the fortifications were sited on its two main features, a hill in the east about 38m high and one 37m high in the west. Work had begun in 1942 installing six 194mm former French Schneider railway-guns in open emplacements. Though comparatively old, these guns were capable of firing an 83kg shell over 18km. Each hill had three guns, each with its own ammunition bunker and personnel shelter. The battery control post was built on the western hill, probably because this waterway was the main entrance to the port of St Malo. The whole island had six ex-French 75mm guns for anti-aircraft defence and several 2cm flak guns. A 15cm naval gun intended for firing illumination rounds was located in the middle of the island.

The mixed garrison of Russian, Italian and German troops was commanded by a naval officer, 47-year-old *Oberleutnant* Richard Seuss. The skill and professionalism with which he commanded the battery reflected the fact that in the First World War he had been a gunner in the German Army and served in the army up to the 1920s. It was not until 1941 that he transferred to the *Kriegsmarine*.

He took command of 'Île de Cécembre'/*Marine-Artillery-Abteilung* 608 on 23 August 1942. In August 1944, his guns engaged US forces during the fighting in St Malo, inflicting substantial losses. For this he was awarded the Knight's Cross. Oak Leaves would be added on 2 September.

With St Malo in Allied hands, Seuss signalled to the Channel Islands that he was low on food, water and ammunition, and that a replacement radio was needed. The little island had expended its stock of 194mm shells, but the 150mm gun could still be supplied from Jersey. Two ships were sent from Guernsey in hazardous night-time missions; one returned but the other went aground off Cézembre and was sunk by the Americans the next day. Two nights later, another vessel was sent from St Helier carrying ammunition, and it was able to take off the crew of the stranded vessel, the wounded and twenty-two unwounded Italian soldiers. Though they were kept supplied, the major problem was sustaining the morale of the mixed garrison, and in fact three Italians managed to steal a boat and reached St Malo, where they surrendered.

From 9 August onwards, the island was shelled from land and sea, and bombed from the air. Thirty-five planes were diverted to Cézembre for the attack on the Citadel on 17 August, creating huge columns of smoke with their napalm strikes. General Macon now authorised Maj. Joseph M. Alexander and two enlisted men, as well as an accredited civilian film camera-man, to demand that the Germans surrender. On 18 August, the party rowed across the St Malo Bay. At Cézembre, an NCO met the boat and conducted Alexander and his interpreter to the fortress commander.

The *US Army in World War II: European Theater of Operations* notes:

Neither arrogant nor boastful, the German commander stated that the last order he had received from higher headquarters instructed him to maintain his defence. Until he received a countermanding order, he would continue to do just that. Informed that the mainland was completely under American control, he declared that he did not understand how that changed his situation. Reminded that Aulock had surrendered the day before, he countered that he had not exhausted his ammunition on Cézembre. After a courteous conversation lasting fifteen minutes, the Americans were escorted back to the beach and helped to launch their boat for the return trip.

With Seuss's refusal, plans were laid for an infantry assault supported by armour. Meanwhile, a major air strike on 31 August by twenty-four P-38s of the USAAF IX Bomber Command carrying napalm, 165 Halifaxes of No. 6 Group and five pathfinder Mosquitos of RAF Bomber Command, with one photographic Mosquito, hit the island. RAF records state that, 'The bombing force flew at 3,000 ft or less over the undefended targets and achieved a good bombing concentration. 1 Halifax lost.' A history of 433 Squadron states that Cézembre 'could well have been the easiest target bombed by heavies during the entire European campaign, yet one aircraft failed to return. Halifax "O–Oboe" suddenly went into a steep dive from which it never recovered. It plunged into the sea, killing its entire crew. The casualties were, Flying Officer K. R. Beveridge, Flt. Sgt. E. C. Harman, Pilot Officer L. S. Guernsey, Flt. Sgt. W. L. Long, Sgt. G. W. Pharis, Sgt. C. W. Garrett, R.A.F., and Sgt. J. R. Hawkins.'

Further strikes against the island were ordered on 1 September, as well as bombardment by the 15in guns of HMS *Warspite*. Seuss now contacted Jersey and informed them that he had some 277 wounded on the island and that they had to be evacuated. The hospital ship *Bordeaux* was sent, but it was captured at first light on 2 September and taken to Portland. Deteriorating weather prevented a resupply run, and this forced Seuss's hand; the white flag appeared over the island, just as the men of F Company, 2nd Battalion, 330th Infantry Regiment, 83rd Infantry Division were getting ready to assault.

Landing craft were sent across, and on 2 September Seuss surrendered along with 232 German, seventy-one Italian and twenty Russian soldiers. Of the German prisoners, 228 belonged to the *Kriegsmarine* and four to the army, who were from a specialist signals unit. Some accounts state that there were four female nurses. At the time of his death on 26 September 1963, Seuss held the rank of reserve lieutenant commander in the West German Navy.

This diverse group had held out fifteen days after the fall of St Malo in a siege that had cost the Germans 300 casualties. By the end of the siege, the island had become the most heavily bombed place in France and even today areas are fenced off because of the presence of unexploded ordnance.

It had been a brave stand that had earned the respect of the Allies. However, the most telling analysis would remain classified for many years. The official report of the British Bombing Survey Unit, drawn from BAU Report 29, states that the surrender of the island garrison was 'due more to lack of ammunition, food and water, than to the destruction caused by the fire to which they had been subjected – in the course of which 4,000 tons of HE bombs were dropped, and an average of 45 bomb strikes (20 tons) per acre achieved over the small island'.

If Cézembre could hold out in the face of this onslaught, what kind of defence could the larger and much more heavily fortified Channel Islands offer?

To the north of St Malo, the little port of Granville had been protected from a seaborne assault by four 12cm guns sited in casemates, with a fire control bunker built forward of the battery, as well as infantry positions and flak defences. Granville harbour consists of an outer mole protecting the Avant Port, a 'drying harbour' that is subject to the marked tidal change (40ft in spring tides) that is a feature of the English Channel and Gulf of St Malo. The inner locked harbour in which ships could remain tied up and afloat once the lock gates had been closed at high tide was known as the Basin à Flot. It had berths for seven ships on a draught of 5m (16½ft) and a maximum length of 328ft. Before D-Day, the skippers of craft using Granville could have a nervous time outside the port, unprotected by the flak batteries, waiting for the tide to be full and a berth to be free.

Before they surrendered, the Germans had undertaken comprehensive demolitions in Granville. Tugs and motorised barges like the *Georges Guynemer*, *Point à Pitre* and *Comptoir 51*, which had been regulars of the supply run to the Channel Islands, had been scuttled at strategic points. In July 1944, the most effective piece of demolition by German engineers was when they blew up the lock gates and sank a barge across the entrance. Even without these demolitions, the lock gate itself presented a challenge to skippers, being 223ft by 50ft, which meant that only ships of 320ft or under could negotiate it.

Though the docks were damaged, happily, unlike St Malo, there was no fighting in the town. Granville consists of the la Haupte Ville, the older upper town built on the Pointe du Roc, the headland that shelters the harbour from north winds. La Haupte Ville, confined within fifteenth-century citadel fortification and with a slab-like barracks at the western end, consists of four narrow streets with small granite houses. The granite church of Notre-Dame du Cap Lihou that dominates the heights was built by the English during the Hundred Years War.

To the north and east is the modern town of Granville, which expanded in the nineteenth century when the port was linked up by railway to Paris, and Parisians discovered the long sandy beach, casino and several spa hotels offering seawater health treatments.

In the autumn of 1944, France was almost secure and the garrison and residents of the Channel Islands realised that they could be left 'to wither on the vine' like some of the heavily fortified Japanese-held islands by-passed in the American 'island hopping' campaign in the Pacific. Despite this, on 1 September 1944 the OKW issued a tactical review of the islands in which they listed, in order of military significance, Guernsey, Jersey and Alderney. Each of the eleven battalions of the 319th Division was allocated 13km of coastline. The review stated that Jersey's large sandy bays were 'now protected by armoured walls'. On Guernsey, the intelligence summary identified the larger bays of L'Ancresse, Grand Havre and Vazon as likely landing sites for 'one or two companies'.

Radio communications with the shrinking Third Reich hundreds of miles to the east were now exclusively through the powerful *Kriegsmarine* transmitters, that had originally been intended to reach U-boats far to the west in the North Atlantic.

With the islands isolated, the opportunity to apply psychological pressure presented itself. In what would turn out to be at considerable personal risk, Maj. Alan Chambers of the Canadian Army Intelligence Corps developed a strategy that was built round air-delivered newspapers aimed at the garrison, and a personal invitation to enter into surrender negotiations aimed at von Schmettow. It was part of the wider Nestegg liberation operation for the islands.

The plan had been prepared, following the fall of Brest, to take a captured German general, given the code name 'Mr John Black', to negotiate with von Schmettow with a view to securing the capitulation of the islands. Mr Black was in fact *Generalmajor* Dipl. Ing. Gerhard Bassenge, a *Luftwaffe* officer with a distinguished career as a fighter pilot in the First World War, who had been captured in North Africa on 9 May 1943.

Copies of a letter inviting von Schmettow to attend a parley at sea, under Article 32 of The Hague Convention, were dropped from aircraft at night, and the mission was illuminated by flares. Prior to this, the islands had been saturated with the propaganda news sheet *Nachrichten für die Truppe*.[2] The news sheets were dropped in the proportion of three to Guernsey, two to Jersey and one to Alderney, and the mode of delivery was bombs, special air burst leaflet. Once the garrison realised the hopelessness of their situation, General Bassenge would telephone von Schmettow on the Channel Islands–Pirou cable, the French end of which was now controlled by the Allies. If his persuasion worked, then the *Befehlshaber* (commander in chief) might be induced to meet Bassenge on a vessel offshore and the islands' garrison capitulate – thus saving numerous lives, both military and civilian.

SHAEF had given the operation its full backing, but with provisos; the surrender must be unconditional and there would be no early return to Germany for the garrison. However, it was prepared to give Nestegg real muscle. If von Schmettow was a fanatic, determined to fight to the end, then *Nachrichten für die Truppe* would be replaced by leaflets demanding surrender, and this would be backed up by an intense and heavy air bombardment – though SHAEF planners insisted that the target should only be Alderney.

Bombs, special air burst leaflet were first dropped on the night of 30/31 August, with Fort Richmond being the aiming point on Guernsey, St Ouen's Manor on Jersey and St Anne in Alderney. On Jersey, Leslie Sinel watched as *Kriegsmarine* ratings gathered the news sheets for destruction before they reached more of the garrison, though some were picked up by the civilian population. Over the next twelve nights, more raids followed, directed at likely troop locations. A total of 218 of these non-lethal bombs were dropped.

On 1 September, this phase of Nestegg was reckoned to be complete, so it was time to deliver a personal message to von Schmettow. At 11 p.m. an aircraft dropped two copies of a letter on SHAEF headed notepaper, addressed to the *Befehlshaber*, urging him to open negotiations over the telephone link to France. From 12–15 September, Chambers and Bassenge waited in France for a telephone call, but the phone did not ring.[3]

On mainland France, the silence was hard to read. However, it appeared that the message had reached its intended destination. On Guernsey, Louis Guillemette, the secretary to the Controlling Committee, noted, 'Last Tuesday night although an allied plane flew over the Island no newspapers were delivered. The plane dropped flares, however, an unusual occurrence; and in the light shed by them many people saw parachutes falling.' On Wednesday morning he learned that a secret letter, which had been opened, was found in the letterbox of the *Befehlshaber* HQ. Guillemette was asked by the Germans if this was a hoax, and though he had no knowledge of it, or its contents, he was able to track down the islander who had found it. After four years of occupation, islanders had a reasonable working knowledge of German and this man established that the letter contained instructions to von Schmettow to contact France by telephone, with a time and date specified. Subsequently, the second letter was found by a German, who delivered it to the HQ.

However, Radio Berlin broadcast that 'the Channel Islands had refused several demands for surrender and were still holding out'. Though this phase of Nestegg did not appear to be going according to plan, Chambers decided that it would be worth delivering a second message proposing a parley. On the night of 21/22 September, the message was parachuted onto the island. It proposed that under the terms of the Hague Convention, von Schmettow should meet with a representative of SHAEF, who would be at a point 4½ miles south of St Martin's Point near St Peter Port in an unarmed boat flying a white flag. The *Befehlshaber* should come in an unarmed boat under a flag of truce.

This time, however, the parachuted message drifted out to sea. The pilot had also dropped flares and reported that he believed the messages had landed in the sea. Chambers decided to keep up the pressure and, accompanied by 'Mr Black', set off on the morning of 22 September, arriving just after midday at the appointed rendezvous, off St Martin's Head. According to Cruikshank, Chambers and Bassenge were in an American civilian launch, 'as it was considered inappropriate to use a naval vessel'; in Chambers' report, the craft is identified as an unarmed RAF air-sea rescue craft flying a white flag.

The launch left Cap Carteret at 10.45 a.m. and took the hazardous course of running along the north coast of Jersey, not knowing if the German gunners had any idea of their mission. Happily, though poor visibility obscured their white flag, it also masked the launch. When they reached the rendezvous, no German vessel was visible, but a white signal flare was fired from the shore, and with no sign of any German emissaries, Chambers decided to take the craft right into St Peter Port and compel the enemy to parley with him. At 2 p.m. a German patrol boat put out from the harbour and drew alongside. Ominously, it was not flying a white flag and all the guns were manned. Chambers boarded it and demanded to see von Schmettow.

After messages had been flashed to the shore and back again, the request for an interview was refused. Chambers returned to the RAF craft and put to sea again, being fired at by the enemy batteries while passing Alderney en route to Cherbourg. A German Army officer who was present was seen to be visibly shaken as the full import of the mission became clear – he evidently thought that a full-scale assault on the islands was in the offing.

Like the after-action reports of the commando raids earlier in the war, the matter-of-fact tone of Chambers' report gives little indication of the danger (see Appendix V).

The refusal by von Schmettow to enter into negotiations – he had sent a robust rebuff to Chambers – was at the time attributed to interception by operatives of the SS, who had kept the general in the dark, while other commentators have suggested influence by the sinister Admiral Hüffmeier. Cruikshank says the fact that von Schmettow 'was simply a loyal soldier who was unlikely to surrender except when all was obviously lost does not seem to have occurred to those on the Allied side'.

Turner expands this idea by highlighting the strategic situation in September 1944. At Arnhem in Holland, the Germans had defeated Operation Market Garden, an Allied airborne operation to outflank the barrier of the River Rhine, and virtually destroyed the British 1st Airborne Division. General Patton's 5th Armoured Division might have liberated Luxembourg and entered the Reich, but it was low on fuel and slowing down, as were other American formations. On the Eastern Front, Soviet forces were dug in at river barriers. The onset of winter would further slow operations. Though V1 launching sites had been captured in France on 8 September, the first V2 ballistic missiles were launched, with one landing on Chiswick in west London. Nazi Germany was playing for time, hoping that there would be a falling out between the Western Allies and the Soviet Union, and that the new *Wunderwaffe* 'wonder weapons' like the radar-equipped Me 262 jet fighter, the V2, tanks with infrared night vision equipment and Type XXI Elektroboote, a U-boat that could operate underwater for sustained periods, would tip the tactical and ulti-mately strategic balance in its favour. The island garrisons were secure behind excellent defences and surrender to the Allies at this juncture would achieve little.

They might be isolated, but in this respect they were not alone. German garrisons held the French ports of Lorient, Saint-Nazaire, La Palisse and La Rochelle, while in the Mediterranean the islands of Milos, Leros and Rhodes, along with the western end of Crete, were also be under their control. German forces would hold parts of Holland and the whole of Norway and Denmark until the end of the war in Europe.

With the benefit of hindsight, Cruikshank is perhaps unduly harsh when he judges the outcome of the first phase of Operation Nestegg: 'The odds against success were heavy, but the impatience with which Chambers acted doomed the operation to failure. The efforts of the R.A.F. were wasted.' More important, the chance of saving the islanders from six months of untold misery were carelessly thrown away. The RAF was keen to know if the hazardous flights over the islands had yielded results and pressed the SHAEF Psychological Warfare Division for news. After waiting for a month and receiving no reply they asked again and were told that Major Alan Chambers had contacted members of the enemy garrison off Jersey [*sic*] who had thanked him for 'the newspapers which were received regularly by the troops'. The leader of the RAF Squadron which had been tasked with the mission of delivering *Nachrichten für die Truppe* felt that the reply to his enquiry was hardly an expression of gratitude but rather a 'strawberry' – one better than a vulgar raspberry. The pilots would have been even more disappointed if they had seen the letter from Edward Le Quesne, head of Jersey's Department of Labour, in which he wrote: 'Planes have been dropping thousands of leaflets in German, presumably for propaganda amongst the troops. We often ask why not some giving us news in English from our own people?'

However, Cruikshank identifies the flaws in the plan and its implementation. It was essential that the second letter should reach von Schmettow before the SHAEF representatives came to Guernsey. However, dropping only two copies was unreliable – on previous air operations, thousands of copies of *Nachrichten für die Truppe* had blown out to sea, so there was a high chance that the critical letters would follow the same route. It would have been better if several copies of the letter had been dropped over a period of a week. 'Chambers should never have left Cap Carteret,' writes Cruikshank, 'until he had reason to believe that the letter was safely in von Schmettow's hands.'

The second flaw in the plan was that the general was required to be at the offshore rendezvous. Clearly, Bassenge would be reluctant to board a German ship, running the risk of capture and possibly execution as a traitor, while von Schmettow might be taken prisoner on an Allied ship. 'Had the dialogue been planned to start at a lower level (as was first envisaged),' writes Cruikshank, 'von Schmettow might have eventually been drawn in.'

With the failure of this phase of Operation Nestegg, it would be nearly seven grim months before the Channel Islands were liberated. As the war had dragged on, to stay alive and enjoy some quality of life the islanders had been obliged to improvise; for 'tea', they used parsnip, sugar beet, green pea pods, camelia leaves, blackberry leaves, lime blossom and carrots – shredded and baked. Parsnips and sugar beet also stood in for coffee, along with chicory, barley, wheat, beans and lupin seeds – roasted and ground. For smokers, the substitutes for tobacco were cherry leaves, sweet chestnut leaves, rose petals, sweet scented butterburr, coltsfoot and clover. Sultana and currant substitutes included sugar beet, diced and dried, and dried elderberries. The lack of salt meant that seawater became the obvious source – however, with the beaches mined and off-limits, water was brought in by road tanker to be collected inland. Tinsmiths were kept busy making simple cooking utensils and oil lamps out of tins and other containers that in peacetime might have been discarded.

Hunger was universal. During the Nestegg negotiations off St Peter Port in September 1944, two German sentries had boarded the RAF Launch 2632. The autumn haze had burned off and in the sunshine, as they lazed on the deck, the Allied crew started eating their rations, that had been supplied by the US Army and included a whole roast chicken each. The two Germans, who like the rest of the garrison had suffered a cut in their rations in August, watched them intently; eventually, feeling common cause with the young soldiers, the crew of 2632 gave them bits of their rations, including cigarettes.

It was not only food that was in short supply. One islander recalled that quite early in the war shops emptied and 'needles, pins, tape, elastic, wool and cotton; kitchen utensils of every kind; all facilities for cleaning anything' could not be replaced. In addition 'tinned foods; beer and spirits; tapioca, rice, sago, pearl barley and the like; pepper, salt, mustard and all other condiments and sauces, coffee, cocoa, chocolate and sweets of all kinds' had disappeared off counters and shelves.

In early December 1944, a letter from a Jersey citizen reached her mother in London and was published in *The Times*. It described how 1lb (453g) of meat bought on the black market was going at the equivalent price today of about £45. Another writer smuggled out a letter which said a bar of Lifebuoy soap had sold for the equivalent of £112.

Like occupied Holland in 1944–45, the islanders faced the grim prospect of a 'hunger winter'. However, in the work of the remarkable Joint War Organisation (JWO) of the British Red Cross and Order of St John, the islanders literally received life-saving support. As early as February 1942, the JWO had sent supplies of medicines, drugs and medical stores to the Channel Islands. A large consignment was dispatched via the International Committee of the Red Cross (ICRC) and reached the islands in June and September 1942. A further consignment of medical supplies arrived in October and November 1943, based on lists from medical officers in Jersey and Guernsey. In December 1943, 100,000 units of insulin were sent to Guernsey. In July 1944, a supply of vitamin D for all the children of the islands was sent via Geneva.

Special individual requirements were even included, such as a surgical boot for an elderly woman, a new truss for a man, special powders for a man who had been badly gassed in the First World War and new equipment for a radiologist.

D–Day had changed everything, cutting off the islands from supplies from France. Cruikshank observes in *The German Occupation of the Channel Islands* that:

> The decline and tame capture of the Wehrmacht in the Channel Islands in May 1945 were due in part to the German troops' failure to become efficient market gardeners and peasant farmers. They could never have become completely self-sufficient, but if they had looked ahead they could have put themselves in a position to survive much longer.

Before the war, the mild climate of the islands had seen them grow a range of early fruit and vegetables that were exported to Britain. The islands' cows enjoyed then, and continue today, an international reputation for their top quality milk and cream, while Jersey new potatoes and the islands' tomatoes, coming early in the year, still attract good prices.

Rations might be in short supply, but sometimes the men of the garrison were lucky. A sailor from Hamburg, based on Guernsey, described how after a diet of oatmeal bread and Swiss chard soup – both of which he described as barely edible – they spotted some drifting lifeboats from a ship that had been sunk by a U-boat. The boats contained a good supply of survival rations and the men of the *Kriegsmarine* were able to enjoy milk drops, biscuits, pemmican (a meat concentrate) and chocolate.

As hunger took hold on the garrison, the Channel Islanders began to live in fear of robberies by hungry soldiers and even hungrier slave labourers. Perhaps most distressing was the theft of domestic pets. In one instance a girl was walking the family Scottish Terrier when a vehicle stopped and the German soldier grabbed the dog and drove off. Cooking cats took time – a German sailor explained that they needed to be boiled for two hours 'in order to get rid of the bugs which cats have'. The cat meat was the basis of a stew made up of root vegetables and nettles, and the surreal touch was that he recalled that it was presented with a silver setting on a white tablecloth with champagne. One of the sailors, who had sworn that he would never eat dog or cat, happily consumed this 'rabbit stew', only to be told by his comrades, with a certain gruesome glee, that he had eaten cat.

A tiny trickle of supplies did get through by air to the garrison, but this was unreliable and hazardous. The plan was to send a minimum of one aircraft a week to the islands. On 6 October 1944, two long-range Heinkel He 111s were tasked with flying rations to Guernsey. One crashed on take-off while the other jettisoned its cargo in the sea off St Malo. Two days later there was success, when two aircraft made it, bringing in addition to rations seven bags of mail – these aircraft were the first for four months.

Mail, which is normally seen as an important boost for soldiers' morale, was now having the opposite effect. As the Third Reich came under sustained attack from the RAF and USAAF, letters contained only grim news of death and displacement. In the later summer of 1943, life became unbearable for an officer from Hamburg, where on leave he had witnessed the devastation of the city following the firestorm. Back in St Helier he became deeply depressed and finally killed himself. Following D-Day, mental health became a serious problem for the garrison; 'Island Madness' was not now the sole preserve of Adolf Hitler. Werner Grosskopf recalled how one of his more reliable NCOs ran out of a bunker, loaded a machine gun and fired off a full box of ammunition out to sea. This triggered an immediate alarm, but when the island HQ demanded that the NCO be arrested an army doctor intervened and said that the man 'probably couldn't help what he did'.

Hunger and isolation began to sap the morale of even the most senior officers. In reply to a broadcast greeting from Dr Joseph Goebbels, the propaganda minister, von Schmettow said:

> In our complete isolation on British soil for many months past we particularly appreciate the broadcast as well as your personal greetings. The three Island fortresses, conscious of their strength, and following the example of other fortresses, will faithfully hold out to the last. With this in mind we salute our Führer and Fatherland.

As Dr Cruikshank notes, the Channel Islands are not referred to as 'former British soil', the official terminology used by the German Foreign Ministry, and in the signal von Schmettow no longer speaks of holding out until final victory.

Hunger undermined health. In a memorandum sent by the Guernsey Bailiff to the commander of the German forces on 31 August 1944, Dr R.N. McKinstry, the medical officer of health, stated of the islanders, 'Many are in a very poor condition, so the extra reduction in food values will have a serious consequence for them.'

The German foreign ministry had proposed via the Swiss that the Channel Islands be evacuated of all civilians except men of military age. For the Germans, this would leave a core civilian population who could be used to farm and so support the garrison. As this memorandum circulated through departments in Whitehall, it was realised that to do nothing would hand the Germans a valuable propaganda weapon. However, when the memorandum reached Churchill, he wrote, 'Let 'em starve. No fighting. They can rot at their leisure.'

In *Outpost of Occupation*, Barry Turner observes that Cruikshank's take on this note is that the British Prime Minister was 'of course, thinking of the Germans'. However, as Turner says, 'there was no "of course" about it. The war leader was focused on a single objective, the defeat of Germany. All else was secondary. Civilians might suffer – they were suffering all across Europe – but that was the price of ultimate victory.'

This uncompromising approach to the fate of the islanders was also to be found in a different quarter. When the bailiffs of both the main islands approached von Schmettow, expressing their concern for the civilian population, Coutanche recalled that he:

> told us we had no idea what other populations had suffered that, by comparison with many other places, the islands had not even felt the breath of war and he finished up by saying that in future it might be necessary for him to draw indiscriminately on our stocks of cattle, flour, potatoes and all other supplies, because Germany did not build fortresses of the kind which Jersey had become in order to surrender them.

The British government reminded the German commander that it was the duty of the occupying authority to feed the civilian population. On 12 November, the German authorities allowed Alexander M. Coutanche, to send a message to the British government giving details of the state of the islands' supplies. Information was also reaching the Allies via escapees who had made the journey from the islands to liberated France.

The Home Office issued a letter on 9 November 1944, proposing that the JWO take definite action to help the islanders. The government would provide facilities for sending food parcels to British civilians on the islands, subject to the same conditions under which parcels were sent to POWs. The ICRC would supervise the supply and distribution of the parcels.

The German government agreed to accept a supply of food to the islands. For the garrison, rations were running low, and on 13 January 1945, out of ninety-nine men on Guernsey who reported sick, twenty-four were suffering from malnutrition.

The JWO estimated it would need to supply 300,000 food parcels and 10,000 diet supplement parcels (for the ill) to the civilians on the islands for the first five or six weeks.

The JWO had several ships operating a shuttle service between Lisbon and Marseilles. The government asked the organisation to provide one of their ships to transport the supplies, and the Swedish ship the SS *Vega* was chosen for the duty. Rumours began to circulate on the islands that a Red

Cross ship would be coming, and on Guernsey Kathleen Nicolle noted in her diary on 3 November 1944, 'I wish it would hurry.'

The Bailiff of Jersey announced in *The Evening Post* on Friday 8 December 1944, 'I am officially informed by the German military authorities that a Red Cross ship was, weather permitting, due to leave Lisbon on Thursday, December 7th, for the Channel Islands. The ship will call at Guernsey first, en route for Jersey.' They were also informed that letters for the Channel Islands' civilian internees in Germany would be collected by the Red Cross ships.

The Red Cross' SS *Vega* left Lisbon in neutral Portugal on 20 December, carrying food parcels and diet supplies. She arrived in Guernsey with her life-saving cargo on 27 December and in Jersey on 31 December. Unloading was supervised by Col Islein of the Swiss Army, representing the ICRC. 'God, we were happy,' remembered Gerald Le Marrec, who was 11 years old at the time when the parcels were unloaded. 'Maple Leaf cheese, Klim milk, cans of salmon, jam, Smiles and Chuckles chocolate … Every person had a parcel. We felt sorry for the German soldiers, though – they had nothing.'

The *Vega*'s cargo was:

119,792 standard food parcels
4,200 diet supplement parcels for the ill
5.2 tons of salt
4 tons of soap
96,000 cigarettes
37cwt of medical and surgical supplies (equivalent to 1,850kg or 3,700lb)
a small quantity of clothing for children and babies

Food parcels were provided from the British Commonwealth supply stores in Lisbon and included 108,592 Canadian-packed parcels and 11,200 New Zealand-packed parcels. The diet supplement parcels were from British Red Cross stocks in the UK and were dispatched to Lisbon. The salt was a gift from a Portuguese donor. The medical and surgical articles were supplied by the Home Office, with the cost being met by the JWO. The cigarettes were New Zealand brands from stocks in Lisbon and the clothing was supplied through Lady Campbell of the British Embassy in Lisbon. On one of the islands, a baby girl born on the day the Red Cross ship docked was christened Vega.

Two ICRC delegates sailed with the *Vega*. They unloaded supplies for the people of Jersey at St Helier. With bureaucratic insensitivity, the German authorities insisted that their troops should unload the *Vega* to ensure that no contraband had been smuggled in aboard the ship. For the soldiers and sailors now on reduced rations, it was demoralising. Farmers from neighbouring districts volunteered to transport supplies from the pier, and mothers with pushchairs collected their family allocations.

Each islander who had a ration book for 1944 received one food parcel every month. It contained 6oz of chocolate, twenty biscuits, 20oz of butter, 2oz of milk powder, a 16oz tin of marmalade, 14oz tin of corned beef, 13oz tin of raisins, 6oz tin of prunes, 4oz tin of cheese, 3oz bar of soap and 1oz of pepper and salt.

The JWO, Canadian and New Zealand Red Cross Societies received a message from the Bailiff of Jersey expressing the heartfelt thanks of the inhabitants:

> for the wonderful gifts which arrived on the last day of 1944. Our doctors and medical services rejoice in the relief afforded by the timely arrival of medical supplies and the entire civil population is overjoyed at the thought of the relief represented by the food parcels and other commodities which compose this truly magnificent New Year gift.

The Bailiff of Guernsey wrote to the JWO to convey the grateful thanks of the inhabitants when the first shipment arrived. He said that the parcels had arrived at the most opportune moment.

The *Vega* sailed five more times. In relief voyages between February and April 1945, she brought mixed cargoes of Red Cross parcels and commodities supplied by the British government. The JWO sent a letter to the Home Office on 9 February 1945, stating the items the ship was carrying:

> standard food parcels
> invalid diet supplement parcels
> standard medical unit parcels
> medical and surgical supplies
> educational material

> books and indoor recreations
> out–door games
> soap and toiletries

Following liberation, the JWO agreed with the Home Office that the *Vega* should make one more journey, clearing the cargo lying at Lisbon and already planned for her to load. On the sixth and final journey, on 31 May 1945, the *Vega* carried:

> 21,232 standard food parcels
> 118 bales of medical supplies
> twenty-three cases of X-ray equipment
> 721½ tons of flour
> 1¾ tons of yeast
> thirty-eight tons of sugar
> twenty-six tons of soap
> 1,888 cases of biscuits
> 502 bales of clothing
> 163 bales of boots and shoes
> 155 drums of paraffin
> seventy-one barrels of diesel oil
> ten cases of honey
> 150 sacks of salt
> two cases of clothing

In total, the *Vega* brought to the islands 456,264 standard food parcels, a combined gift from the JWO and the Dominions Red Cross Societies. The ship also carried 22,200 invalid diet supplement parcels.

Islanders showed their gratitude after the *Vega*'s mission with remarkable generosity. When a Red Cross fund was opened in Jersey it had reached £125,000 (the equivalent today of £4,426,526), while Guernsey raised £46,000 (£1,628,961), by October 1945. The letter from the islanders that accompanied the cheque explained that they were, 'trying to show their undying gratitude to the British and Empire Red Cross Societies for the great and timely aid which they had received from them'.

For the islanders who had endured four years of occupation, there was a certain satisfaction seeing the envious looks of the German servicemen, whose main midday meal now consisted of horse meat sausage with potato and green vegetable soup. One islander recalled that an officer swapped his binoculars for a Red Cross parcel, and many soldiers no longer had watches since they had been traded for food.

Malnutrition and declining morale were worrying for the German command on the island, but there was worse – insurrection. It took two forms on Jersey. Disenchanted soldiers began circulating leaflets that read very like the morale-sapping propaganda in *Nachrichten für die Truppe*:

> Hitler wanted to conquer the world. Hitler began this war. He wanted to pulverise English towns. He wanted to exterminate whole populations. The entire guilt of this insane visionary and his accomplices has been avenged … We have only him and his Nazi clique to thank for the immeasurable sorrow that has been cast over the whole world, and above all, over the German people.

Jersey was also the island on which a different kind of protest was manifested. In late February, two officers issued orders to a couple of hundred men under their command to paint swastikas on buildings in St Helier. The officers said that the motive for this 'political protest' was their National Socialist principles. Von Aufsess was furious and noted that, 'It was such criminal fools who plotted the "crystal night" in 1938, which triggered off the storm of hatred against the Jews.' It has been suggested that the swastika daubing was an attempt to goad the population into a reaction that would allow the garrison to adopt severely repressive measures. If it was, it did not work. One man hung an empty picture frame around 'his' swastika, another wrote 'England for ever' by his, while a third converted the graffito into a decoration for merit and courage.

With France no longer occupied, the opportunities for escape were now greatly improved, and on 8 January 1945 Captain Ed Clark and Lt George Haas of the USAAF escaped from the POW camp at Mount Bingham, Jersey. They were assisted by local residents, and in particular Deputy W.J. 'Billy' Bertram BEM, who with other members of his family had settled at East Lynne farm, Fauvic, close to the coast. They successfully avoided recapture by the Germans, and on the night of 19 January made their way to Grouville Bay, then, dodging the beams of searchlights on nearby Fort Henry, moved through a gap in the minefields and boarded a small boat. After an arduous fifteen-hour crossing in bad weather, they landed near Carteret on the Cotentin peninsula.

As the war in Europe drew to a close, the Channel Islanders and the British government would be haunted by the fear that Hüffmeier might refuse to accept orders from Berlin and a make a last stand. If this had happened, they could have suffered the fate of the German island and naval base of Heligoland, which on 18 April 1945 was hit by a massive RAF air raid of 617 Lancasters, 332 Halifax and twenty Mosquito bombers. When, following the attack, the surviving inhabitants emerged from their deep air-raid shelters, they discovered that their island home had been reduced to an unrecognisable, stinking, cratered, smoking moonscape of pulverised earth and concrete.

It was a fate that the Channel Islands only just escaped.

Notes

1 In 1944, *Bordeaux* a *Lazarettschiffe* was already a veteran, having been launched and commissioned in 1912. Remarkably, she would remain in use until 1951, when she was broken up and scrapped.

2 *Nachrichten für die Truppe* (News for the Troops) was the brainchild of Sefton Delmer, Britain's master black propagandist. It contained a mix of factual news and subversive propaganda and was put together daily by a joint team of British and American journalists, and air-dropped onto German troops on the Western Front. The front page accurately reported the war situation on all fronts, usually before German troops received the news from their own sources. The inside pages generally dealt with the situation on the home front, covering the corruption of the Nazi bosses (*Bonzen*), how they avoided military service, lived in luxury outside the cities, safely away from the bombing, received extra 'diplomatic' food rations and basically profiteered from the war. Meanwhile, soldiers' wives were shown to be in peril through overwork in munition factories, dodging the air raids and suffering with poor diet and diseases coming from the east. *Nachrichten* also had a pin-up girl and even gave details of German Army promotions and awards.

3 There are some interesting parallels with the surrender negotiations in the Falklands nearly forty years later. The islands had been invaded by Argentina in April 1982 and a British Task Force sent from the United Kingdom to liberate them landed in strength at San Carlos Bay on 21 May.

15

ENDGAME: *KOMMANDO-UNTERNEHMEN GRANVILLE*, 8–9 MARCH 1945

It was on the night of 8/9 March 1945, only two months before Nazi Germany's unconditional surrender, that an amphibious raiding force set sail from the Channel Islands. Their objective was the port of Granville in Allied-controlled France, and their aim was to take the war to the enemy, bring back supplies, liberate POWs and capture or kill Allied servicemen. Bar local counter-attacks in mainland Europe, the raid is probably one of the last significant offensive operations undertaken by German forces in the Second World War.

In the last months of the war, a US Army-administered POW camp had been established at Granville on the west coast of the Cotentin peninsula, an area which by late 1944 was 500 miles safely behind enemy lines. Just before Christmas 1944, a naval artillery midshipman, *Fänrich der Marineartillerie* Leker, and four paratroopers, who had been captured at Brest, escaped from the camp. They had attached themselves to a working party in the harbour area, passing themselves off as interpreters, and on 21 December slipped away under cover of darkness and located an American landing-craft LCV(P), which they contrived to take out on the evening tide. With only a pocket compass and a sketch map to guide them, they reached Le Maître in the Minquiers group, where the German observation post, having first signalled 'Under attack by English landing craft', opened fired on them, and then, when their identity had been established, directed them on to St Helier.

The POWs reported that the harbour at Granville was in full opera-tion. There were usually about five ships there, most of them discharging coal. These ships came over in a convoy from Falmouth every other night, escorted by one escort trawler of the Plymouth Command Auxiliary Patrol. A US Navy patrol craft (PC) was also stationed at Granville, usually anchored outside the tidal harbour.

The winter of 1944–45 was particularly cold, and though there were coal mines in eastern France there was fighting in some of these areas, while in others the rail transport links were so badly damaged by the Allied air forces and German demolitions that coal could not be moved from the pitheads around the country. To help France to recover, the British began sending coal to the continent, and Granville was selected by Commander-in-Chief Plymouth, along with St Malo, Morlaix and St Brieuc, as one of the ports that could handle these deliveries from coasters sailing from South Wales. Despite the German demolitions, Granville had been cleared of many of the obstructions and the first collier entered the harbour in September 1944. It was in order to monitor these shipping movements that the German com-mand on the Channel Islands had established the observation post on Le Maître in the Minquiers group.

The POWs said that a unit of the US Army was billeted in the barracks near the old town on the high ground overlooking the harbour. They would not have known the numbers, but the force was a half company – some fifty-two men of the US Army's 156th Infantry Regiment, whose HQ was 20 miles to the north of Granville at Barneville. At Granville the only heavy weapon available for the US soldiers was one M1 57mm anti-tank gun. One hundred and thirty second-line French troops, armed with captured light German weapons, were stationed in the barracks overlooking the port. This rather bleak accommodation was known as 'The Rock' – a name more com-monly associated with Alcatraz, the grim high-security Federal penitentiary in San Francisco Bay. Finally, there was a battalion of US Army labour troops armed with carbines, whose principal function was to guard and supervise the Germans POWs working in the docks. While not all of this would have been known to the Germans on the islands, they would have had a detailed knowledge of the layout of harbour, since Granville had been used through-out the war as a resupply base.

There was a signal station on the south pier of the headland at Granville, and a radar station on the coast a short distance to the north. It would emerge later that the German defences had been dismantled or were no longer manned.

Following the D-Day landings, the Channel Islands had collected a small but effective naval force. Some of the ships had been based in the French ports along the Gulf of St Malo, and following the liberation of Normandy had made a run for literally the closest safe haven. On the islands, many were now laid up due to lack of fuel.

On the basis of the intelligence from the POWs, *Generleutnant* Graf von Schmettow decided to seize the chance of hitting back at the enemy while incidentally raising the morale of his own men, which was suffering almost as much from lack of action as from lack of food. The plan was to put Granville harbour out of action, capture a coal ship to help the desperate fuel situation in the Channel Islands and destroy the rest of the shipping. In addition, staff officers who were believed to be billeted in the hotels would be captured. It was calculated that all this could be achieved in sixty minutes. Though the initial planing for *Kommando-Unternehmen Granville* was the work of von Schmettow's staff, with the passage of time the credit would be hijacked by his successor.

The early commanders of the occupying forces under von Schmettow were reasonable men: they aimed to have a collaborative rather than coercive relationship with the population, so much so that prayers for the British royal family were even permitted to be said in services in the island churches. But in the closing stages of the war, after the failure of the July 1944 bomb plot against Hitler, and as Western and Russian armies approached the German heartland, extremists took over everywhere within the Third Reich.

Von Schmettow was replaced on 29 February 1945 by 47-year-old *Vizeadmiral* Friedrich Hüffmeier, who had come to the islands in June 1944 as *Seekommandant Kanalinseln*, or *Seeko-Ki*, to take over a command that had been established at the end of July 1942 and held by the highly efficient *Kapitän zur See* Julius Steinbach.

Hüffmeier was a former captain of the battle cruiser KMS *Scharnhorst*, a post in which he had proved incompetent and unpopular. In *Death of the Scharnhorst*, John Winton describes the crew's impression of their commander:

It took only a short time for *Scharnhorst*'s ship company to decide, to a man that 'Poldi' Hüffmeier was a walking disaster area. They believed he owed his appointment more to social influence than to ability, and he quickly showed himself a poor seaman, with almost no talent at all for ship handling.

Under Hüffmeier's command, the *Scharnhorst* had run aground off Hela at 26 knots; an Arado reconnaissance aircraft was catapulted off the ship before the engine had been opened up, and when it ditched only the observer was recovered alive; the *Scharnhorst* wrapped a buoy cable around the starboard screw while leaving Gdynia harbour, requiring dockyard repairs; and in August 1942 collided with the newly commissioned Type IXC U-boat U 523 while on manoeuvres in the Baltic. The latter accident led to further repairs. Despite this dismal record, Hüffmeier liked to be associated with the *Scharnhorst*, a ship that had sunk or captured twenty-two merchant ships in its role as a commerce raider. He even cultivated the rumour that he had been on the bridge when she made the daring Channel Dash in February 1942. In fact, the skipper of the battlecruiser was Capt. Kurt Hoffman, who two months after the remarkable operation was promoted Rear Admiral, and it was then that Hüffmeier took command.

Interestingly, as late as 1985, Hüffmeier's version of events still had the power to mislead. Michael Ginns MBE, the author of the recently published authoritative *Jersey Occupied: The German Armed Forces in Jersey 1940–1945*, writes of Hüffmeier in *After the Battle No 47*, 'he was nonetheless a competent deck officer, having commanded the battlecruiser *Scharnhorst* in its famous dash up the English Channel in February 1942'.

Unusually for the *Kriegsmarine*, Hüffmeier was an ardent Nazi, who controlled the only radio link powerful enough to reach Berlin. Before the liberation of France, communications had been transmitted from the islands by telephone, teleprinter or radio to the Corps HQ at St Lô on the mainland, and thence relayed to Berlin.

The formal handover of command was announced at 6.35 a.m. on 27 February 1945, when the *Oberbefehlshaber West* sent a signal jointly to *Marineoberkommando West* (MOK West) Naval High Command West and the 319th *Infanterie-Division*:

With immediate effect *Generleutnant* Graf von Schmettow, Commander of the 319 Division and Commander-in-Chief, Channel Islands, is transferred for health reasons to the Supreme Command of the Army Officers' Pool and *Vizeadmiral* Hüffmeier, Naval Commander, Channel Islands, is appointed Commander-in-Chief, Channel Islands. A new commander for the 319 Division will be ordered by personnel division. Generalleutnant Graf von Schmettow is to be despatched at once without awaiting arrival of new Divisional Commander.

For Hitler, following the July plot in 1944, the *Kriegsmarine* was now the only arm in which he had any confidence. The plot had been the work of army officers, and the *Luftwaffe* was discredited as it failed to stop the Allied air offensive against the Reich. Hüffmeier could be trusted in Berlin because he had attended the *Nationalsozialistiche Führungsstab der Kriegsmarine*, the National Socialist Leadership School of the Navy.

Descriptions of this officer vary. Some accounts say he was a gaunt, rather sinister figure with a weak smile and a long admiral's greatcoat that gave the impression of a cowl, and that he stalked around his tiny command carrying a large, bulging briefcase. King says of the *Vizeadmiral*, 'in spite of his avuncular appearance he was a ruthless *Kriegsmarine* Nazi determined to hold the Islands at all costs, and deeply suspicious of the existing generals whom he saw as being too close to the Island rulers'. The Woods write, 'Tall, burly, with something of the Goering build, his geniality masked a hint of fanaticism.' They are perhaps a little generous, as some fellow officers on the islands who could observe him closely simply thought that he was mad.

Von Aufsess made the most perceptive assessment of the *Vizeadmiral*:

> Two things strike me about him, his round shoulders, typical of the bookman rather than the man of action, and his high forehead, typical of the thinker. The army officers must find him a puzzling alien being. He belongs to that category of Nazi who are so carried away and bemused by their own oratory that they can never reckon to be dealing honestly either with themselves or with others. The Admiral would not be out of place as an evangelical pastor speaking from the pulpit. Certainly he could not proclaim his political, as against his religious, beliefs with more fervour or conviction.

Turner comments in *Outpost of Occupation*, 'It was a shrewd assessment. After the war Hüffmeier found God and turned to the church.'

But now, in March 1945, at the height of his powers, *Vizeadmiral* Hüffmeier announced his self-appointed promotion in the *Deutsche Inselzeitung*:

> As from 12 noon on 28.2.45 I have taken over as Commander-in-Chief, Channel Islands, and Fortress Commander, Guernsey from *Generalleutnant* Graf von Schmettow, who has been recalled to the Fatherland for reasons of health. I know only one aim, to hold out until final victory.
> I believe in the mission of our Führer and our people, I will serve them with unflinching faithfulness.
>
> *Heil* to our beloved Führer
> (signed) HÜFFMEIER
> Vice-Admiral and Commander in Chief

On the islands, the German POWs who had escaped from Granville were treated as heroes. Signals were exchanged with Berlin and a Heinkel He 111 made the hazardous flight across Allied-controlled Europe to collect them for a triumphant parade in the German capital. In a fast turnaround, it landed at 12.40 a.m. on 25 December and took off for the return flight at 3.42 a.m. On board were *Fregatten Kapitän* Breithaupt, *Oberleutnant zur See* Pauli, a wounded naval rating and the escaped POWs, *Fänrich* Leker and three of the four paratroops. However, their aircraft was picked up by a USAAF night-fighter and shot down near Bastogne – probably the result of Ultra decryption of signals traffic from the islands to Berlin. All on board were killed and are buried at the *Kreigsräbersttätte* at Recogne-Bastogne, Belgium. When, on 5 January, news of the interception reached the islands, Hüffmeier announced the death of Breithaupt, an officer 'whom the enemy never managed to touch in all his time at sea'. Flags were ordered to be flown at half mast on the islands.

In December 1944, Hüffmeier put his proposals for a raid on Granville in a private letter to *Admiral* Theodor Krancke, commander-in-chief of Navy Group Command West. Krancke decided that the enterprise had a good chance of success and gave it the go-ahead.

Interestingly, this would not be the first time that Hüffmeier had been involved in an amphibious raid. The one episode during his command of the *Scharnhorst* that reflected creditably on him was on 8 September 1943, when *Admiral* Oskar Kummetz led Operation *Sizilien* (Sicily), a naval surface attack on the British- and Norwegian-manned weather stations at Barentsburg and Longyearbyen at Spitzbergen. After departing the Alta Fjord in Norway, the battleship *Tirpitz* (*Kapitän zur See* Hans Meyer) and the battlecruiser *Scharnhorst* bombarded the two settlements, while the destroyers Z 27, Z 29, Z 30, Z 31, Z 33, *Erich Steinbrinck*, *Karl Galster*, *Hans Lody* and *Theodor Riedel* landed a battalion from Infantry Regiment 349 that wrecked various installations and took prisoners.

In January 1945, on the Channel Islands, selected volunteers were given special training. Among them, Paul Sommerfeld, a soldier in Infantry Regiment 584, recalled that the men selected had combat experience. Training was undertaken away from public view and the men were accommodated at Le Chalet Hotel in Fermain Lane, Guernsey. Allied signals intercepts had picked up that 400 hand-selected men were being given commando training, but when this intelligence reached London it was not taken seriously.

The men were transferred to Jersey and billeted in a hotel near Gorey harbour. They were kept apart from the garrison and forbidden to talk to civilians. They checked their weapons and equipment and waited for the right tidal conditions for a raid. It was established that at 11.30 p.m. on the night of 6/7 February there would be a high tide in Granville harbour, and so the raid was on.

A flotilla of craft[1] left St Helier on the night of 6 February, but fog closed in, a swell developed and *Kriegsfischerkutter* war fishing cutter VP 229 developed engine trouble, slowing down escorting ships, and so the expedition was recalled. According to the US Navy history, the decision to cancel the raid was an encounter by an E-boat with PC-552, commanded by Lt James Spielman USNR. The patrol boat had been stationed outside the harbour to protect seven merchant ships in the Granville roadstead. The PC-552 opened fire and chased the E-boat for 20 miles to a point east of Cape Fréhel, and then west to the Minquiers, but the superior speed of the German craft allowed it to make the safety of Jersey. The E-boat was S 112, which had taken up a patrol position to screen the convoy – the chase by PC-552 was exactly what the German raiders planned, since it took the US Navy boat away from its duties outside Granville.

Three patrol boats carrying the diversionary party and a tug did not receive the recall order. The patrol boats came to within 250m off the shore, so close to Granville that their crews said they could hear the music from the Americans in the Hôtel des Bains and Hôtel Normandie. Only then did they realise that the rest of the force had returned to St Helier. They withdrew, undetected by the American radar station. On the return journey, the LCV(P) that had been captured by the five escaped POWs foundered on rocks south of Jersey and had to be abandoned.

As an early part of the operation, S 112 had laid mines in the northern approaches to St Malo. The mines were in fact British parachute mines, dropped by the RAF in the entrance to St Peter Port harbour as part of air operations supporting the D–Day landings. It had been feared that the Channel Islands might be used as a base for U–boats, which would have been able to attack the huge concentration of Allied shipping off the coast. The mines were spotted by the Germans at low tide and disarmed by *Leutnant (Waffen)* Heinz Kass and then recovered. Rearmed, they were loaded onto S 112 and their deployment would be the only success in the first attack on Granville.

Berlin had confirmed Hüffmeier as the new commandant of the Channel Islands. He now set himself to work on a new raid on Granville, no doubt encouraged by the fact that it appeared that no ships had been detected by Allied radar in the first attempt. Training exercises were carried out by 800 men on Guernsey, the island furthest away from the French coast, and away from the civilian population. As a further security precaution, no joint training was undertaken between the ships and assault forces in case observers deduced what was planned.

At the end of the first week of March 1945, the German observation post on Les Minquiers reported that a number of Allied ships were headed for Granville. The weather was fair and so Hüffmeier decided that the moment had come to launch the attack. The assault force marched down to the docks at St Helier and, on the evening of 8 March, the ships moved off into the darkness. This time *Kommando-Unternehmen Granville* was on.

However, it might not have been. On 7 March, just a day before the raid was launched, there was a fire and explosions at the grand Palace Hotel at

Bagatelle near St Helier. Some historians have assumed this was sabotage – an indication of the declining morale of the island's garrison. The truth is more intriguing. Within days of the occupation, the hotel had been commandeered, initially as a communications centre, then later as an officers' training school. It was here that much of the planning for the Granville raid had taken place, so when a small fire broke out in a ground floor room that had been used to store explosives, the Germans attempted to control it themselves. Had the St Helier fire brigade been called, it was feared that they would see the maps and orders related to the raid, which might compromise the plan.

As the fire took hold, in a risky move, on the orders of *Leutnant* Hans Kiegelmann, demolition charges were placed on three floors in an attempt to create a firebreak. In the ensuing explosions, nine soldiers were killed and many injured, and much of the hotel was destroyed. Most of the burned and blasted shell was later demolished. A wing of the hotel did survive and in October 2007, researching the fate of the Palace Hotel for the BBC Radio 4 series *Making History*, Vanessa Collingridge travelled to Jersey and met historian Michael Ginns, who took her to the site. The indicators that the fire was sabotage are reinforced by the fact that, on the same day, fire damaged a German stores building, and a week later a fuel dump was set ablaze.

On 7 March, men of the US 9th Armored Division, 1st Army captured the damaged but intact Ludendorff railway bridge across the Rhine at Remagen. The Allies now had a lodgement on the east bank of the last major obstacle protecting the western borders of the Third Reich. In the east, the Red Army entered Kolberg and the Soviet High Command announced the capture of 8,000 men in a large pocket south of Schievelbein. German counter-attacks in the Lake Balaton sector of Hungary were repulsed. On 8–9 March, the heavily bombed city of Bonn fell to the US 1st Infantry Division. The Third Reich, which Hitler had promised would last for a thousand years, now only had months to live. However, on the Channel Islands, *Vizeadmiral* Hüffmeier was in denial and final orders were issued for *Kommando-Unternehmen Granville*.

The raid was led by 41-year-old *Kapitänleutnant* Carl-Friedrich Mohr,[2] and the full-scale commando raid flotilla comprised four large M-class minesweepers, the M412, M432, M442, and M459, with their masts removed in order to reduce their radar reflection; three *Artilleriefährprahm* or AFP (artillery ferry) armed craft mounting 8.8cm guns, AF65, AF68 and AF71;[3] three fast motor launches; two small R Type minesweepers; and the *Diecksand*, a seagoing tug. Embarked on the ships were eight army assault detachments totalling ten officers and 148 men, and thirty-four men in three naval assault groups with two officers. The *Luftwaffe* provided a flak crew of six, who were to give supporting fire when they landed.

The raiders were divided into five assault groups, numbered 1a, 1b, 2, 3 and 4:

> Group 1a, the minesweepers, the M412 and M452. Both ships carried soldiers and naval personnel tasked with demolition of the port facilities and radar station. The soldiers were commanded by *Oberleutnant* Jagmann. The sailors would crew the captured ships for their return journey to the iIslands. Mohr had selected M412 as his command ship.
>
> Group 1b, M432 and M442. The minesweepers were to take up position to shell the landward approaches to the harbour and so prevent reinforcements reaching Granville.
>
> Group 2, AF65, AF68 and AF71. The artillery ferries commanded by *Oberleutnant zur See* Otto Karl would draw off the Granville guard ship and intercept any ships that might be sent from St Malo. Finally, as the force withdrew they were to destroy the Grand Chausey lighthouse to make navigation difficult for any pursuers. Destruction of the lighthouse would also make routine naval operations more difficult for the Allies.
>
> Group 3, commanded by *Kapitänleutnant* Lamperdorff and *Oberleutnant zur See* Meyer. The fast *Hafenschutz* boats, the FK01, FK04 and FK56, would land the diversionary force under *Hauptmann* Schellenberg. They were to raid the two spa hotels Hôtel des Bains and Hôtel Normandie, where it was expected staff officers would be housed.
>
> Group 4, the auxiliary minesweeper M4613 and the cutter FL13. These would screen the Cotentin passage.

Embarked on the vessels were the eight army assault groups, who were on the ships in Groups 1a and 3; also in Group 1a was the six-man *Luftwaffe* flak crew. The three naval assault groups were on the ships in Group 1b.

Inside the harbour on the night of the raid were five coastal steamers, the *Kyle Castle*, *Parkwood*, *Eskwood*, *Nephrite* and *Helen*, and outside were the coastal steamer *Gem*, HM Trawler *Pearl* and PC 564.

The US Army radar station at Coutainville had picked up the German task force at 9.49 p.m., not long after it had left St Helier. The contact report was sent to the US Naval HQ in Cherbourg, the 156th Infantry Regiment at Berneville – who were put on standby – and, significantly, to the officer-in-charge at Granville. According to the *History of US Naval Operations of World War II, Part XI*, the officer regarded these reports as only 'interesting information' and consequently he did not order an alert. Ultra intercepts had also picked up that a raid was in the offing, and this information was passed on to the Americans at Granville. However, as with any Ultra intelligence that was disseminated to lower levels of command, the language in which it was couched was guarded and vague to conceal the priceless source – so it was not taken seriously.

There were other indicators that a raid was in the offing. A firm in Guernsey had been instructed to make scaling ladders, and these preparations came to the attention of the French consular agent on Guernsey, M. Lambert. He sent a warning to the Allies in France via M. Golivet, a French *Todt* worker who was planning to escape with the help of fishermen in St Peter Port.

Late on Thursday 8 March, word of the approaching task force had been passed to the US Navy submarine chaser PC 564, commanded by Lt Percy Sandell USNR. He had only been in command of the vessel for twelve days and had a scratch crew. At the same time, the Plymouth-based Asdic trawler HM Trawler *Pearl*, which had been escorting the *Gem*, a small collier, to Granville, was ordered to join PC 564. For some unexplained reason, the trawler skipper ignored the repeated requests to assist PC 564. The Cherbourg-based PT 458 and PT 460 were ordered south to support PC 564, but then were halted to cover the approaches to Cherbourg in case the Granville attack was a feint to draw off naval forces prior to an assault on Cherbourg.

This left Sandell and PC 564 as the only Allied ship guarding Granville. Without hesitating, he set course to intercept the convoy west of the Chausey Isles, but in so doing played into the hands of the Germans.

It was just before 11.59 p.m. that the American ship fired three starshells and closed for action, but after firing one round her 3in gun jammed. Now, as German starshells floated down in the spring night, the heavily armed AFP artillery ferries closed in and an 8.8cm shell hit the wheelhouse, killing everyone in it except Sandell and Lt Klinger, his gunnery officer. More shells and 2cm tracer fire hit the little craft, starting a fire and knocking out the secondary armament. Though the fire had been extinguished, Sandell knew that the situation was hopeless and gave the order 'stop engines and abandon ship'. Fifteen men went over the side and took to a small life raft. At the time they were listed as missing, presumed killed; in fact, with one exception, they were rescued by the Germans and would spend six weeks in the POW camp on Jersey.

Now, with half the crew dead, wounded or missing, at Klinger's suggestion the surviving crew restarted the engines and headed for the Pierre d'Herpin lighthouse, where they beached the patrol boat. The following morning, aboard the *Pearl*, Jack Yeatman, a radio telegrapher, noted in his diary:

> We searched along the coast for the PC and found her near Pierre de Herpin. An awful sight – guns blown away and bits of her crew all over the deck – men we'd got to know quite well. 10 killed, 11 wounded evacuated to Rennes by ambulance, and about a dozen missing. There are also 11 more known to be adrift in a life-raft, not seen since 0030. They never really knew what hit them.

French fishing boats also arrived to help the wounded, and the next day, PC 564 was towed into St Malo harbour and then to Plymouth for repairs.

As the raiders approached Granville at 1 a.m., they saw that the harbour lights were burning, which suggested that there was some activity there. The three AFP took up position between the Ile Chausey and St Malo to cut off any Allied patrols in that area, and two of the minesweepers stationed themselves between Jersey and the Cotentin peninsula for the same purpose. Another two of the minesweepers were to be the spearhead of the attack. Their plan was to sail straight into the harbour, and when challenged by the signal station, simply to flash back the same challenge in the hope that this would throw the defenders momentarily off their guard and allow them to get in safely; a similar ploy was used by the British in the raid on Saint-Nazaire in 1942. On the night, the Americans thought the signaller had got the reply to the challenge muddled and gave him the benefit of the doubt.

The radar station on the western end of the Pointe du Roc had picked up the tracks of approaching unidentified ships, so Maj. Brown, the port commander, ordered a blackout and that the work party of seventy-nine German

POWs who were about to start unloading the colliers should be secured in a stockade.

Before anyone realised what was happening, the German ships were into the harbour and seventy men equipped with demolition charges had poured onto the quayside, covered by the *Luftwaffe* crew.[4] It was here that the neap tide that would prevent the raiders from capturing all but one of the colliers would also cause the one serious loss of the raid. M412 ran aground at the harbour entrance and, after the tug had transferred the troops on board and landed them, the crew of the *Diecksand* attempted to pull M412 clear – but she was stuck. *Kapitänleutnant* Mohr abandoned his command ship and transferred to the M452. The minesweeper M412, which was later identified inaccurately as *De Schelde* – Allied intelligence officers had found the plate with the shipyard's name *De Schelde* and assumed it was the ship's name – was blown up using the ship's depth charges.[5] Demolition specialist Paul Sommerfeld, who had originally been tasked with the destruction of a fuelling station in Granville, was rapidly assigned to this task.

In the harbour, the raiders demolished nine of the eighteen newly installed cranes and a locomotive. The third pair of minesweepers was left outside the harbour to provide covering fire, the three motor boats made straight for the bathing beach by the Hôtel des Bains and Hôtel Normandie to land their party, and the tug moved slowly towards the harbour entrance to give the leading minesweepers time to secure themselves. The assault parties were ashore and had established themselves in positions from which they could control the approaches to the dock area. For an hour and a half they remained in command of the situation, in spite of fierce counter-attacks by the Americans.

The local American forces were now on full alert, but the men of the 3rd Battalion of the 156th Infantry Regiment, some military police and the French light infantry company were no match for the heavy volume of German automatic weapons fire.

On La Haute Ville, or The Rock, Maj. Brown and Capt. T. Wilkinson were rallying their troops. Since the American soldiers were only armed with their personal weapons, they were outgunned by the firing from M432 and M442. The two American officers attempted to rouse the French troops in the barracks, but their officers thought that this was merely a realistic test exercise and it took considerable efforts by the Americans to get the French troops out along the wall, parallel and above the harbour, where they opened a desultory and inaccurate fire on the raiders.

It was different at the western tip of The Rock, where US soldiers were manning the radar station. Armed only with their personal weapons, they defended the site with such vigour that they not only drove off the raiders but killed *Leutnant zur See* Scheufele, the officer in command of the raiding party. The attack on the radar station failed in part because the boats covering this part of the operation found that the tide was so low that they could not get close enough in to provide adequate covering fire.

The Germans had assumed that a reasonable number of vessels in the harbour would be afloat and could therefore be taken under tow or taken out under steam. In fact, the tide was now so low that of the four ships in the harbour, three were firmly aground and only the 1,200-ton *Eskwood* was afloat, loaded with only 122 tons of coal. With the tide ebbing, time was against the assault force. Both Charles Cruikshank and Barry Turner say that the Germans miscalculated the way in which the tide would affect the operation.

However, Michael Ginns makes an interesting observation about this aspect of *Kommando-Unternehmen Granville*:

> In an account written in 1952 Vizeadmiral Hüffmeier made it clear that the timing of the raid depended upon two factors; one of them was a moonless night with a high tide at a time which gave as much cover of darkness as possible. High tide, with no moon, was at midnight on the night of March 8/9 but it was a neap tide with a height of only 31 feet. Still it was a risk that had to be taken.

Ginns explains that an additional factor was that the Red Cross ship *Vega* would be making a delivery to the population of Jersey, and there were fears that her master might see indications that an operation was in the offing and pass this on to the British. Ginns writes, 'In their assumption the Germans were correct as surviving documents show that the captain did indeed pass on information about anything he saw in the Channel Islands' harbours.'

In Granville, the engines of the three grounded ships – *Kyle Castle*, *Nephrite* and *Parkwood* – and the Norwegian merchantman *Heien* were severely damaged by explosive charges, and the port installations – cranes, locomotives, wagons and fuel dumps – were systematically demolished. It had been intended that the tug should tow away any vessel that was captured, but in the event it was not needed. Capt. Wright, the master of the *Eskwood*, had been killed in the indiscriminate shooting, but there was still a crew aboard made up of chief engineer Bill Woodhead, first officer John Campbell, second engineer George Harrison, firemen Robert Dick and James Blair and donkeyman Joseph Sworda.

Since it was a policy to arm merchantmen to give them protection against *Luftwaffe* bombers and U-boats, the *Eskwood* was a defensively equipped merchant ship (DEMS) and had a gunner on board, Lance Bombardier James Mattock of the Royal Artillery. It was these men who took the *Eskwood* out of the harbour under her own steam. According to the account written by Hüffmeier in 1952, 'The crew took a sportsmanlike view of the proceedings and worked their ship.' In reality, the men were reluctantly crewing the ship under the barrels of German guns. When Michael Ginns contacted Bill Woodhead in 1984, he noted in his article on the Granville raid for *After the Battle Number 47*, 'If the language used by Mr Woodhead … is anything to go by, his appreciation of the whole situation was anything but sportsmanlike!'

Fifty-five German POWs were liberated. There are suggestions that it was as high as seventy-nine, but twenty-four contrived to be recaptured, preferring the comfort of a US Army-run POW camp to the insecurity and rigours of life on the Channel Islands.

The diversionary assault on the Hôtel des Bains and Hôtel Normandie was completely successful. The fast patrol boats slowed to a halt about 250m offshore, inflatable assault boats were launched and the raiders paddled to the sandy beach. It had been cleared of barbed wire, and though there is a seawall there is also a slipway close to the casino that allowed the men easy access.

The raiders under *Hauptman* Schellenberg had enough time to spread out into roads south of the hotels, roads that now bear the names Avenue de la Libération and Rue General Patton. In this part of the town, the owners of the small shops and flats, hearing the explosions from the docks, the sound of gunfire and shouted orders in German, opened their windows.

Their curiosity proved fatal – bursts of automatic fire killed six Frenchmen and women, and 40-year-old dockworker Marcel Guilbert was killed as he ran for cover up the Rue General Patton. Writing in the mid-1980s, Ginns noted that bullet scars could still be seen around some of the windows in the streets adjoining the hotels.

Two US Navy sailors were killed at the turreted and half-timbered Hôtel des Bains, which is only a few metres away from the slipway, and though the Hôtel Normandie was slightly less accessible there was little resistance in either location. Nine Americans were taken prisoner, among them Capt. R.H. Shirley, First Lt W. Wendell Heilman and bespectacled First Lt Newell Younggren. They had only arrived in Granville that evening and had no idea that the Channel Islands were still in enemy hands. Younggren had been sent a pair of pyjamas by his mother as a Christmas present, but in December 1944 he was caught up in *Unternehmen Wacht Am Rhein*, Operation Watch on the Rhine, the surprise German offensive through the wooded Belgian Ardennes. Now, on 8 March 1945, in a hotel that he was sure was miles from the front line, he had settled into bed in his pyjamas. Now, with jackets over their pyjamas, they were hustled down to the beach.

After the exhilaration of the liberation, it seemed that some of the French had grown tired of the behaviour of some of the rear echelon US forces and remembered the 'correctness' of the German occupiers with nostalgia. It is reported that some of the hotel staff assisted the raiders, showing them the rooms where American officers were staying. Writing later, von Schmettow recalled that the raid captured six officers and 43-year-old John Alexander, a principal welfare officer with the United Nations Relief and Rehabilitation Administration (UNRRA).[6] Alexander was in Granville to liaise with US Army officers and arrange accommodation for displaced persons (DPs) who were expected to be arriving in the town.

The most senior captive, Lt Col Anderson, had not been caught napping. Hearing the gunfire, he and his driver, Private Mark Layman, had jumped into a Jeep and driven rapidly down to the harbour to investigate. They arrived in time to be captured by the raiders and ushered down to the beach and on to a *Haffenschutz*. In a wry comment in his report on the raid, von Schmettow noted that some of the officers in the hotels were not alone in bed, but the raiders 'left the girls behind'.

One Royal Navy officer, Lt Frederic Lightoller RNVR,[7] who had been the port commander at Granville, and five of his men died during this attack. Earlier in the war, as a skipper of MGB603 and 613, Lightholler had been awarded the DSC and received two mentions in despatches. In 1945, he was on the staff of the shore establishment HMS *Odyssey*, the naval parties' accounting base at Ilfracombe. With the war in Europe drawing to a close, Granville was a secure posting and he was looking forward to rejoining his wife, Marcia, and their daughter.

It is an indication of how low the US garrison at Carteret had seen the threat from the Channel Islands that, on the evening of 8 March, some of the officers from the 156th Infantry Regiment (Separate) had thrown a party. Among the guests were two US Army nurses, Angeline 'Angel' F. Paul and Ellan J. Levitsky, of the 164th General Hospital, who had slipped out through a gap in the perimeter fence of the hospital without booking out.

Now, as the raid exploded in Granville, none of the US soldiers in the area knew what they were up against, so the two nurses were hurried upstairs by their escorts, covered with blankets in a wardrobe and told to remain silent. Through the night, the girls heard shouting, vehicles speeding around and even gunfire. With the dawn, US Army roadblocks barred the route back to La-Haye-du-Puits, and so they did not reach the hospital until late afternoon. 'Angel' was frantic because no one had signed out, and Ellan feared that her sister Dorothy, a nurse at the 164th General Hospital, would be worrying about her. Safely back at the hospital, as Ellan reached to hug her sister, Dorothy burst into tears, yelling, 'What was I going to tell Mother?', and gave her a resounding slap.

The German raiding force left Granville at 3 a.m. Ships of the Royal Navy and men of the US 156th Infantry Regiment reached the port about an hour later. On their way back to Jersey, as planned, the Germans attacked the lighthouse and signal station on the Grand Île de Chausey. On Jersey, observers saw that the light in the lighthouse at Cartert 14 miles away had been lit. Fearing that this might be to assist Allied naval units that could intercept the raiders on their return journey, the gunners in the *Haesaler* and *Schlieffen* batteries opened fire at 4.30 a.m. After shells had fallen around the lighthouse it was turned off.

All the German vessels, except the minesweeper and three dinghies, returned safely. The German losses were one missing (taken prisoner), fifteen wounded and three killed, including the leader of the radar station demolition team, whose body was left behind. The bodies of 29-year-old *Oberfeldwebel* Josef Kunkel (Grenadier Regiment 584) and 20-year-old *Obergefreiter* Paul Pfahler (Grenadier Regiment 583) were brought back to Jersey and buried with full military honours at St Brelade's Cemetery. In 1961, the *Volksbund Deutsche Kriegsgräberfürsorge*, the German war graves commission, dismantled the cemetery and the bodies were moved to Mont-de-Huisnes near Mont-Saint-Michel in Normandy.

The Allied losses were estimated at nine dead , with thirty confirmed wounded and sixty-seven POWs, who were taken back to the Channel Islands. Among the men of the Merchant Marine who are buried at Bayeux are 20-year-old fireman George Bell, the ship's master William Fraser and 33–year-old able seaman Charles Olsson, who despite his Scandinavian name came from Penarth, Glamorgan, and served on the Liverpool-registered SS *Kyle Castle*. On the London-registered SS *Nephrite*, 22-year-old able seaman Gordon Wills was killed and is also buried at Bayeux. On the Goole-registered SS *Eskwood*, the 43-year-old master Andrew Wright of County Antrim, Northern Ireland, died in the fighting. Acting able seaman John D. Cullen from the *Kyle Castle* and acting able seaman Richard Lees from the *Nephrite* were killed and are listed as Royal Navy casualties serving aboard DEMS. Cullen's name appears as Gollen in some accounts, and he is listed as a Royal Artillery gunner. It is probable that Cullen and Lees were the gunners aboard the ships and would have manned and maintained a bow-mounted gun.[8]

The prisoners were some of the first English-speaking strangers to be seen in the islands for five years, and according to some accounts the young ladies of Jersey society threw gifts and blew kisses across the barbed wire. Some of the Americans caused irritation by their reaction to the gifts. 'One,' write the Woods in *Islands in Danger*, 'presented with a set of underwear, sent back a message the he never wore anything except silk; another, given a rare present of Virginia cigarettes, asked for blended next time.' There may have been a little bit of licence in this account, since Ginns reports that the prisoners were housed in the old military prison at South Hill, overlooking St Helier. Forty years after his capture, Newell Younggren, now a grandfather, returned to Jersey for the first time. Accompanied by his grandsons, he visited the cell in which he was held and presented the Channel Island Occupation Society[9] with the very pyjamas he was wearing when he was captured, along with a chess set he had used as a POW.

Since he had taken command of the islands, *Vizeadmiral* Hüffmeier had held regular meetings with Alexander Coutanche to discuss how many POWs were being held on the islands to ensure that they received Red Cross parcels. During one such meeting, Coutanche had joked, 'Truth is, we are both prisoners of the Royal Navy.' Following the raid, Hüffmeier sent a message to the Bailiff, 'Beg to report, there are now thirty more of us who are prisoners of the British Navy.'

In the years after the war, and up to his death in 1974, and despite having found God, Hüffmeier would be happy not to dispute the version of the Granville raid that credited him with its planning and execution. However, at 8.04 a.m. on 9 March 1945 - just an hour after the raiders had disembarked at St Helier – his *Kriegsmarine* radio operators transmitted a long and detailed after-action report, that began:

> From: *Befehlshaber, Kanalinseln* to *MOK West*
> Emergency – Preliminary Report
> *Raid on Granville (including harbour destruction) planned by Generalleutnant von Schmettow and broken off 7/2 was replanned and, at my request, repeated under his control during the night.*

In a ceremonial parade, the raiders received decorations for their part in *Kommando-Unternehmen Granville*. Their commander, *Kapitänleutnant* Mohr, was awarded the Knight's Cross on 13 March 1945,[10] and eight days later *Oberleutnant zur See* Otto Karl, skipper of artillery ferry AF65, learned that he too had been awarded this high decoration. According to Admiral Ruge, 'Boldness, a sound plan, thorough preparation and complete secrecy had enabled the Channel Islands to strike a shrewd blow. Compared with the battle in Germany it was no more than a pin prick, yet it was the best they could do for their suffering country.'

The German-controlled *Guernsey Evening Press* reported on 12 March:

> German assault troops of the Channel Island garrison, under the command of Lieut. Capt. Mohr which had been landed by patrol vessels of the German Navy

carried out a coup de main on the enemy supply harbour of Granville, situated in the Gulf of Saint Malo, in the night preceding March 9th. They destroyed the locks, set the town and harbour on fire and made numerous prisoners including a Lieut/colonel and 4 further officers. 55 German soldiers were liberated from captivity. Furthermore, one American patrol boat was sunk, 5 supply vessels of together 4,800 gross registered tons destroyed, and one supply steamer captured.

Supplementing the report of the attack on Granville, Radio Berlin announced on Saturday night that troops from Guernsey and Jersey took part and that men of the French and American garrison were taken by surprise. The German prisoners of war who were liberated were found while they were shovelling coal. Before the alarm could be raised, the raiding force had returned to their ships, bringing twenty-eight prisoners with them. The supply steamer was captured and carried off as a prize as she was entering Granville harbour. 'Although,' concluded the radio commentator, 'the Channel Island troops are completely isolated, this enterprise bears testimony that their fighting spirit is in no way impaired.'

The raid was important enough to merit a reference in the situation briefing on 10 March held in Berlin by Grand-Admiral Karl Doenitz:

Channel Islands
During the report on the successful raid on the port of Granville by the forces stationed on the Channel Islands, the Commander-in-Chief, Navy, states that the newly-appointed commander of the Channel Islands, Vice-Admiral Hueffmeier, is the heart and soul of this vigorous action.

These were brave words, but with the benefit of the hindsight of history, in *Outpost of Occupation*, Barry Turner puts the raid in context:

The Granville raid was audacious and bravely executed but it achieved little of substance, except to provide the Channel islands with an extra delivery of coal. It made no contribution to the German attempt to hold the Allies at its borders until a peace deal had been brokered, and while a boost to garrison morale was badly needed, there is no suggestion that it won over any of those who doubted Hüffmeier's sanity.

In Berlin, another man with a limited grasp on reality, William Joyce, 'Lord Haw Haw', speaking of the Granville raid in a broadcast on 9 April 1945, said, 'The BBC is compelled to admire the strength of the German resistance in the West.'

In reality, though the raid had been audacious it did not cause a significant amount of damage to shipping or the port installations.

The 1,049-ton SS *Parkwood* had one boiler destroyed and a hole blown in her starboard side. The little 927-ton SS *Nephrite* had a boiler destroyed and a mine detonated in the fiddley (the hatch around the smokestack and uptake on the weather deck of a ship for ventilation of the boiler room) and No. 2 hatch.

The 845-ton SS *Kyle Castle* had charges detonated in the engine room and the hull was holed below the waterline. Capt. William Fraser, the master of the *Kyle Castle*, a tough 46-year-old Ulsterman who had joined the merchant navy at the age of 16, had refused to co-operate with the raiders and had been killed. Richard Reed hid along with another member of the crew until the Germans retired and then he took over as captain. He managed to repair the damaged hull, but with engines unusable, he then floated *Kyle Castle* out on the ebb tide and, with the hatch covers as improvised sails, managed to make the Channel and was then towed into Plymouth. Capt. Fraser, who along with the other casualties of the raid is buried at Bayeux, had been awarded the MBE in 1944 for gallant and meritorious service.

Lastly, the SS *Heinen* had suffered the modest damage of a bullet hole through the wheelhouse window. Significantly, only two days after the raid, three of the four damaged ships were operable again.

In the port, of the five portal cranes on the North Quay, Nos 1, 2 and 3 were repaired in a day; No. 4 was, however, badly damaged, but No. 5 was operable. Of the six portal cranes on the South Quay, No. 1 was repaired in a day, though Nos 2 to 6 were badly damaged. Of the six crawler cranes, three were seriously damaged, whilst three could still be operated. One 22-ton Kearing crane was badly damaged. Three stiff leg derricks were listed as being in 'fair working condition', while one shunting locomotive was destroyed and the raiders destroyed a US Navy Jeep when they threw a grenade into the vehicle.

Hüffmeier would assert after the war that there was additional damage, including an ammunition bunker and eight trucks destroyed. The American report on the raid makes no mention of this damage, and moreover states that the port was back in action within two days of the raid, albeit at a reduced capacity. However, the Americans conceded that 'the enemy had fire superiority … which enabled him to set off demolitions at will … In fact he had complete control of the Granvillle area and were his objective that of conquest, he was the conqueror.'

There would be one more raid from the Channel Islands, on 5 April 1945, when an eighteen-man German sabotage squad sailed from Jersey via Alderney in the vessel M4613. The M4613 was a drifter that had been modified as a minesweeper and consequently could have been mistaken by the Allies for a French fishing boat.

The raiders' mission was to disrupt the rail links from Cherbourg by blowing up the bridge at Le Pont. The team was named the 'Maltzahn Demolition Party' after Lt Maltzahn, the officer who had trained the men and would lead them on the operation. Though the sabotage team was drawn from engineers in the army garrison of the islands, it had a *Kriegsmarine* signaller, *Funkergefreiter* Bernd Westhoff, attached – dressed in army uniform. Each man carried his personal weapon and ammunition, rations and 16kg of explosives.

Westhoff had a simple code with short signals that began with the message that, decoded, read 'raid failed'. In what was good psychology but bad staff work, the commander of the 46th *Minensuchflottille*, *Kapitänleutnant* Armin Zimmerman,[11] changed the order of the messages so that the first signal on the list read 'raid successful'. However, he failed to record this change.

The men embarked on M4613, commanded by a very experienced and reliable chief petty officer, *Obersteuermann* Koenig, on 4 April – Westhoff's birthday – and made a successful covert landing by inflatable assault boats on Cape de la Hague on 5 April, though one man fell overboard and lost his kit. Westhoff noted that the inflatable assault boats were left on the beach, with no attempt to conceal them. The raiders made their way through an old German minefield and, marching by night and laying up by day, made their way towards Cherbourg. Passing an American billet, they could hear US soldiers singing and laughing. Westhoff recalls they were 'apparently celebrating; to them the war seemed far away'. Hiding in undergrowth, they watched 'an enormous and endless stream of U.S. Supply trucks passing by'.

Westhoff set up his radio and transmitted a brief signal confirming that the party had landed safely – it was acknowledged promptly by the Naval HQ in Guernsey. It was at this juncture that the engineers realised that their demolition stores were insufficient for the task of destroying the railway bridge, so Lt Maltzahn instead decided to attack tracks and rolling stock at Cherbourg. During the night the men marched openly along roads, with the officer answering in French when challenged in English and vice versa. The bluff worked.

Close to their target, Westhoff and his mate, who had carried the radio batteries, lay up at an agreed RV. They heard gunfire and, after an interval, only Maltzahn returned – they waited and, realising that the raid had failed, started to make their way back to the coast. They transmitted the first coded message on the pad and at the Naval HQ on the Channel Islands there was delight that the railway link had been cut. It was at this point that Zimmerman remembered that he had changed the order, and the cluster of numbers and letters actually meant 'raid failed'; he was able to alert *Vizeadmiral* Hüffmeier before he transmitted a triumphant signal to Berlin. The Americans were now on full alert, searching for the raiders. Westhoff had received instructions from the HQ on Guernsey that he was to destroy his radio set and codebooks.

Maltzahn left the two radio operators hiding in a barn but failed to tell them where they could be picked up by minesweeper M4613, and when four Jeeps mounting Browning .50 machine guns surrounded the barn, the sailors knew they would have to surrender. Ironically, as they climbed down the ladder, the first GI to enter the barn was so nervous when he saw them that he put his hands up.

The US Army intelligence officers who interrogated Westhoff and his fellow radio operator used coercive techniques, including pointing a Colt 45 in their faces and the offer and then instant denial of food. Westhoff was taken to the naval prison at Cherbourg, where he caught 'flu, and was then moved to a ward in the naval hospital, where there were twenty seriously ill men but no medical support. The questioning continued, with the Americans insisting that he repair his radio so that negotiations could begin with Guernsey to arrange a surrender. Westhoff explained that he was a radio operator and not a technician.

He was then sent to a POW camp for 'trouble-makers' that was run by the French. It was a short but unpleasant stay that ended when he was transferred to the UK, and then on 23 February 1946 he was released and repatriated to Münster.

It was while he was in the UK, at Featherstone Park POW camp, that he learned what had happened to Maltzahn. The young officer made his way to the RV, a point 15km west of Cherbourg and just within the 18km range of the guns on Alderney. The minesweeper was waiting offshore. An inflatable assault boat was sent to collect him, and Maltzahn, who Koenig noted was 'dirty and hungry', bleeding from several wounds and limping, was helped on board. The officer was still carrying his MP40 sub-machine gun. The skipper of the minesweeper was not happy that Maltzahn had abandoned the signallers and, worse still, not told them the location of the RV.

Back on the Channel Islands, Westhoff was awarded the Iron Cross First and Second Class, but when Koenig raised the situation of Westhoff with Hüffmeier, the admiral ordered that Westhoff be promoted to *Funkmaat*. After the war, Koenig made strenuous efforts to track down Westhoff and they met in 1948.

Elated by the success of the Granville raid, *Vizeadmiral* Hüffmeier was already planning another attack on the port – reasoning that the Americans would not expect a repeat attack. A group of volunteers would take the SS *Eskwood*, loaded with concrete blocks, and sink her at the entrance to the harbour, while another team would block the harbour at St Malo using a freighter that had been laid up in the Channel Islands. The blockship crews would then be evacuated by high-speed launches. The date set for the great attack was to be 7 May, but Admiral Karl Dönitz, whom Hitler had named in his will as the new national leader, ordered *Vizeadmiral* Hüffmeier not to launch any offensive operations. In fact, it was on 7 May that the unconditional surrender of Nazi Germany was signed in Rheims – the attack on Granville would be the last major raid.

The Channel Islanders' leaders, in these last months, dreaded the possibility that Hüffmeier might attempt to hold out after a German capitulation. To capture and liberate the islands would have involved an Allied bombardment and the destruction of everything, and of everyone whom they had worked so hard to save. Fortunately, they became aware that they had allies amongst the Germans themselves. There was resentment by soldiers at having a naval officer as commander-in-chief, fear and dislike of Nazism by men like Baron von Aufsess and Baron von Helldorf, who had never been Nazi Party men, and finally troops who had been stationed for years on the islands felt more in common with the civilian populations than with 'outsiders' like Hüffmeier.

A month before the war ended, *Vizeadmiral* Hüffmeier had addressed a mass meeting in the Forum Cinema, St Helier, Jersey, where he explained the importance of defending the Channel Islands. It was stirring stuff – an attack by the British and Americans might happen at any moment and put them in the front line. They must prepare for this hour spiritually and materially; the more desperate the times, the more united they must be. It was reported by the rather incongruously named *Deutsche-Guernsey Zeitung* on 19 March 1945:

> Vice-Admiral Hüffmeier left no doubt in the minds of his audience that, with firm, unshakable faith in the victory of our just cause, he is determined to hold as a pledge, to the very end, the Channel Islands which have been entrusted to him by the Führer. A settlement of accounts with the Anglo-Americans, arms in hand, is quite possible, and perhaps not far ahead … Those who kept within their hearts the ideal of National Socialism, in its original purity, would have the upper hand.

On Hitler's birthday, troops were assembled in the Regal Cinema in St Peter Port, Guernsey, to hear a similar message, and the admiral even took it to the garrison of Sark. For the men on the tiny island, he had 'inspiring' words – if they did not resist an Allied attack they would be sent to the Eastern Front, a front that was now inside the borders of the Third Reich.

Key installations on the islands were rigged with demolition charges, among them the new jetty at St Peter Port, where some 207 big 27cm shells were removed from the concrete piles following the liberation.

On 3 May, news of Hitler's death reached the Channel Islands. The German-controlled *Jersey Evening Post* ran the headline 'Adolf Hitler Falls at His Post', and on public buildings on the islands swastika flags flew at half mast. It was three days after Hitler had shot himself in the bunker in Berlin, and though the paper said that he 'met a hero's death' fighting 'the Bolshevik storm flood', even then it was widely suspected that he had committed suicide.

On 8 May, as Churchill formally announced the unconditional surrender of Nazi Germany, a similar demand was put to Hüffmeier. His representative, a nervous young naval officer, Armin Zimmerman, kept the rendezvous with the destroyers HMS *Bulldog* and HMS *Beagle*. His journey to and from the warships was slightly humiliating, from a minesweeper trawler in a three-man inflatable dingy rowed by *Kriegsmarine* ratings. On board, he took a deep breath and told the British he had been authorised to discuss an armistice, not a surrender. His hosts replied that it was surrender or nothing. Zimmerman took another deep breath and said his instructions were that the British must withdraw or they would be fired on.

The two ships withdrew out of range. That night, saner voices pressured *Vizeadmiral* Hüffmeier to change his mind. The ships returned; Hüffmeier threatened to open fire when they arrived ahead of the designated time. Since Hüffmeier could not bring himself to attend the surrender negotiations, *Generalmajor* Heine, Hüffmeier's deputy, signed the surrender document. Ironically, the vessel that transported Heine to HMS *Bulldog* was M4613 *Kanalblitz*, the minesweeper that had landed the Maltzahn sabotage patrol on mainland France.

The final act was left for von Aufsess to announce, at a hastily convened meeting of Channel Island elders: '*Der Krieg ist zu Ende, und in den Kanalinseln auch*' ('The war is over, and in the Channel Islands too').

Only a small number of people within the Admiralty knew that HMS *Bulldog* had already won herself a place in history – but one that would remain secret until the early 1970s. On 9 May 1941, she was responsible for the capture of U110, Sub Lt David Balme finding the Enigma code machine ciphers and, critically, the current codebooks. U110 was taken in tow and *Bulldog* kept her afloat for seventeen hours, then let the towline slip. The intention was to tow U110 into Iceland, but the Admiralty realised this would have been a massive error of judgement. In the event, allegedly, U110 resolved the matter herself by sinking.

At 3 p.m. on 8 May, Churchill announced to the world, 'Our dear Channel islands will be freed today.'

The *Beagle* returned on 12 May, and the British took Hüffmeier into formal custody. His last order was that when they came ashore his men should greet the British with Nazi salutes. Most ignored him, since by now they were too drunk to bother.

Hundreds of illicit wireless sets were brought into the open for the people of Jersey, Guernsey and Sark to learn from Churchill that nearly five years of occupation were almost over. A German soldier climbed to the top of a crane in Jersey harbour to fly the Union flag. British soldiers were mobbed, and on Guernsey, a British colonel's bald head was coated in ersatz lipstick. Aboard HMS *Bulldog*, after endorsing the surrender document, Coutanche smoked real tobacco for the first time in years and washed his hands in real soap (see Appendix VI).

The Nestegg had finally hatched.

The work of quiet heroes could now be made public. On Jersey, the heroism of physiotherapist Albert Bedane could be acknowledged. It was to his house that Erica Richardson, a Dutch Jew, fled after she had given her German guard the slip in June 1943. The Germans combed St Helier for her, and Bedane risked execution by hiding her until the island was liberated. He also sheltered an escaped French prisoner of war and Russian slave labourers, on the principle, in his words, that he 'might as well be hanged for a sheep as for a lamb'.[12]

Besides the award of the OBE by the British government for his courageous conduct, Wilfred 'Billy' Bertram, a former corporal in the Canadian Army, was also awarded the United States Medal of Freedom by the US government after the war for the help he gave the USAAF air crew in their escape. In *Outpost of Occupation*, Turner observes that the award of an OBE to Bertram was 'the only nod in the direction of the resistance' by the British government, which was embarrassed by what had unjustly been perceived as the comparative passivity of the population during the occupation.

Another person who was not island-born but gave valuable support to escapers, was Irishman Dr Noel McKinstry. He was one of the few islanders who was prepared to help Soviet slave workers, and had the resources and contacts to provide them with identity and ration cards. He was one of a network of islanders who provided safe houses and encouraged them to adopt English names, such as Bill, George or Tom, and to learn English in order to avoid detection. With papers and a command of English, they were able to find work and so become self-sufficient. McKinstry was awarded an OBE in the occupation honours.

Remarkably, on Jersey, the mother and aunt of the youthful Stella Perkins, Augusta Metcalfe and Claudia Dimitrieva, were both Russians who had come to the island as refugees following the Bolshevik revolution in 1919. Islanders knew that they were Russian, so escaped Russian slave labourers would be referred to them as a safe house. Escaped Russians would sometimes simply call in to have a chance to talk in Russian about their homeland in a domestic setting. As Stella recalled, these meetings – with enemy soldiers marching past on the street below – were 'one in the eye of the Germans'.

One Russian, Georgio Kozloff, was a gymnast and when Stella made him some swimming trunks out of an old pullover, he went down to the open air swimming pool at St Helier and did some spectacular dives. Stella was with him and she was terrified that he might be spotted by men of the *Feldpolizei*, whose HQ at Silvertide guest house overlooked the pool.

Some, however, would only be honoured in the memory of the islanders. Louisa Gould hid Fyodr Polycarpovitch Burriy, an escaped Russian slave labourer whom she took in because she had lost a son in the war and was determined to do an act of kindness 'for another mother's son'. Named 'Bill', Burriy lived with her for two and a half years before Louisa was betrayed by a neighbour. While the Russian escaped, she was arrested and, on 22 June 1944, sentenced to two years' imprisonment for 'failing to surrender a wireless receiving apparatus, prohibited reception of wireless stations and abetting breach of the working peace and unauthorised removal'. The unauthorised removal was sheltering 'Bill'. She was found guilty and sent to a concentration camp along with her brother, Harold Le Druillenec.

Louisa was gassed in Ravensbrück concentration camp and Harold would be the only British survivor of the notorious Bergen–Belsen concentration camp, a place that he recalled as 'the foulest and vilest spot that ever soiled the surface of this Earth'.[13]

The German soldiers on Alderney surrendered a week after the main Channel Islands. Their commander, *Oberst* Schwalm, ordered that the camps that had housed the forced labourers be burned to the ground, and destroyed all records connected with their use before the island was liberated on 16 May.

On Thursday 10 May, a party of British soldiers crossed from Guernsey to Sark. The small detachment marched up from the harbour surrounded by excited islanders, and then along the Avenue, throwing sweets and cigarettes to the delighted crowds, and accepted the surrender of the *Kriegsmarine* lieutenant left commanding the little garrison. However, for the next week, the governor, Seigneur Dame Sybil Hathaway, was left in command of the German troops.

To the west of Alderney, on the Casquets, on 17 May two officers and twenty men were taken off the lighthouse, but Trinity House left six prisoners on the rock to continue the maintenance of the lighthouse until they could be replaced by British lighthouse keepers.

The very last *Wehrmacht* soldiers to surrender on the Channel Islands were the small detachment manning the observation post on the tiny island cluster of the Minquiers. A French fishing boat, skippered by Lucian Marie, approached the islands and anchored offshore. A fully armed German soldier came down to the jetty from the fishermen's cottages on Le Maître, the largest island, and shouted across to the Frenchman, 'We've been forgotten by the British, perhaps no one on Jersey told them we were here, I want you to take us over to England, we want to surrender.'

It was 23 May 1945.

The war in Europe had been over for three weeks.

> This is the way the world ends
> This is the way the world ends
> Not with a bang but a whimper.
>
> T.S. Eliot, 'The Hollow Men'

Notes

1   It consisted of eight *Heer* assault detachments (mainly the 319. Infanterie-Division) consisting of nine officers and 148 men; two *Kriegsmarine* naval detachments of one officer and twenty men; as well as the following naval vessels:

S112, a fast motor torpedo boat or *Schnelleboot*. This craft, commanded by *Leutnant zur See der Reserve* Nikelowski, had escaped from Brest. Nikelowski, in peacetime a whaler captain, was a skilled seaman.

Four M40-class minesweepers of the 24th *Minesuchflottile*, M412, M432, M442 and M452. Commanded by *Kapitanleutnant* Mohr, these ships were armed with one 10.5cm SK c/32 ship's gun and numerous 3.7cm and 2cm flak guns.

Two auxiliary minesweepers of the 46th *Minesuchflottile* and 2nd *Vorpostenflottile*, commanded respectively by *Kapitanleutnant* Zimmermann and *Fregattenkäpitan* Lensch.

Gruppe Karl, three 'artillery carriers' or *Artillerie-Träger*, AF65, AF68 and AF71, survivors of the 6th *Artillerieträgerflotille*. Originally based at Cherbourg, the vessels were commanded by *Oberleutnant zur See* Otto Karl.

V228, V229 War Fishing Cutters (*Kriegsfischerkutter*, KFK) of the 2nd *Vorpostenflottille*.

FK01, FK04, FK56 Harbour Protection Vessels (*Hafenschutzboot*) of the *Hafenschutzflottille Kanalinseln*.

FK60, a captured Allied LCV(P). The prefix FK stands for *Frankreich Kanalinseln*, or French Channel Islands. The ships were commanded by *Kapitänleutnant der Reserve* Lamperdorff.

2 Carl-Friedrich Mohr (10 May 1907 – 29 January 1984) was a career naval officer who had commanded 24th *Minensuchflottille* Karl Friedrich Brill.

3 The *Artilleriefährprahm* or AFP (artillery ferry) was a gunboat derivative of the *Marinefährprahm* (MFP), the largest type of landing craft used by the *Kriegsmarine* during the Second World War. These ships were used for escorting convoys, shore bombardment and mine laying. They were fitted with two 8.8cm guns and 2cm AA guns. The AFP were mainly built in Belgian yards and converted in Holland.

4 The six men of the *Luftwaffe* may have been the crew of a 2cm flak 30 or 38 anti-aircraft gun. The weapon weighed 450kg (992lb) and could therefore have been manhandled into position on the dock. In a direct fire role, the 20mm shells fired at close range would have been devastating against soft targets.

5 The M412 minesweeper (*Minensuchboot*) was built in the 1940s by N.V. Koninklijke Mij 'De Schelde' shipyard located in Vlissingen, the Netherlands, as a minesweeper or escort vessel for the *Kriegsmarine*. It had a transverse frame of steel construction, which was partly welded, and also had eleven watertight compartments and a double bottom with hard-chine foreship and tug stern. The superstructure, bridge etc. was armoured up to 10mm in thickness. The propulsion system installed in these vessels was two vertical three-cylinder triple expansion engines. When used as minesweepers, the Kabel Fern Raum Gerat (KFRG) system was employed, which used generators producing 60V, 20kW to power the magnetic sweeping gear.

6 John Alexander, who would be the only UNRRA official to be captured during the war, was very much a man of peace. He had been warden at Oxford House educational settlement, Risca, Monmouthshire. Oxford House had been established during the 1920s, when the Lord Mayor of London made an appeal to help people impoverished by industrial strife. In response, the Mayor of Oxford's Mining Distress Committee was formed to organise and dispatch aid to coalmining areas, including Risca. Some public utility works at Risca were subsidised and relief in other forms was contributed. Alexander took over

as warden from the pioneering Mr and Mrs David Wills, who had been joint wardens. After the war, Alexander became warden of the Mary Ward Centre, the adult education establishment in Bloomsbury, and he held this post until his retirement in 1971. He died on 2 December 1981.

7   Lightoller was the oldest son of Charles Herbert Lightoller, the second officer on the RMS *Titanic* who was the most senior surviving member of the crew to survive the disastrous sinking in 1912. In the First World War, he would serve with distinction in the Royal Navy, winning a bar to his DSC. In the Second World War, as a civilian, along with his son, Frederic, he took a 'little ship' to Dunkirk in 1940 to assist with the evacuation of the BEF. His youngest son, Brian, a bomber pilot in the RAF, had been killed on the first day of the war in a daylight raid on Germany. Frederic is buried at the Commonwealth War Graves Cemetery at Bayeux, Normandy.

8   A variety of armaments were fitted to merchant vessels, typically a 4in deck gun at the stern, sometimes a 12pdr (3in shell), usually at the bow, mounted as either LA (low angle) for use against surfaced U-boats or surface raiders, or HA (high angle) for anti-aircraft use. Initially, the light machine guns were manned by 500 men of the Royal Artillery, Light Machine Gun sections, who were taken on and off vessels as they arrived and departed from British ports. The effectiveness of these army gunners was quickly realised, and the Maritime Anti-Aircraft Regiment Royal Artillery was formed in 1941, renamed the Maritime Royal Artillery (MRA) in January 1943.

9   The Channel Island Occupation Society was formed in 1961. However, it can trace its roots back to 1956, when two Guernsey schoolboys, Richard Heaume and John Robinson, formed a club to collect occupation relics. In defiance of their elders, including their headmaster, they explored bunkers and tunnels on the island, recovering helmets, gas masks and other items of equipment. By 1961, Richard Heaume's collection had outgrown the attic of the family home and the club, named The Society for the Preservation of German Occupation Relics, was no longer confined to the pupils of Elizabeth College. The name was shortened to The German Occupation Society in 1963 and, seven years later, the word 'German' was dropped. Today there are two branches, one in Jersey and the other in Guernsey.

10 Mohr, who prior to the Granville raid had commanded 24th *Minensuchflottille* 'Karl Friedrich Brill', would survive the war and die at the aged of 76 on 29 January 1984 at Bodenbach.

11 In 1972, Zimmerman would become the first naval officer to hold the rank of Inspector-General of the West German Armed Forces, the *Bundeswehr*, serving in this post until 1976.

12 Albert Bedane (1893–1980) was born in Angers, France, and lived in Jersey from 1894. He served in the British Army from 1917 to 1920, and was naturalised as a British subject by the Royal Court of Jersey in 1921. On 4 January 2000, Albert Bedane was recognised as 'Righteous Among the Nations', also known as 'Righteous Gentile', by the State of Israel. In 2010, Bedane was posthumously named a 'British Hero of the Holocaust' by the British government. A plaque marks the house where he sheltered the escapees.

13 In May 1965, the Soviet Union recognised the courage of the Channel Islanders who had sheltered Soviet slave labourers and awarded them twenty gold *Poljot* brand (the Russian word for 'flight') watches, made by the First Moscow Watch Factory. Recipients were Albert Bedane, Claudia Dimitrieva, François Flamon, Ivy Forster, René Franoux, Royston Garret, Louisa Gould and Dr McKinstry (posthumously), Leslie Huelin, John Le Breton, Norman Le Brocq, Mike Le Cornu, Harold Le Druillenec, René Le Mottée, Francois Le Sueur, Bob Le Sueur, Augusta Metcalfe, Oswald Pallot, Leonrad Perkins and William Sarre.

APPENDIX I

FORTIFICATION ORDER OF 20 OCTOBER 1941

1 Operations on a larger scale against the territories we occupy in the West are, as before, unlikely. Under pressure of the situation in the East, however, or for reasons of politics or propaganda, small-scale operations at any moment may be anticipated, particularly an attempt to regain possession of the Channel islands, which are important to us for the protection of sea communications.

2 Counter-measures in the islands must ensure that any English attack fails before a landing is achieved, whether it is attempted by sea, by air or both together. The possibility of advantage being taken of bad visibility to effect a surprise landing must be borne in mind. Emergency measures for strengthening the defence have already been ordered, and all branches of the forces stationed in the islands, except the Air Force, are placed under the orders of the Commandant of the islands.

3 With regard to the permanent fortification of the islands, to convert them into an impregnable fortress (which must be pressed forward with the utmost speed) I give the following orders:

(a) The High Command of the Army is responsible for the fortifications as a whole and will, in the overall programme, incorporate construction for the Air Force and the Navy. The strength of the fortifications and the order in which they are erected will be based on the principles and practical knowledge gained from building the Western wall.

(b) For the Army: it is important to provide a close network of emplacements, well concealed, and giving flanking fields of fire. The emplacements must be sufficient for guns of a size capable of piercing armour plate 100 mm thick, to defend against tanks which may attempt to land. There must be ample accommodation for stores and ammunition, for mobile diversion parties and for armoured cars.

(c) For the Navy: one heavy battery on the islands and two on the French coast to safeguard the sea approaches.

(d) For the Air Force: strong points must be created with searchlights and sufficient space to accommodate such AA units as are needed to protect all important constructions.

(e) Foreign labour, especially Russians and Spaniards but also Frenchmen, may be used for the building work.

4 Another order will follow for the deportation to the continent of all Englishmen who are not natives of the islands, i.e. not born there.

5 Progress reports to be sent to me on the first day of each month, to the C-in-C of the Army and directed to the Supreme Command of the Armed Forces (OKW) – Staff of the Führer, Division L.

Signed: *Adolf Hitler*

APPENDIX II

OPERATION DRYAD ORDERS

Intelligence Doc

Operation Dryad, 2–3 September1944
Plan:- To take prisoners on Isle Casquets
Force:- MTB 344, twelve officers and ORs, SSRF
Force Commander:- Major G.H. March-Phillips DSO, MBE
Command:- Commander-in-Chief, Portsmouth
The Casquets:
Admiralty Charts 60 & 2669
Channel Pilot, Part II, 10th Ed.
Tidal Streams of Channel Islands and adjacent coast of France (HD 347)

Intelligence Docket
Situation:
The Casquets group of islets and rocks lies with the largest and highest islet about 6 miles westwards of the western extremity of Alderney in Lat. 49° 43'N., 2° 22' W.

The distance from Weymouth is 54' direct.

Description:
The group has the appearance of a helmet or cap. The largest and highest islet, which elevates 90 ft., forms with the rocks close off its northern and southern sides, the central mass. On it are the light tower and two other stone towers. At low water the central mass is nearly connected and from it other rocks extend 2½ cables eastward and westward.

Within 1½ cables eastwards of this central mass are six high detached rocks, separated by narrow gullies through which the tidal streams rush with great velocity.

Point Colotte, the eastern rock, is 33ft high.

The southern and eastern sides of the group are steep-to, but on the northern side between Point Colotte and the light-tower, and about a quarter of a cable off-shore, are two small detached heads which dry.

L'Auquiere rock, about three-quarters of a cable westward of the western extremity of the central mass (Lat. 49° 43'N., Long 2° 23'W.), is 44 feet (13m 4cm) high. Rocks which dry extend about 70yd (64m) northward, north-westward and south-westward; and half a cable southward of L'Auquiere. There is a boat channel between this rock and the central mass, but it is very narrow owing to the rocky ledge, which dries 11 feet (3m 4cm) in the middle, and should only be used in the cases of necessity.

Noire Roque lies about 1¾ cables south-westwards of L'Auquiere; it is 12 feet (3m 7cm) high, craggy, and unapproachable. The Ledge with a depth of 8 feet (2m 4cm) over it, lies a cable west-south-westward of Noire Roque; its position is generally indicated by a strong ripple, and with any swell, the sea breaks on it. A rock, with a depth of 4 feet (1m 2cm) over it, lies midway between Noire Roque and L'Auquiere; no vessel should attempt to pass between them.

Approaches:

For description of outlying banks and dangers see *Channel Pilot*, P.226–228 and Charts.

For description of Ortac Channel, with dangers and directions and Burhou Island, with adjacent rocks and dangers, see *Channel Pilot*, P.228–232.

Caution:

The great rates attained by the tidal stream in neighbourhood of the Casquets renders approach to them in thick weather hazardous. Vessels should never approach them with the tidal stream in such circumstances but should wait for slack water, or until the stream in its usual rotary changes turns in the desired direction; or should get leeward of the rocks and approach them against the tidal stream. If a shoal sounding should be obtained while approaching the

Casquets in thick weather the vessel should at once turn against the tidal stream; after which she should haul out cautiously into deep water.

Tides:
At the Casquets:- Chart 60
Springs 18½ft.
At Alderney:-
Springs 20¼ft.
Neaps 15¾ft.
Mean Level 11¾ft.
For tidal streams in the neighbourhood of the Casquets, see *Channel Pilot*, P 228–229, Chart 60, and 'Tidal Streams of the Channel Islands and Adjacent coast of France' (H.D. 347).

Anchorage:
Anchorage can only be attempted off the south-eastern side of the Casquets during the south-west-going stream, and only by stream vessels. The best berth is, in depths of about 15 fathoms (27m 4cm), fine sand, with the north-eastern tower on the the Casquets bearing 319°, and the northern extremes of Fort Albert, Alderney in line with the southern extreme of Ortec rock (page 228) bearing 087°, and seen between L'Equet and Foutquis rocks.

Landing Points:
Little Casquet Rock, about three quarter of a cable southwards of the light-tower, is 53 feet (16m 2cm) high, and affords shelter to a landing place for boats on the main rock at an inlet named Petit Havre. There is another landing place on the north-eastern side of Little Casquet; and a third in a rocky bight on the northern side of the main group.

   The possibility of effecting safe landing at either of these landing places is indicated by a flag displayed at the flagstaff between the towers.

Signal Signification:
A blue square flag, landing can be effected at Petit Havre.

A white square flag with a red St George cross, landing can be effected on the north-eastern side of Little Casquet.

A red square flag, landing can be effected at the northern landing place. When no flag is displayed landing is not considered to be safe anywhere.

Objective:

It is reported that six German personnel are in occupation of the Lighthouse (Major Gwynne).

Careful enquiries have been made, but the report has not been confirmed, denied or amplified. (N.I.D.I.)

Some lighthouses in the area are known to be manned by Germans, others by Frenchmen.

It is probable that some Germans are at the Casquets, and six would be a reasonable number, although it can not be confirmed.

A small W/T set is believed to be on the Casquets, by means of which it receives instructions as to operating its lights.

The Casquets is not, however, a signal station in the proper sense of the term.

The Casquets exhibits its light at an elevation of 120 ft., from the white western tower, 75 ft. in height situated on the highest rock of the Casquets.

A fog signal is sounded from the north-east tower on this rock; and a W/T fog signal is transmitted. Distress signals are made from this light-tower. (C.P.)

Defences:

No defences are known to be located on the Casquets. (N.I.D.I., H.F.)

It should be assumed that the lighthouse personnel will be adequately armed.

Enemy Order of Battle:

No enemy forces are known or believed to be located on the Casquets other than the lighthouse personnel. (N.I.D.I. H.F.)

The nearest point, from which reinforcements can be expected, other than patrol vessels, is Alderney, 6' away.

Enemy Patrols (Sea):
Two small patrol vessels of armed trawler type are believed to maintain a continuous patrol in the Alderney vicinity. (N.B. It must be borne in mind that there is a possibility of meeting 'E' or 'R' boats on the passage.)

Inter-Island traffic and convoys to and from the mainland may be encountered most nights off Alderney; the route followed may be to the west of the Casquets.

Convoys on the Cherbourg-Brest route proceed irregularly and infrequently. They are escorted by two to four patrol vessels (usually armed trawlers but occasionally M-type minesweepers with a speed of 15 knots).

Mines:
A British ground magnetic Mine has been dropped in error in approximate position 49° 44'N., 02° 34'W (to the west of the Casquets).
Other mines are not known in the area affected by the operation.

German Air Force:
The nearest German Air Force bases are:-
  (i) Alderney (Landing Ground) 66' away.
  (ii) Guernsey/Le Bourg (Aerodrome) 17' away.

The following interpretation report relating to SORTIE S/455 of 31.5.42, Photographs 18-19 have been prepared:-
The largest island is about 280yd long x 150yd broad. It is a rock, flat at the western end, with a ridge rising to 90 ft. on the eastern end, on which are three towers. The most westerly of these is the lighthouse. The north-east corner appears to be most inaccessible for landing, the remainder of the shore being low cliffs up which, trained men could scramble.

On the southern side is a smaller rock joined to the GRAND CASQUETS by a narrow neck which may be covered at high water. There is a narrow inlet some 70 ft. wide between this rock and the main mass which would afford a sheltered anchorage to small craft. This is known as PETIT HAVRE.
There are no signs of any defences or military activity.

Outline Plan Dryad

Intention:

To carry out a raid on the Casquets Lightouse, west of Alderney, in latitude 49° 43'N., 2° 22' W., capture prisoners and bring away code books and documents.

Force Taking Part:

Two M.L.s

Twenty-two Officers and other ranks of S.S.R.C. personnel.

Outline of the Plan:

It is intended that the force shall sail from Portland to within half a mile of the Casquets Rock where the M.L.s will heave to and launch two landing craft each containing six raiding personnel and a crew of five. These boats will push into which ever of the landing places is considered suitable in the prevailing conditions and stand off the rock while the landing party is ashore. Every attempt will be made to ensure surprise.

> (a) In the event of the enemy opening fire before the party lands, the boats will push back on the prearranged signal at the discretion of S.S.R.C.
>
> (b) If fired on while landing, attempt will be made to reach the objective at the direction of S.S.R.C.
>
> (c) If the landing is unopposed the party will collect, under cover, at one of the entrances and attack immediately.

Intelligence:

Date of Operation:

The operation will take place on the first night considered suitable by C. Portsmouth after 10th June.

Withdrawal:

After not more than 1½ hours ashore or on the completion of the operation, if that is earlier, landing craft will be called in by signal from the shore and the raiding party and prisoners will be transferred to the M.L.s.

Landing craft must leave shore not later than 1 hour before the start of nautical twilight. If at dawn, no signal is seen and the landing craft are not visible, the M.L.s will proceed to their base under senior Officer of M.L.s.

In the event of fire from the rock or appearance of enemy surface craft, the senior Officer of M.L.s will at his discretion, order a retirement out of range but will endeavour to contact the landing craft one mile south–west of the rock or on such a bearing as wind and tide direct to be notified during the operation.

Allocation of Responsibility:

S.S.R.C. will be responsible for cancelling the operation during passage if enemy action or weather conditions made it necessary to do so. Unless special circumstances dictate otherwise, the operation is to be cancelled if the force is sighted by enemy aircraft during the approach.

Reports:

S.S.R.C. is to forward a report on the operation to both C in C Portsmouth and C.C.O.

Senior Officer of M.L.s is to forward his report through S.S.R.C.

APPENDIX III

THE COMMANDO ORDER

Der Führer SECRET No. 003830/42 g.Kdos.OKW/Wst F.H. Qu 18.10.

12 Copies Copy No.12

1 For a long time now our opponents have been employing in their conduct of the war, methods which contravene the International Convention of Geneva. The members of the so-called Commandos behave in a particularly brutal and underhand manner; and it has been established that those units recruit criminals not only from their own country but even former convicts set free in enemy territories. From captured orders it emerges that they are instructed not only to tie up prisoners, but also to kill out-of-hand unarmed captives who they think might prove an encumbrance to them, or hinder them in successfully carrying out their aims. Orders have indeed been found in which the killing of prisoners has positively been demanded of them.

2 In this connection it has already been notified in an Appendix to Army Orders of 7.10.1942 that in future, Germany will adopt the same methods against these Sabotage units of the British and their Allies; i.e. that, whenever they may appear, they shall be ruthlessly destroyed by the German troops.

3 I order, therefore:

From now on all men operating against German troops in so-called Commando raids in Europe and Africa, are to be annihilated to the last

man. This is to be carried out whether they be soldiers in uniform, or saboteurs, with or without arms; and whether fighting or seeking to escape;
and it is equally immaterial whether they come into action from Ships
or Aircraft, or whether they land by parachute. Even if these individuals on discovery make obvious their intention of giving themselves up
as prisoners, no pardon is on any account to be given. On this matter a
report is to be made in each case to Headquarters for the information of
Higher Command.

4   Should individual members of these Commandos, such as agents, saboteurs, etc., fall into the hands of the *Wehrmacht* through any other means
– as, for example, through the Police in one of the Occupied Territories
– they are to be instantly handed over to the SD. To hold them in military
custody – for example in POW camps etc., – even as a temporary measure,
is strictly forbidden.

5   This order does not apply to the treatment of those enemy soldiers who
are taken prisoner or give themselves up in battle, in the course of normal
operations, large-scale attacks; or in major assault landings or airborne
operations. Neither does it apply to those who fall into our hands after
a sea fight, nor to those enemy soldiers who, after air battle, seek to save
themselves by parachute.

6   I will hold all Commanders and Officers responsible under Military Law
for any omission to carry out this order, whether by failure in their duty
to instruct their units accordingly, or if they themselves act contrary to it.

(Signed) *Adolf Hitler*

[Perhaps conscious that this order breached the rules of war, *Generaloberst*
(Lt Gen.) Alfred Jodl, chief of the operations staff of the *Oberkommando der
Wehrmacht* – OKW (Armed Forces High Command) – classified his cov-
ering note to the Commando Order 'Secret'.]

HEADQUARTERS OF THE ARMY SECRET *No 551781/42 g.k.*
Chefs W.F.St/Qu F.H. Qu19.10.42 22 Copies

The enclosed Order of the Führer is forwarded in connection with destruction of enemy Terror and Sabotage-troops. This order is intended for Commanders only and is in no circumstances to fall into Enemy hands. Further distribution by receiving Headquarters is to be most strictly limited. The Headquarters mentioned in the Distribution list are responsible that all parts of the Order, or extracts from it, which are issued are again withdrawn and, together with this copy, destroyed.

Chief of Staff of the Army (Signed) Jodl

ORDER OF BATTLE OF 319TH DIVISION

The 216th Division would go on to fight with distinction on the Eastern Front, but after suffering heavy losses would be disbanded in 1943. In contrast, the men of the 319th Division would earn the dubious nickname of Kanada Division, since it was seen as destined for POW camps in Canada.

The order of battle of the 319th was:

Commanders:

    Generalleutnant Erich Müller (19 November 1940 – 1 September 1943)

    Generalleutnant Rudolf Graf von Schmettow (1 September 1943 – 27 February 1945)

    Generalmajor Rudolf Wulf (27 February 1945 – 8 May 1945)

Area of operations:

    Germany (November 1940 – May 1941)

    Channel Islands (May 1941 – May 1945)

Order of battle (1943–1945):

Stab der Division (Headquarters in Guernsey)

Grenadier-Regiment 582 (*Ost-Bataillon* 643 incorporated as IV. *Bataillon* on 19 April 1944) (Regiment based in Jersey)

Grenadier-Regiment 583 (*Georgisches Infanterie-Bataillon* 823 incorporated as IV. *Bataillon* on 19 April 1944) (Regiment based in Guernsey)

Grenadier-Regiment 584 (Regiment based in Guernsey)

Artillerie-Regiment 319 (Regiment headquarters in Jersey; I. and II./AR 319 based in Jersey; III. and IV./AR 319 based in Guernsey; 11./AR 319 based in Alderney)

Pionier-Bataillon 319

Panzerjäger-Abteilung 319 (11 x 4.7cm *Pak (t) auf Geschützwagen* R-35 (f); based in Jersey)

Schnellen Abteilung 450 (11 x 4.7cm *Pak (t) auf Geschützwagen* R-35 (f); based in Guernsey)

Nachrichten-Abteilung 319

Versorgungseinheiten 319

Attached units:

MG-Bataillon 16 (based in Jersey)

Panzer-Abteilung 213 (*Abteilung* headquarters in Guernsey with 2 x Renault Char B1 bis command tanks; 2. *Kompanie* with 12 x Renault Char B1 bis tanks and 5 x Renault Char B1 bis flame-throwing tanks in Jersey; 1. *Kompanie* with 12 x Renault Char B1 bis tanks and 5 x Renault Char B1 bis flame-throwing tanks in Guernsey)

NESTEGG REPORT

TOP SECRET
SUPREME HEADQUARTERS ALLIED EXPEDITIONARY FORCE
Psychological Warfare Division
24 September 1944

SUBJECT: OPERATION 'NEST EGG'
TO: Brigadier General R.A. McClure, Chief, PWD/SHAEF.
FROM: Major Alan Chambers

Further to my report on the above dated 15 September 1944.

1   On 18 September 1944 it was decided at SHAEF (FORWARD) to postpone the PWD plan to bring our German General (Mr. Black) into contact with Lt. General von SCHMETTOW Commander of the German garrison in the CHANNEL ISLANDS until after the fall of BREST.

2   On 21 September 1944, BREST having fallen and the meteorological forecast being favourable for the ensuing 24 hours period it was decided to proceed with the attempt.

3   Accordingly I notified the USN Chief of Staff at CHERBOURG (Captain CLARK) to alert the craft and arranged with the Leaflets Section to make a night drop, with flares, of a letter to von SCHMETTOW (in duplicate). (See Appendix 'A'). This letter stated that, under article 32 of the Hague Convention of 18 October 1907 I, as accredited representative of the Supreme Command accompanied by two companies would arrive at a point 4½ miles South of ST. MARTINS HEAD, 142 degrees

(True North) at 1100 hours (GMT) on 22 September 1944. It invited von SCHMETTOW to come to the same point at that time. It was further stated that our party would travel in R.A.F. sea air rescue craft No. 2632, flying a white flag and completely unarmed, and that our course would be due west from the mainland at CAP GARTERET to the point specified.

4   The air drop having been arranged to take place at approximately 2300 hours on 21 September 1944 on the enemy H.Q. at ST. PETER PORT – GUERNSEY I left for France in the afternoon to complete arrangements with Major Lord ABERFELDY and Mr. BLACK, arriving at GRANVILLE at 1930 hours.

5   At 0150 hours on 22 September 1944 Captain FOX (Leaflets Section) telephoned from LONDON to advise that our pilots reported the result of the drop to be poor. That it was just possible that the letters had been received but that due to drift they more probably had fallen in the sea off ST. PETER PORT.

6   I advised my companions forthwith and after discussion it was agreed unanimously to take the chance that one of the letters had been received.

7   Accordingly at 0845 hours on 22 September 1944 we drove to CAP CARTERET and from the beach went aboard R.A.F. sea air rescue boat No. 2632 (F/O Robert CHANDLER, R.A.F.) and left for the rendezvous at 1045 hours.

8   From my first report dated 15 September 1944, it will be recollected that our plan was to proceed to the rendezvous and if the enemy did not appear after a reasonable interval I was to go in alone in a dinghy with an outboard motor under a white flag with the object of forcing the enemy to receive me. Our plan then was that I should endeavour to speak to von SCHMETTOW and tell him that a high ranking German Officer (Mr. BLACK) was in our boat and that he wished to confer with him. It was hoped that I might then persuade von SCHMETTOW to come out to our vessel – Mr. BLACK made it plain that he would not personally land but that von SCHMETTOW must come to him.

9   About 25 minutes after leaving CARTERET we sighted the north east coast of JERSEY and ran due west along it at about 16 knots. Visibility was poor and it is certain that the enemy could not see our white flag and probably not even our craft. The enemy batteries took no action.

10 At 1200 hours on the same course we sighted SARK, visibility was still poor. The enemy took no action.

11 At 1240 on the same course we sighted ST. MARTINS HEAD Island off GUERNSEY and arrived at the rendezvous 4½ miles to the south of the Head at 1246 hours, being then 46 minutes late. There was no sign of anyone so we proceeded in at about 10 knots and prepared to drop our dingy overboard.

12 We continued to move in at reduced speed and stopped at 1320 hours in the roadstead of ST. PETER PORT (the enemy H.Q.) about 1½ miles off shore at SARDRIER BUOY. At 1325 hours the enemy fired one white very light and we replied with two very lights. We did not know what this signal meant but naturally took it to be an invitation to come in.

13 Accordingly we proceeded further in and then launched the dinghy at 1335 hours. I got in with one seaman and a white flag. Unfortunately in spite of repeated efforts by several of the hands the outboard motor refused to start.

14 At 1350 hours I decided to take our craft in further and row the dinghy to shore – accordingly we started up again and moved in towards ST. PETER PORT inner harbour.

15 At 1355 hours an enemy motor boat fully armed without a white flag put off from the inner harbour and approached at speed with her guns manned. We continued to move in and made contact at 1400 hours by hailing in German over our loudspeaker.
[There is no Point 16]

17 The enemy boat contained a naval full Lieutenant (Oberleutnant See MEYER-LOTTING) an Army 2nd Lieut. – interpreter – and a crew of eight. I told them my orders were to contact von SCHMETTOW personally. They invited me aboard and I went aboard alone.

18 In his cabin MEYER requested my authority and my mission. I produced my written authority (Appendix 'B') signed by Lt. General MORGAN on behalf of the Chief of Staff, Supreme Headquarters, Allied Expeditionary Force and he then communicated the exact German text by light signal to the Admiral on shore about one mile away. I then suggested we should proceed in, in his boat. He said 'not until I have permission'. Adding, 'if you

have come about a surrender let me tell you now that is useless'. I replied that I had nothing to discuss with him and that my orders were to contact von SCHMETTOW personally. I asked MEYER why no one had been at the rendezvous to meet us. He stated that they had no knowledge we were coming. I asked if they had seen our drop the night before. He said 'Yes, I was on sea patrol last night and saw two parachutes fall in the sea about one mile east of ST. MARTINS HEAD.'

19 At about 1425 the reply came out by light signal from the Admiral acknowledging my credentials and asking my business. At my request Lt. MEYER replied by the same means that I wished to speak personally to von SCHMETTOW.

20 At about 1455 hours the reply came back 'specifically what matter does Major CHAMBERS want to discuss'. At this point I had to make the decision whether to answer that I had a high ranking German on my boat and disclose my full purpose to the occupants of their boat and the Admiral, and his staff, as well as to von SCHMETTOW. This I was pre-pared to do if it seemed at all possible that von SCHMETTOW would come out to talk to him. (BLACK, as described above, would not go in) I saw no purpose in disclosing my hand unless there was a reasonable chance of attaining my objective. There was also the possibility that they might have ordered BLACK brought in by force. As they were fully armed and we had no arms such an order could have been carried out. BLACK would have been no great loss but it would [if] he made a good story for GOEBBELS. I conferred over the ship's rail with Major Lord ABERFELDY and we agreed that my answer should be that I wished to discuss the 'general military situation' with von SCHMETTOW, hoping that they would let me in when I would be able to persuade von SCHMETTOW to talk to BLACK.

21 At 1520 hours the reply came back 'Lt. General von SCHMETTOW is fully informed as to the military situation and therefore declines any discussion' and ordered MEYER to break off and return to ST. PETER PORT, forthwith. I requested a written copy of this last communication and append it hereto (appendix 'C'). I then asked MEYER if he as well as von SCHMETTOW understood the full import of this refusal. He said he was sure they all did. I repeated my question slowly and solemnly

in English to the Army 2nd Lieutenant and again in German so that all might hear. He also agreed, but was quite visibly shaken. I then left and went aboard our craft.

22 The events described above took place in full view of a number of interested civilians in and about ST. PETER PORT approximately 1 mile off shore – and would also of course have been clearly visible to our people on SARK.

23 At 1530 hours we got underway and set a course for CHERBOURG (as the breeze was increasing) by way of LITTLE SARK, BLANCHARD BUOY and FORAINE TOW without interference from the enemy.

24 At 1700 hours in the RACE of ALDERNEY when abeam of ALDERNEY[,] distance 6 miles approximately[,] the enemy batteries fired a salvo at us, scoring a near miss, the burst falling to port and starboard simultaneously, distance from 10 to 50yd. Only prompt evasive action by our skipper F/O Robert CHANDLER, R.A.F. saved the craft and occupants. Some damage to hull on both sides and one slight casualty. Ammunition was identified from fragments as 8.8cm. We arrived at CHERBOURG at 1840 hours. (At appendix 'D' is a sketch of our course).

25 REMARKS:

The following notes are the result of joint observations and from my conversation on board the enemy craft held during the intervals between the despatch and receipt of messages to shore:

(a) It was clear that we were not expected and from remarks on the boat that we had probably not been seen at all until close to ST. MARTINS HEAD. Their watch was apparently poor.

(b) From the behaviour of the crew, the conduct of the two German officers and their remarks it would appear that the enemy will to resist is not unanimous.

(c) The Army Officer indicated by his conversation that as the Division had been on the islands so long their relations with the civilians were very friendly. The troops regarded themselves as prisoner of war in effect already and saw no reason why we should not leave them that way.

(d) It was noticeable that their craft was poorly found – except for their weapons. Their uniforms were threadbare and ordinary supplies like cigarettes and sugar etc. were lacking.

(e) We saw no sign of mines or underwater obstacles anywhere.

(f) Major Lord ABERFELDY, Mr. BLACK and I agreed that it seemed probable that von SCHMETTOW (like the other remaining German commanders still holding out in the West) had received a definite order not to treat with the Allies and to refuse all demands for surrender. Compliance with this order being assured by control in Germany of the families of the officers.

(g) We agreed however that it was quite possible that MEYER's communication to shore had been dealt with by the SS and that von SCHMETTOW had not been entirely in the picture.

(h) We agreed that force would be necessary to get a surrender but that not much force would be required.

26. CONCLUSION:

(a) In view of the above I believe that no further specifically Psychological Warfare attempt should be made except in conjunction with a show of force.

(b) May I be instructed please to discontinue nightly air dropping of information leaflets (NACHRICHTEN) on the Islands.

Signed *Alan Chambers Major, G.S*

ARTICLES OF SURRENDER

Signed by Major General Heine of the German Forces and Brigadier Snow of the British Forces in HMS *Bulldog* off St Peter Port[,] Guernsey.

9 May 1945

1. Terms of unconditional surrender for Channel Islands
    'The Commander, German Forces, Channel Islands, hereby announces uncon-ditional surrender of the Forces under his command to the Supreme Commander, Allied Expeditionary Force. The Supreme Commander, Allied Expeditionary Force, accordingly announces the following Terms of Surrender with which the Commander, German Forces, Channel Islands, undertakes to comply.

    1   German Forces have ceased hostilities on land, sea and air; the German Commander has issued instructions to all forces under his command to cease hostilities at 0001 hours DBST on 9 May 1945.

    2   (a)   All German armed forces and organisations equipped with weapons shall completely disarm themselves at once.

        (b)   German forces and all civilians accompanying the German forces will remain in their present position pending further instructions.

        (c)   All German forces shall be declared prisoners of war.

    3   All aircraft shall remain grounded.

    4   All German shipping and all shipping of the United Nations at the disposal of the Germans will remain in port. Crews to remain on board pending further instructions.

5   (a)   The German Commander will hold intact and maintain in good condition and will hand over to the Allied representative at such time and places as may be prescribed:-

          (1)   All arms, ammunition, military equipment, stores and supplies, aircraft, naval vessels and merchant shipping and all other war material, together with records pertaining thereto.

          (2)   All military installations and establishments and all factories, plants and other civil institutions, together with plans and records thereof, as required.

          (3)   All transportation and communications facilities and equipment, by land, water or air, and records thereof.

          (4)   All livestock, crops, food, wines, spirits, fuel and water supplies under his control.

          (5)   All submarine cables, telephones and telegraph installations to be handed over in full working order.

    (b)   The German Commander shall provide all facilities for movement and land communications of Allied troops and agencies; he will maintain all transportation in good order and repair and will furnish the labour services and plant necessary therefor.

6   (a)   The German Commander will release to the Allied representative in accordance with procedure to be laid down, all prisoners of war belonging to the forces of the United Nations, and will furnish full lists of these persons indicating the places of their detention. Pending release of such prisoners of war, the German Commander will protect them in their persons and property and provide them with adequate food, clothing, shelter and medical attention in accordance with their rank or official position.

    (b)   The German Commander will likewise provide for and release all other nationals of United Nations who are confined, interned or otherwise under restraint, except any confined for purely civil crimes, unconnected with the war. Records of all such prisoners will be presented to the Allied representative when requested.

(c) The German Commander will be responsible that no harm of any kind shall be inflicted on inhabitants or their property or possessions.

7 (a) The German Commander shall furnish to the Allied representative full information regarding German armed forces and within twenty-four hours of surrender shall furnish information concerning numbers, locations and dispositions of such forces.

(b) Similarly, complete and detailed information will be furnished by the German Commander concerning mines and obstacles to movement by land, sea or air; all safety lanes will be kept open and clearly marked; as far as possible all mines and minefields and other dangerous obstacles will be rendered safe, and removed. German unarmed personnel and equipment will be made available subsequently and utilized for the final removal of mines, minefields and other obstacles as directed by the Allied representative.

8 The German Commander will prevent destruction, removal, transfer, concealment or damage to all archives and records except as directed by the Allied representative.

9 All forms of communication including Radar under German control shall cease operation except as directed by the Allied representative.

10 The German Commander will afford all facilities to such advance parties which the Allied representative may send into the Channel Islands to make arrangements for the entry of Allied forces and for other purposes.

11 The German Commander will accept and execute any and all orders which may be issued by the Allied representative for the purpose of furthering the execution of these terms of surrender, of obtaining information, of improving the general situation in the Islands, of facilitating Allied occupation of the Islands, and of aiding in the Allied assumption of control over the Islands and German forces.

12 This Instrument will enter into force and effect immediately upon its acceptance by the Allied representative. In the event of failure

on the part of the German forces promptly and completely to fulfil their obligations the Allied representative will take whatever action may be deemed to be appropriate by him under the circumstances.

13 These terms of unconditional surrender are expressedly [*sic*] subject to any Instrument of total surrender which may later be imposed by the United Nations on Germany.

14 These provisions are drawn up in the English and German languages. The English text is authoritative. In case of any question as to the meaning of the provisions the decision of the Allied representative will prevail.

Signed in HMS *Bulldog* off St Peter Port
this ninth day of May 1945 at 0715

2. (a) All German armed forces and organisations equipped with weapons shall completely disarm themselves at once.

(b) German forces and all civilians accompanying the German forces will remain in their present position pending further instructions. All German forces shall be declared prisoners of war.

3. Orders for German TPS [troops] as PW [prisoners of war]

1 (a) German troops (except as in (b) and (c)) will NOT CROSS bounds of the area to be evacuated by German Forces (except under escort). See marked maps Appendix 'A'.

(b) Liaison HQ Staffs as detailed separately will remain confined to the HQ building.

(c) German troops posted as sentries over stores will NOT leave their Sentry Areas except on orders of a British Officer.

2 (a) Any PW attempting to pass the boundaries stated, except under escort, after once being warned and disregarding that warning, are liable to be fired on.

(b) If called to Halt, any PW will halt, raise his hands, and NOT move until further orders.

3 All PW, officers, and OR [other ranks] will comply with all orders issued by officers, guards, escorts and sentries placed over them.

4 (a) Any PW guilty of disobedience to orders or any act prejudicial to safety, good order or discipline, will be punished.

    (b)   Deliberate disobedience coupled with resistance or appre-
hended resistance, or other conduct of a mutinous or riotous
kind, will, if necessary, be dealt with by force of arms.

5   PW will NOT converse with any person other than another PW,
or a British Officer or soldier in the performance of his duty.

6   (a)   Officer PW will salute all officers of equal or higher corre-
sponding rank to their own.

    (b)   OR PW will salute all officers.

7   Personal baggage is limited to one suitcase, or equivalent.

8   PW may retain badges of rank and decorations.

9   No intoxicating liquor may be possessed or consumed.

10   The senior German Officer in each location will be responsible for
the strict observance of discipline in each such location.

BIBLIOGRAPHY

Bonnard, Brian, *Alderney at War* (Stroud: Alan Sutton, 1993)

Briggs, Asa, *The Channel Islands Occupation and Liberation 1940–1945* (London: BT Batsford, 1995)

Bunting, Madeleine, *The Model Occupation* (London: HarperCollins, 1995)

Cruikshank, Charles, *The German Occupation of the Channel Islands* (Guernsey: The Guernsey Press, 1975)

Durnford-Slater, Brigadier John, *Commando: Memoirs of a Fighting Commando in World War Two* (London: Greenhill Books, 2002)

Falla, Frank, *The Silent War* (London: Leslie Frewin, 1967)

Forty, George, *Channel Islands at War: A German Perspective* (Shepperton: Ian Allan, 1999)

Franks, Xan (ed.), *War on Sark: The Secret Letters of Julia Tremayne* (London: Webb and Bower, 1981)

Ginns, Michael, *The Granville Raid* (London: After the Battle Number 47, 1985)

Harris, Roger, *Islanders Departed Part 1* (Jersey: Channel Islands Specialists Society, 1980)

Howarth, David, *Dawn of D-Day* (London: Collins, 1959)

King, Peter, *The Channel Islands War 1940–1945* (London: Robert Hale, 1991)

Martienssen, Anthony, *Hitler and his Admirals* (London: Secker and Warburg, 1948)

Messenger, Charles, *The Commandos 1940–1946* (London: William Kimber, 1985)

Ramsey, Winston G., *The War in the Channel Islands Then and Now* (London: After the Battle, 1981)

Stephenson, Charles, *The Channel Islands 1941–45: Hitler's Impregnable Fortress* (illustrated Chris Taylor) (Oxford: Osprey, 2006)

Stroobant, Frank, *One Man's War* (Guernsey: Guernsey Press Ltd, 1967)

Toms, Carel, *Hitler's Fortress Islands* (London: New English Library, 1967)

Turner, Barry, *Outpost of Occupation* (London: Aurum, 2010)

Winton, John, *Death of the Scharnhorst* (London: Antony Bird, 1983)

Wood, Alan and Mary, *Islands in Danger* (London: Evans Brothers Ltd, 1955)

Young, Peter, *Storm from the Sea* (London: William Kimber, 1958)

INDEX

Visit our website and discover thousands of other History Press books.